INTERMEDIATE GRAMMAR

From Form to Meaning and Use

TEACHER'S BOOK

INTERMEDIATE GRAMMAR

From Form to Meaning and Use

TEACHER'S BOOK

CHERYL PAVLIK WITH ELLEN BALLEISEN
AND SUSAN KESNER BLAND

Oxford University Press

Oxford University Press
198 Madison Avenue
New York, NY 10016 USA

Walton Street
Oxford OX2 6DP England

OXFORD is a trademark of Oxford University Press.

Oxford New York

Auckland Cape Town Dar es Salaam Hong Kong
Karachi Kuala Lumpur Madrid Melbourne
Mexico City Nairobi New Delhi Shanghai Taipei
Toronto

With offices in

Argentina Austria Brazil Chile Czech Republic
France Greece Guatemala Hungary Italy Japan
Poland Portugal Singapore South Korea Switzerland
Thailand Turkey Ukraine Vietnam

ISBN 978-0-19-434367-1

Editorial Manager: Susan Lanzano
Art Director: Lynn Luchetti
Production Manager: Abram Hall
Project Manager: Jane Sturtevant

Content Editor: Tünde Dewey
Production Editor: Janice L. Baillie
Designer: Alan Barnett

Cover design by: John Daly

Realia by: Claudia Kehrhahn

Printing (last digit): 10 9 8 7 6 5 4

Printed in China.

Contents

Introduction

The Characteristics and Needs of Intermediate-Level Students

As its name states, the Student Book for *Intermediate Grammar* was written with intermediate students in mind — students who may vary considerably from one another in their wide range of skills and knowledge of English grammar. One of the most salient defining characteristics of an intermediate class, therefore, is that it is rarely homogeneous. Since most intermediate students have used different course books with different syllabuses, they do not all have a uniform knowledge of English. Some may have followed a functional course and never have studied grammar formally before at all. Others may have had a teacher who emphasized writing and are therefore weak in informal conversational structures. Still others may have very little formal study and have simply picked up English on the street or in the workplace. With their varied backgrounds, the only thing that can be said of an intermediate class is that they are ready to learn to express themselves more effectively without relying on translation or memorization, but the grammatical structures that they bring to this task will vary from student to student.

Intermediate students have other defining characteristics. One of the most notable is the fact that, although they have met the main functions and structures of English before, they often have difficulty sustaining accuracy. An intermediate student may use a structure correctly one day, only to make basic errors in the same structure the next. This stage has been called the "intermediate plateau," because intermediate students often feel frustrated at their lack of measurable progress. In addition to their lack of homogeneity and their sometimes high level of frustration, intermediate classes may also present another challenge for teachers — the problem of boredom. On any given day, at least one, and more often, many, students in the class will already have studied what you are going to present. While they probably have not learned all there is to know about the structure, they may think they have, and the challenge is for the teacher to keep them involved in the lesson.

The *Intermediate Grammar* Teacher's Book helps teachers of intermediate students overcome these problems by:

> providing structure-by-structure assessment quizzes to inform teachers of their students' areas of strength and weakness;

> emphasizing the importance of elicitation, a more student-centered approach to teaching and an approach that particularly benefits from the differences in skills and knowledge found in an intermediate class;

> helping students to analyze familiar grammatical structures from the more unfamiliar and challenging perspectives of meaning and use;

> allowing students to consolidate their knowledge by providing a large number of varied exercises and extension activities;

> combating boredom and other signs of "I've studied that already" with exercises that engage students' intellect, judgment, creativity, and problem-solving skills.

⮕ Philosophy

The aim of the *Intermediate Grammar* Teacher's Book is NOT to provide teachers with a step-by-step guide to working with the text in class. This is so for two reasons. First, the exercises and activities in the text are self-explanatory, and even relatively inexperienced teachers will not have problems using them. Exercise titles, for example, make it easy for teachers to relate the exercises to the points in the Form or the Meaning and Use boxes. This one-to-one correspondence offers teachers of intermediate students the flexibility they need for choosing which exercises their students can handle at a particular time. Second, the most useful information in teacher's books is often lost in a lot of mechanical, step-by-step instructional filler.

In order to make the text as useful as possible, we have tried to give guidance where it is the most beneficial — in the presentation of structures and ideas for extension activities. In this way, even experienced teachers searching for new ways to present structures will find the Teacher's Book a valuable aid.

Parts of the Teacher's Book notes

Introduction	• A brief overview of the unit that points out possible problem areas for the students and pitfalls that teachers should avoid.
Using the Preview	• Ideas for using the Student Book Preview material in class.
Examining Form/ Meaning and Use	• Suggested presentations for the material in each Form and Meaning and Use box in the Student Book.
Using the Conversation Notes	• In certain chapters, ideas and dictations (where appropriate) to use along with the Conversation Notes in the Student Book.
Troubleshooting	• In certain chapters, advice on handling particular problems that may arise during the presentation of the Form or Meaning and Use material.
Additional Activities	• Extension activities including real-world assignments, writing, songs, and short stories that provide well-contextualized examples of the target structures.

The remainder of the Teacher's Book

Diagnostic Quizzes	• Structure-by-structure pre-tests.
Achievement Quizzes	• Chapter quizzes that compare and contrast the form, meaning and use of the material covered in the chapter.
Quiz Answer Key	• Suggested answers to all quizzes.
Student Book Answer Key	• Suggested answers to all of the exercises in the Student Book.

⮞ Methodology

The philosophy of the *Intermediate Grammar* Teacher's Book is based on one predominant concept: Intermediate students already know quite a bit of grammar. Therefore, teachers should elicit as much as possible from students and then build on their students' knowledge, filling in the gaps and clearing up confusion where necessary. Hence, almost all the presentations use variations on the same basic steps:

1. Students are given a task to complete, individually, in pairs or in groups.

2. Their answers, which are expected to be somewhat incorrect or incomplete, are presented to the rest of the class.

3. The class looks at the information in the relevant box and revises their answers as necessary.

We realize that this type of student-centered approach may not suit all classes and teachers. And, even in classes where teachers and students are comfortable with this approach, it will not always be desirable. Sometimes students may not know enough to even begin to answer. At other times, the diagnostic quiz may show that most students already have a fairly good grasp of the target structure. Therefore, two alternate methods may be desirable.

For students and teachers who are more comfortable with direct instruction and for less able classes:

> Work directly from the boxes to present the Form or Meaning and Use material to the students. Use the ideas suggested in the Teacher's Book as a guide when presenting the material, modifying them to eliminate almost all but the most basic elicitation.

For students who already have a good grasp of the target structure:

> Skip the Form or Meaning and Use boxes and go directly to the exercises. Use the information in the boxes to clear up any problems that students encounter as they work through the exercises.

> It is more likely, however, that students may have a good grasp of only some of the points in the Form or Meaning and Use boxes, and they may still need to refine their knowledge of some of the other points. After completing an exercise, have the students generalize about the form, meaning, or use points that are relevant to the exercise and use the appropriate box to confirm their generalizations.

The *Intermediate Grammar* Student Book itself is designed for flexibility and ease of use. This enables teachers to tailor their classes to the needs of their students by using selected sections of each chapter. The following describes the sections of the Student Book and gives some suggestions of how they can be used.

Parts of a chapter in the Student Book

Preview
- The first page of each chapter. Describes and gives examples of the meanings and uses of structures in the chapter.

- Assign it for before-class preview of structures or use it for presentation.

Form box
- Displays, describes, and explains the forms of a given structure.

- Use it with form exercises to confirm or revise students' conclusions about form.

  Students can use it as a reference for study and review.

Meaning and Use box	• Gives the *what*, *where*, *when*, and *why* of meaning and use.
	• Use with meaning and use exercises to revise, confirm, and expand students' understanding of meaning and use.
	Students can use it as a reference for study and review.
Conversation Note	• Describes a special feature of pronunciation or usage. It often contrasts spoken and written language.
	• Use it as a springboard for discussion of the differences between spoken and written language and what "correctness" is.
Focus on Vocabulary	• Presents vocabulary associated with a specific structure. There are seven in the book.
	• Use it to focus instruction on grammar problems related to vocabulary.
	Students can use it for study and review.
Summary	• A comprehensive, at-a-glance display of form, meaning, and use for each structure in the chapter.
	• Use it as a detailed table of contents for the chapter when planning lessons and writing tests.
	Students can use it for reference and review.
Exercises	• Early exercises for each structure are strictly on form and are quite controlled. Later exercises focus on meaning and use, and become more open-ended.
	• Each chapter has exercises appropriate for diagnostic use, interactive practice, dictation, homework, and review.

In the back of the Student Book

Appendix	• Spelling and pronunciation rules, word lists, and explanations related to specific structures.
	• Use it to teach these grammar-related topics and to supplement basic vocabulary supplied in the chapters.
	Students can refer to it when writing or doing exercises.
Glossary	• Definitions and examples of all grammar terms used in the book.
	• Use it as a ready source of examples.
	Students can refer to it for study and review.

Index

- Lists structures, alternate terms, common language functions and uses, grammar terms, and words and phrases related to specific structures (for example, *haven't, how long, guess, generally*).

- Find which structures in the book fulfill a given language function or use.

  Students can use almost any related word to look up a structure.

⇒ Teaching Techniques

ELICITATION

Elicitation is one of the most useful teaching techniques when teaching grammar to intermediate-level students. However, some teachers and students may be uncomfortable asking or answering questions on "new" material. It is important to remember that, especially with intermediate students, what is new to one student may not be new to another. In addition, students should be made to understand that they are not being tested. You should explain that errors are not only expected, they are crucial to the learning process. Correct answers only show you what the students know; incorrect answers do much more. They allow you to pinpoint the areas that students have not yet mastered, they give you insight into the way your students are thinking about the target material, and they help to guide your teaching.

ERROR CORRECTION

In the accuracy-fluency continuum, much of grammar practice is often considered a high-accuracy activity. You should, nevertheless, do everything possible to lower the error anxiety level in your classroom. This is particularly important in the elicitation phase of the lesson. Comments such as "That's an interesting error," or "I can understand why you said that, but we would normally use a different structure," can help students see their errors in a less judgmental light and encourage them to guess and try out new structures that they are not sure of.

The *Intermediate Grammar* Teacher's Book carefully points out that the difference between "correct" and "incorrect" grammar is often not black and white. Even though many of the errors that your students make are different from native speaker "errors," you can help your students become more linguistically mature by using the examples in the Conversation Notes to show them that native speakers also violate the "rules" under certain circumstances. This should help them begin to understand that grammar rules are not absolutes but merely products of custom and habit.

INTERMEDIATE GRAMMAR

From Form to Meaning and Use

TEACHER'S BOOK

CHAPTER 1

Expressing the Present: The Simple Present, the Present Continuous, and Stative Verbs

Most intermediate-level students have studied the simple present and the present continuous in earlier courses. Use this chapter as an opportunity to get to know your students. Do not spoonfeed them. Step back and let *them* show you what they know.

Using the Preview

➠ Tell the students to open their books to the Preview on page 1. Ask them to circle examples of the simple present and underline examples of the present continuous in the sample dialogues.

Give them one or two minutes. Then call on different students to read the sentences aloud.

Ask the students to tell you as many uses as they can think of for the simple present. If they are unsure of what you mean, give them an example. Write their answers on the board. Do not correct the answers. Next, ask them to tell you the uses of the present continuous. Write statements on the board.

Tell the students to read the two paragraphs at the bottom of the page. Ask them to compare the information on the board with the information in the book.

The Simple Present

Examining Form

➠ As an example for the students, talk about yourself in the simple present making several general statements. (For example: *I like cats. I enjoy dancing. My favorite color is red. I live in Los Angeles. I have two children. I don't have any grandchildren. I don't own an airplane.*, etc.)

Tell the students to write five statements about themselves. Tell them not to repeat any verbs and that they should include at least one negative statement. Ask

them to begin each statement with *I*. Give them two minutes. Then call on two or three students to read one of their statements. Write the sentences on the board.

Use the sentences you have elicited from the students to review the form of the simple present. Ask what form of the verb they used. *(The simple form.)*

Erase the pronoun *I* in one of the sentences and replace it with *she* or *he*. Ask the students what else needs to be changed in the sentence. *(The verb needs an -s on the end.)* Make the change on the board. Then call on different students to make the changes in the other sentences on the board. Refer the students to the Appendix on spelling and pronunciation rules for third-person singular forms at the back of their Student Books.

Call on a student to come up to the board and transform a sentence into a *yes/no* question. Have another student answer the question. Encourage the student to give a short answer using a contraction in the negative statement. Call on a second student to transform another sentence into an information question with *where*, *when*, *why*, or *how*. Call on a third student to transform another sentence into an information question with *who* or *what* as subject. Have the students compare the structures of the two information questions.

Examining Meaning and Use

➠ Bring to class some newspapers, magazines, comic books, and other reading material. Pair the students and let them look for examples of the simple present. Ask them to write down at least five statements and analyze the use of the simple present. Give the pairs ten minutes to work.

Then ask the students to look at the Meaning and Use box on page 5 in the Student Book. Have the pairs give you examples of as many different uses as they can from the examples they wrote down earlier.

The Present Continuous

Examining Form

➠ Make several statements about yourself using the present continuous. (For example: *Right now I'm standing in front of the classroom and thinking about how to get more students to participate in class. Today I'm wearing a blue shirt. This week I'm not watching as much television as I normally do. This semester I'm teaching three classes.*, etc.)

Tell the students to write three similar statements about themselves. Tell them not to repeat a verb and that one statement must be negative. Ask them to begin their statements with *I*. Give them a minute. Then call on two or three students to read their statements. Write some of the statements on the board.

Direct the students' attention to the sentences on the board. Ask them what the verb phrase in each of these sentences is. *(Be + verb + -ing.)* Underline the verb phrase.

Next change the subject in one of the sentences from *I* to *we*. Ask the students what other change needs to be made. **(Am needs to be changed to are.)**

Ask a student to come to the board and change the subject of one of the sentences to *he* or *she*. Ask what form the verb will take. **(Is + verb + -ing)**

Call on a second student to come up to the board and transform a sentence into a *yes/no* question. Then call on a third student to transform another sentence into a nonsubject information question, and call on a fourth student to transform a sentence into an information question with *who* or *what* as subject.

Using the Conversation Notes (page 10)
Give the students two minutes to look over the information. Ask them to close their books and tell you what they found out. Write their answers on the board. Then let them compare their answers with the information in the book.

Examining Meaning and Use

➟ Pair the students and have them look at the Meaning and Use box on page 12 in the Student Book. Without the others hearing, assign each pair one of the six points in the box. (Note: Point 6 is the most subtle and should be assigned to the most able students. Point 7 should not be assigned at this point. This use of the present continuous is discussed and practiced in more detail in Chapter 2.)

Tell the students to write a short conversation illustrating the point they have been assigned. Circulate as they are working to help out as necessary.

Then call on the pairs to perform their conversation for the class. Let the other students guess which point each pair was assigned. Make sure that all six points are covered by the students who perform.

➟ The following activity is optional. It combines the present continuous and the simple present. Tell the students to look back at the simple present and the present continuous statements they wrote about themselves. Ask them to choose the most interesting statement of

each type and write them on a piece of paper. Emphasize that they should not choose negatives and that they should not write their names on the paper.

Collect the papers and redistribute them among the students. Tell the students to read and memorize the statements. Ask them to go around the room asking *yes/no* questions based on the statements until they find the person who wrote them. (For example: *Do you like snakes? Are you half Turkish? Are you learning to play the violin?*) Encourage the students to use short answers and contracted forms.

After everyone has found the person they were looking for, ask them to take their seats. Then tell them to make information questions based on the statements. They should make only one question using *who*; the rest of the questions must include other *wh-* words. (For example: *What animal does Rosa like? Who is half Turkish? What instrument is Sara learning to play?*) Let the students direct their questions to the whole class. If no one knows the answer, the original writer should answer. (For example: *I like snakes. I'm half Turkish. I'm learning to play the violin.*)

Stative Verbs

Examining Meaning

➟ Make the students aware of what they know about stative verbs by letting them analyze sentences. Write these sentences on the board:

I am having a car.

She is studying English.

We are practicing karate.

He is looking like my brother.

Tell the students that two sentences are wrong. Ask them if they know which two. *(The first and the last.)* If no one knows, tell them to look at the Meaning box on pages 15–16 in the Student Book.

If anyone knows, ask them if they know why. *(Because the verbs are stative and do not usually take the continuous form.)* As students tell you which statements are incorrect, place an asterisk next to these sentences. Ask the class to tell you of any other stative verbs they know. They may not be familiar with the grammatical term, but they may know the concept. Write all their answers on the board, correct and incorrect.

Then ask the students to compare the list on the board with the list in the Meaning box on pages 15–16. Erase any verbs that do not appear in the box.

Tell the students that they should use this list for reference when they are doing the exercises.

Examining Meaning and Use

➡ To make the students aware of what else they know about stative verbs, let them provide a context for the following sentences. Write them on the board. Assign pairs one sentence each. Give them about five minutes to think of a situation in which their sentence could occur. Call on the pairs to tell the class their situations:

I smell smoke.

I am smelling the tea to see what kind it is.

I see Bill in the yard.

I am seeing Bill.

I taste cinnamon in this tea.

I am tasting the chili to see if it's hot.

I weigh 140 pounds at home and 145 here.

I am weighing myself right now.

➡ Next write the following pairs of sentences on the board. Tell the students to look at the Meaning and Use box on pages 18–19 in the Student Book to find out if the meanings of each pair of sentences are the same or different. If they are different, ask them to explain the difference in meanings:

The bite itches.	The bite is itching.
He's being so stubborn.	He's so stubborn.
She is having a baby.	She has a baby.

Additional Activities

1. Newspaper search. Ask the students to bring to class a daily newspaper. Working in groups, they should find and copy headlines using verbs in the simple present continuous or the simple present. Tell them to underline the subject of the verb and write what pronoun would replace the subject. (Note: Use this as a form exercise only. Simple present and present continuous headlines may express meanings related to past, present, or future time.)

2. Dictation. Use items 4, 5, and 6 of Exercise 16 (Student Book page 20). Read the conversations aloud at normal speed as many times as students need to hear them in order to get them on paper. It is important to keep word groups together as you would in natural speech. (For example: *ham'ndeggs.*) This will help make the students aware of the contracted and unstressed words that they tend to omit in writing because they do not hear them.

3. Making generalizations. After doing Exercise 5 (Student Book page 7), ask the students to make general statements about the people in their class, the people from their country, the people in the city in which they are living at the moment, and so on.

4. What do you know about your classmates? As a class or in groups, one student asks another a simple present or present continuous question about a third classmate. If the student does not know the answer, he then asks the third classmate. For example:

A: What is Maria thinking about at this moment?
B: I don't know. What are you thinking about at this moment, Maria?
C: I'm thinking about lunch.

5. Writing about photographs. Bring in several magazines with full-page photographs and/or illustrations. Tell the students to write a paragraph about what is happening in the pictures at this moment. Ask them to use their imaginations and write sentences in the simple present that describe the likes/dislikes, daily routines, and family situations of the people in the pictures.

6. Writing about a short story. Ask the students to all read the same short story. Ask them to write sentences about both what is happening to the characters at the time of the story (the present continuous) and about the characters' personalities and routines in general (the simple present).

Then ask them to write comprehension and/or discussion questions about the story in the simple present. Have the students share their questions with the class. Write some questions on the board, asking different students to answer them.

Short stories
"Boxes" by Raymond Carver (in *Where I'm Calling From* by Raymond Carver, Vintage, 1986)
"My Father Sits in the Dark" by Jerome Weidman (in *Short Shorts*, edited by Irving Howe and Ilana Weiner Howe, Bantam, 1983)

Songs
"Here Comes the Sun" by George Harrison
"It Amazes Me" by Cy Coleman and Carolyn Leigh
"Tom's Diner" by Suzanne Vega

CHAPTER 2

Adverbs of Frequency, *There is* and *There are*, and Imperatives

Adverbs of frequency, *there is* and *there are,* and imperatives should be familiar to most students. Therefore, elicitation should work quite well in most classes. Try to get as much information as you can from the students. When they have told you what they know, you can fill in the gaps or correct any misconceptions.

Using the Preview

➠ Students should have their books closed. Write the heading *adverbs of frequency* on the board and say to the students *I eat out occasionally.* Write the word *occasionally* on the board under the heading. Next ask the students *How often do you eat out?* Tell them to think of a different one- or two-word answer such as *occasionally.* List their answers on the board. When the students have given you as many adverbs of frequency as they can come up with, tell them to look at the Preview on page 25 in the Student Book.

Adverbs of Frequency

Examining Meaning

➠ To elicit adverbs of frequency, talk about courtship and marriage customs. First draw a vertical arrow on the board with 100% on top of the arrow and 0% underneath it. (Refer to page 26 in the Student Book.) Ask the students questions. (For example: *Do men in your country propose marriage to women? Do women ever propose to men? Do parents in your country allow teenaged girls to go out with boys? Do women get married before their twentieth birthday? Do men date many women before they get married? Do marriages end in divorce?*) Students should answer using adverbs of frequency.

As students answer, ask them to come up and write the adverb of frequency in its proper place on the scale on the board. Ask the class if they agree before moving on to the next question and answer. If a student uses an adverb of frequency that is already on the board, give her a chance to think of an alternative if there is one. If she cannot think of another, let the class help.

Stop when you think you have enough adverbs up and down the scale or when students are unable to think of any more. Then ask the students to compare the list on the board with the list in the Meaning box on page 26 in the Student Book and tell you any adverbs they have left out.

Examining Form

➠ The rules governing the placement of the adverbs of frequency are fairly straightforward and serve as a good structure for students to analyze. With lower-level students, this can be done as a whole-class activity. With more advanced students, it can be done in groups of three or four.

Write the following sentences on the board and use them to elicit from the students rules for the placement of the adverbs of frequency. If they need help, tell them to look at the positions of the adverb of frequency, the main verb, and the auxiliary if there is one. Write the rules on the board as the students tell you. If a rule is incorrect, point to a sentence on the board that contradicts it. If the students want to include sentences that are not listed (for example: *Sometimes I go too. Is he always late?*), tell them that they are only giving rules for the type of sentences that are on the board at the moment:

1. She is often here.
2. He never goes out.
3. I don't always go.
4. She isn't often angry.

When you are finished writing the rules the students give you, tell them to compare their rules on the board with the rules in the Form box on pages 27–28 in the Student Book. Ask them if they would like to make any changes to the rules on the board. Ask them which points in the Form box are not included in their rules (*yes/no questions in point 3, and all of 4, 5*).

Examining Use

➠ Get the students to notice the use of the adverbs of frequency by asking them to think about the difference in these two exchanges:

Mary is so thoughtful. She always gives me presents.
I wonder what Mary wants from me. She's always giving me presents.

Ask the students to tell you which statement sounds more negative. *(The second sentence.)*

Ask them to find out the reason by looking at the Use box on page 29 in the Student Book.

Working in pairs, the students should write two short conversations. In one conversation they should use adverbs of frequency with the simple present. In the other, they should complain about something and use adverbs of frequency with the present continuous. Then call on different pairs to share their conversations with the class.

There Is and There Are

Examining Form

➡ If you would like, you can ask the students to read about *there is* and *there are* in the Preview section on page 25 in the Student Book before they come to class.

➡ Elicit *there is* and *there are* by having the students describe a section of town near your school. On the board, draw a simple map of the area including street names. Call on different students to come up to the board and mark places on the map as they talk about them. (For example: *There's a dry cleaner at the corner of Main and High. There are two gas stations on Green Street.*)

Next have students ask you and then each other questions about neighborhoods. (For example: *Is there a pharmacy in your neighborhood?*)

Troubleshooting: Some students might have difficulty distinguishing *there*, *their* and *they're* when they hear these phrases. Go over the meaning of each of these phrases, and tell the students that all three are pronounced the same way. Then dictate funny sentences using *there, they're* and *their*. (For example: *Their books are over there. They're there, near their coats. There is their dog.*)

Examining Meaning and Use

➡ Write the words *announcement, description,* and *fact* on the board as column headings. Then give the students three minutes to read the information in the Meaning and Use box on page 34 in the Student Book. With books closed, ask the students to write an example of each use of *there is* and *there are*. Call on different students to read their examples to the class.

Imperatives

Examining Form

➡ (Before class, you might want to ask the students to read the conversation in the Preview on page 25 in the Student Book and find out what an imperative does.) In class, to practice the imperative, do an imperative chain with the students. Start by instructing a student to do something. The student does what she was told and then tells another student to do something, and so on. Every student must use a different verb.

➡ Write the word *imperative* on the board with an example sentence. (For example: *Wait here.*) Ask what the difference between an imperative and other sentences is. *(An imperative usually has no stated subject.* **You** *is implied. An imperative uses the simple form of the verb, for example,* **be, have, look,** *etc. This means the verb does not change form.)*

Examining Meaning and Use

➡ To practice the meaning and use of imperatives, have the students write conversations. Start by telling the students to familiarize themselves with the information in the Meaning and Use box on page 37 in the Student Book.

Then assign pairs a category — *commands, requests,* etc. Do not assign the category *signs*. Each pair must write a conversation that contains at least two imperatives in their assigned category.

➡ As a homework assignment, ask the students to look for and write down five examples of signs using imperatives. In class the next day, have some students write their examples on the board. Try to get as many different ones as possible. Tell the students to underline the simple form of the verb. If students give any incorrect examples (for example: *No smoking. You must be eighteen years old.*), put a line through them and discuss why these are not imperatives. If they do not provide incorrect examples, you can supply a few.

Using the Conversation Note (page 37)
Call on a student to read the information aloud. Make sure the students understand that they should still leave out *you* when they are doing the exercises.

Additional Activities

1. Descriptive writing. Ask the students to write a paragraph describing the city or town where they live. Tell them to use *there is/there are* and adverbs of frequency in as many sentences as possible. (For example: *There are always a lot of cars in the streets of New York City. People rarely pay attention to traffic lights*.)

Then have the students write a paragraph describing an ideal place they would like to spend a vacation. (For example: *There are many beautiful sandy beaches in Rio de Janeiro. The water is always clean and the waves are never dangerous*.)

2. Favorite recipes. Ask the students to share with the class favorite recipes for dishes that are typical in their countries.

3. Writing about different customs. Ask the students to give written instructions to a group of American students visiting their countries. The American students are worried that they will offend people because they do not know local customs. (For example: *In Japan, don't leave your chopsticks in your rice bowl*.)

4. Writing advice. Ask the students to write advice to a friend who is about to get married.

5. Reading. Have the students read the short story listed below. They should pay special attention to the uses of imperatives. Ask them to write two or three examples of the different uses of imperatives. Then have the students share their examples with the class.

Short story
"Girl" by Jamaica Kincaid (in *At the Bottom of the River* by Jamaica Kincaid, Penguin, 1992)

Song
"Yakety-Yak" by The Coasters

CHAPTER 3

Expressing Past Time: The Simple Past, *Used to,* and the Past Continuous

Most intermediate-level students will be quite familiar with the simple past and the past continuous. However, many students will probably still make errors when making questions and negative statements in the simple past. You may want to have students memorize irregular past tense verb forms if they do not know them well. Make sure the students know that there is an irregular-verb list in the Appendix at the back of their Student Book.

Students probably will have problems deciding when to use the simple past and the past continuous. Some students may never have encountered *used to,* and initially most probably will confuse it with *be used to. Would* will also cause confusion for some students because they are most familiar with it in polite phrases such as *Would you like a cup of tea?*

Using the Preview

➡ Give the students two or three minutes to read the Preview on page 43 in the Student Book. This will give them enough time to acquaint themselves with the material and the grammatical terms in this chapter. Then ask the students to find all the simple past sentences, past continuous sentences, and sentences with *used to.* Call on different students to read the sentences aloud. (Do not let them leave out the sentences with the past form of *be*.)

Ask the students if there are any verb forms that they have never seen before. Make a mental note of those students who are coming to the material without any background.

The Simple Past

Examining Form: The Simple Past of Regular and Irregular Verbs

➡ The following activity will help students to review the form of the simple past. Students should have their books closed. Write the words *regular* and *irregular* as column headings on the left side of the board. Make two statements about yourself using one regular and one irregular verb. (For example: *I worked for three hours yesterday. I ate lunch at noon.*) Write the verbs under the proper column.

Now call on four or five students to make two statements about themselves using one regular and one irregular verb. Write the verbs in the correct columns exactly as the students use them in their statements. Each time, ask the class whether the verb form is correct. If it is not, ask them to tell you how to correct it. Tell the students to look at the irregular-verb list in the Appendix. Remind them to use this list as a reference when doing the exercises. You may also decide to give a quiz or quizzes on this material if the students need more time to practice.

Next choose one irregular and one regular verb and use them in two sentences beginning with *I*. (For example: *I took a taxi to the airport. I played tennis yesterday.*) Write these sentences on the board. Underneath *I* write all the subject pronouns *(you, he, she, we, they)* except *it*. Ask the students which pronouns require a different verb form. *(None of them.)*

➡ To analyze the negative and question forms, write these incorrect sentences on the board:

Did he went with you?

She didn't wanted it.

What did he saw?

Who did left?

Ask the students what these sentences have in common. *(They are all incorrect.)* Mark each one with an asterisk. Then let the students tell you why these sentences are wrong. Ask them to correct the sentences. Write the students' corrected versions on the board exactly as they tell you. If they make mistakes in their corrections, do not tell them at this time.

Now ask the students to look at the Form box on pages 44–45 in the Student Book to check their answers. Let them tell you what corrections, if any, need to be made.

Using the Conversation Notes (page 45)

As the students follow along in their books, read over the information. Make sure that you read the spoken forms aloud in an informal conversational style so that the students will hear the consonant changes and notice the elisions.

Then give them this short dictation. Tell the students that you are going to read the spoken form but that they should write the full written form:

Spoken Form	Written Form
Didja leave early?	Did you leave early?
Did'e do it?	Did he do it?
When'd he finish?	When did he finish?
Who'ja get?	Who did you get?

Examining Form: The Simple Past of *Be*

➡ To elicit the simple past of *be*, ask the students to close their eyes and try to remember a place from their past. It can be where they once lived, or a place that they visited. The most important thing is that it be in the past.

Give them one or two minutes to see the place in their minds. Then call on different students to talk about the place. If they seem reticent, tell them about a place in your past. As they talk about their place, write down only the sentences that contain the past of *be*. (For example: *It was a very beautiful place. It wasn't very big. There were a lot of trees. We weren't very happy there.*) If a student gives you a sentence with an incorrect verb form, write it on the board and go back to it later. If a student makes another kind of error, simply say it aloud correctly and write it on the board. Stop when you have elicited *was/wasn't/were/weren't*.

Tell the students to write down one *yes/no* question and one *wh-* question that they would ask another student about his special place.

Call on different students to ask their questions. Write several on the board. Remind the students to use the Form box on pages 50–51 to make sure that the sentences on the board are correct.

Examining Meaning and Use

➡ Begin analyzing the meaning and use of the simple past by using the information in the box on page 53 in the Student Book. Go over the first three points one by one. After each point, give students a minute to think of a sentence that illustrates that point. Call on different students to say their sentences aloud.

As the class works in groups of three or four, tell the students to write short skits that practice the different uses of the simple past. Give them ten to fifteen minutes to complete the task. Emphasize that they should incorporate as many uses of the simple past as they can. Tell them to think soap opera!

Call on as many groups as you have time for to perform for the class. Students may feel disappointed if they are not able to perform. Therefore, consider devoting some time to performances over the next few classes.

Focus on Vocabulary: Prepositions of Time

➧ Write some time phrases on the board. (For example: *2010, the 1990s, Wednesday, the summer, May 19, the afternoon, 8:30 A.M.,* etc.) Mix them up. Ask the students what prepositions to use with each word or phrase. If they are unsure of what a preposition is, write *in, at,* and *on* on the board.

Write the preposition next to the phrase as the students tell you. Do not correct. If there is any controversy, simply write a question mark next to the preposition.

Tell the students to look at the chart on page 60 in the Student Book to check the information on the board. Let them tell you what corrections need to be made. (Note: You might want to point out to the students that the inverted pyramid illustrates how the prepositions *in, on,* and *at* go from larger time periods (the wide part of the triangle) to smaller, more specific time at the narrow part of the triangle.)

Used to

Examining Form

➧ Use dictation to begin the analysis of *used to.* Dictate these sentences:

I used to live alone.

She didn't use to like me.

Did he use to study here?

Where did they use to work?

Who used to teach him?

Call on different students to write the sentences on the board. Do not hesitate to call on students whom you think will have problems. One of the purposes of this exercise is to make students aware of the difficulty in distinguishing between *use to* and *used to.* Tell the students that many native speakers also confuse the two.

Ask the students to look at the Form box on pages 62–63 in the Student Book to check their sentences. Go over the sentences one by one and make corrections as they tell you.

Examining Meaning and Use

➧ To illustrate the use of *used to,* talk about yourself as an example and compare your life ten to fifteen years ago with your life now. Write two statements about yourself on the board. One statement should be in the past. It should not include *used to,* but you should be able to transform it into that structure. Give the transformed example. (For example: *When I was younger, I wore my hair long. Now I have short hair./ I used to wear my hair long.*)

Now tell the students to think about the differences between their lives now and their lives in their native countries. (If the students are still in their native countries, ask them to compare life fifty years ago with life now.) Tell them to write two sentences with *used to* and two with *didn't use to.*

Call on different students to read their sentences aloud. If there are any problems, note them on the board and ask the students to correct them using the information in the Meaning and Use box on page 64 in the Student Book.

➧ To introduce the students to the use of *would* for past habit, tell them of a memory from your past. (Alternatively, read them the one in point 4 in the Meaning and Use box on page 64 in the Student Book.)

Ask the students to write a short paragraph (three or four lines) detailing a memory. They should begin the paragraph with *used to* and continue with *would.*

Ask the students where they have heard or seen *would* before. (*In polite requests and offers. For example: Would you please close the window? Would you like some water?*) Point out that this *would* is spelled and pronounced the same but it has a very different meaning.

The Past Continuous

Examining Form

> **Troubleshooting:** The past continuous is often taught in conjunction with time clauses beginning with *when* and *while*. However, *when* and *while* clauses are not presented until Chapter 5. Therefore, do not use *when* and *while* in your examples. If the students ask questions regarding the use of *when* and *while*, tell them those structures will be covered in Chapter 5.

➡ You must set this activity up before class. Ask two or three colleagues to come to your classroom. Give them each an activity to mime. (For example: dancing, cleaning, swimming, horseback riding, etc.) You should also participate. Two guests should be miming the same action at the same time. (If no other teachers are available, ask students to help.)

Let the guests do the activity in front of the class for thirty seconds to one minute. Then stop the activity. Ask the students to describe what they saw. Try not to ask in the past continuous. However, if they give you answers in the simple past, ask them very pointedly *What was everyone doing?* Write the answers on the board.

➡ Ask the students to think of a time from the day before (for example: *3:00 P.M., 7:11*). Call on different students to ask each other what they were doing at that time.

Note any problems on the board. Tell the students to look at the Form box on pages 67-68 in the Student Book. Go over any points that still seem problematic.

Examining Meaning and Use

➡ Describe a scene to demonstrate the meaning and use of the past continuous. Tell the students that the class as a whole is going to write a story. First, however, they must set the scene.

Together, choose a place. (For example: *A park on a sunny day, a haunted mansion late at night, a crowded party,* etc.) Tell the students that to set the scene you are going to describe everything that was happening as the story began. Give them a sentence to start. (For example: *It was a dark and stormy night. It was a bright and sunny afternoon.*) Call on a volunteer to continue with one sentence. (For example: *The wind was blowing.*) Write the sentences on the board. If there are verb form errors, ask the class for the correct

form. If there are other errors, correct them yourself and go on. When adding a new sentence, each student must repeat the sentences that came before. After five or seven sentences, stop the activity. Ask the students to write down the sentences.

Tell the students to look at the Meaning and Use box on page 69 in the Student Book to check the sentences they wrote down.

Additional Activities

1. Examining a short story. Have the students read a short story that is narrated in the past tense. Tell them to look for examples of the simple past, the past continuous, and *used to*. Ask them to explain why the author chose these tenses.

2. Comics search. Ask the students to bring to class a copy of a local newspaper. Tell them to read the comics and circle examples of the simple past, the past continuous, and/or *used to*. Ask them to explain why these tenses were used.

3. Listening for errors. Read aloud one or two paragraphs of a short story. Make four or five errors with past tense forms. These errors could include missing -*ed* endings, -*ed* endings on irregular verbs, *didn't* + verb + -*ing*, or *used to* + verb + -*ed*. Tell the students to listen for the errors. Then ask them what the errors were and have them give you the correct forms.

4. Dictation. Use items 1 and 2 in Exercise 3 in the Student Book (page 47); items 2 and 3 in Exercise 4 (page 48); and items 2 and 3 in Exercise 16 (page 63).

CHAPTER 4

Expressing Future Time: *Be Going to*, *Will*, the Present Continuous, and the Simple Present; Connecting Sentences

Most students will have already been introduced to *be going to* and *will*. However, many will not have a clear idea of the different ways that they are used. In addition, the concept of using the present continuous and the simple present to express future time may well be new to most students. Sometimes the differences between these forms are very subtle. Therefore, many students may require further exposure to English in order to attain a thorough understanding of their uses.

Using the Preview

➡ The students should have their books closed. On the board make four columns and number them 1 through 4. Ask the students to listen for sentences that refer to the future. Read the three Preview examples on page 75 in the Student Book one at a time. (When reading the conversation, stop after each speaker.)

After you read the first example (the recorded announcement), have the students identify the future sentence. Ask a student to write it on the board in the first column. Continue until you have one or more examples of different future forms in each column.

Tell the students that there are four different future forms. Ask the students to identify them. Underline the forms and write the names of the forms on the top of each column: *will*, *be going to*, *present continuous*, and *simple present*.

Then give the students three or four minutes to read the material in the Preview as a follow-up.

Be Going to

Examining Form

➡ To introduce *be going to*, use your and the students' weekend plans. The students should have their books closed. Write a sentence on the board stating your

plans for the weekend. (For example: *I am going to go to the movies this weekend.*) Call on various students to tell you about any plans they have for the weekend. Most students should have no problem doing this. As they answer, call on other students to write the answers on the board. Make sure that they write their answers in the third-person singular. (Elicits *he*, *she*, or the person's name.)

Call on a student to tell you what plans he and his friends have for the weekend. Ask that student to come to the board and write down the sentence. (Elicits *we*.)

Ask another student to tell you what plans she and her friends have for the weekend. Call on a different student to write this sentence on the board. (Elicits *they*.)

Call on students to tell you how to transform the sentences on the board into negative statements. Make sure that both ways are represented wherever they are possible. (For example: *She isn't going…/She's not going….*)

➡ To practice question formation, use interview questions. Tell the students to choose a famous person and write interview questions about that person's future plans. Everyone must write at least two *yes/no* questions (one with *is*, another with *are*) and five information questions with different *wh-* words. Make sure the students write at least one question with *who* or *what* as subject.

Give the students five minutes to write. Ask them to work in pairs and exchange their papers. Tell them to look at the Form box on pages 76–77 in the Student Book to check the question forms. They should point out any errors, but not correct them. Circulate as they are working to help as needed. Then tell the students to return the papers to their partners. Give everyone two minutes to make corrections.

Call on students to read their questions aloud. Write examples of the different question types on the board.

Focus on Vocabulary: Future Time Phrases

➡ Before class, familiarize yourself with the time phrases given on pages 78–79 in the Student Book. In class, elicit as many of the time phrases as you can. The students should have their books closed. First ask the students to tell you as many ways as they can think of to answer the question *When are you going to _____?* Change the verb to elicit different phrases. (For example: *When are you going to hand in your homework? Tomorrow. When are you going to finish this course? In two weeks.*)

Write on the board the phrases as they are given. Divide up the board so that you can display the information as it is shown on pages 78–79.

Then tell the students to look at the time phrases on pages 78–79. Ask them to find any phrases that are not on the board. If the class has come up with phrases that are not on these pages, you can suggest that the students add them.

Examining Meaning and Use

➡ Write the following sentences on the board. Do not write the numbers in parentheses:

Sara can't come to the party. She and Fred are going to go to Las Vegas for the weekend. *(#2)*

What a waste of time! Everyone knows this plan isn't going to work. *(#3)*

My future is all set. I'm going to join the army! *(#1)*

Something wonderful is going to happen tonight. I just know it! *(#3)*

Working in pairs, the students should match the sentences with the points in the Meaning and Use box on page 80 in the Student Book. Go over their answers as a class (answers shown after each sentence above).

Will

Examining Form

➡ Have the students analyze incorrect sentences to introduce the correct form of *will*. The students should have their books closed. Write these sentences on the board. Ask students what they have in common. *(They all use **will** and they are all incorrect.)* Place an asterisk next to each sentence:

She willn't do it.

Will come he? Yes, he'll.

How long you will need it?

He will leaves tomorrow.

Tell the students to work in pairs and look at the Form box on page 82 in the Student Book. Ask them to use this information to correct the sentences.

Using the Conversation Notes (page 83)
Give the students two minutes to read over the Conversation Notes. Then read the simple present and future sentences in an informal, conversational style. Ask the students if they hear a difference. Read the

other examples of spoken form at a normal conversational rate.

Then dictate the following sentences to help the students focus on the difference between verbs with and without *will*:

We'll go with him every day.

They work very hard.

You'll have to leave.

They'll work very hard.

You have to leave.

We go with him every day.

Examining Meaning and Use

➡ Contrast sentences with *will* and *be going to* to introduce the meaning and use of *will*. Write these pairs of sentences on the board:
a. She'll   have a baby soon.
   She's going to
b. I'll   drive carefully.
   I'm going to
c. She'll probably   be here on time.
   She's going to
d. The mayor will   give a speech tomorrow.
   The mayor is going to
e. I'll   be in Chicago next week.
   I'm going to
f. That's a great idea.   I'll   do it.
                                    I'm going to

Ask the students to tell you the differences, if any, between the sentences. Make short notes of their ideas on the board.

Divide the class into groups of three. Let them look at the Meaning and Use box on pages 85–86 in the Student Book. Tell them to match the *will* sentences above with the points in the box *(a. 3; b. 1; c. 3; d. 5; e. 7; f. 2)*. They may also want to look back at the Meaning and Use box for *be going to* on page 80.

The Present Continuous as a Future Form

Examining Meaning and Use

➡ Divide the students into groups. Tell them to look back at the Preview on page 75 and find a sentence with the present continuous as future. *(I'm taking the hotel van to the airport at 12:30.)* Write it on the board. Tell the students to look at the Meaning and

Use box on page 94 in the Student Book and explain why the present continuous is used as a future form in this sentence. Then write the following sentences on the board. Ask the students if they are all correct. *(The second sentence isn't possible because of point 2.)* Place an asterisk next to the second sentence:

We're going shopping.

I'm winning the lottery.

He's going to Florida.

They're having breakfast with us.

Then tell the students to come up with short two-line conversations with the three correct sentences. Give the students three to five minutes to do this activity.

Call on different groups to read their conversations. Ask the students to relate the points in the box to the conversations.

Note: If students have problems with the present continuous forms, ask them to review the Form box on pages 9–10 in the Student Book.

The Simple Present as a Future Form

Examining Meaning and Use

➡ Read aloud these sentences. Have the students tell you which simple present verbs probably refer to the future:

The movie starts at 8:10 on Wednesday evening. *(yes)*

My car starts every morning.

The new mall opens this month. *(yes)*

The store always opens at 9:00 A.M.

He arrives at 3:00 P.M. all the time.

He arrives at 3:00 P.M. tomorrow. *(yes)*

Tell the students to the look at the Meaning and Use box on pages 95–96 in the Student Book to check their answers.

Note: If students have problems with the simple present forms, ask them to review the Form box on pages 2–3 in the Student Book.

Connecting Sentences

Examining Form: *But*

➡ The students should have their books closed. Have them combine sentences to introduce the form of state-

ments with *but*. Write these pairs of statements on the board:

Sam skis.	Becky doesn't ski.
Their class is big.	Our class isn't big.

Ask the students to combine the sentences. If they use *and*, tell them to use *but*. If they do not use the auxiliary alone in the second clause *(Sam skis, but Becky doesn't ski.)*, ask them how to reduce the clause. If they do not know how, show them.

Ask the students to look at the box on page 98 to find out when they cannot use the auxiliary to replace the second verb phrase. *(When the verb phrase is different. For example: Their class is large, but our class is small. Sam skis well, but Becky is a beginner.)*

Examining Form: *And...Too/And...Either*

➡ The students should have their books closed. Use combined statements to examine the forms of these phrases. Write two combined statements on the board. *(For example: I like coffee, and you do too. He doesn't study, and I don't either.)*

Ask the students to tell you what two statements were combined to make each of the sentences on the board. *(For example: I like coffee. You like coffee./He doesn't study. I don't study.)*

Tell them to look at the Form box on page 99 in the Student Book to check their answers.

Examining Form: *And So.../And Neither...*

➡ The students should have their books closed. Use *and...too/and...either* as a springboard for introducing *and so.../and neither...*. Write two sentences with *and...too/and...either*. *(For example: He went, and I did too./Mike can't go, and we can't either.)*

Ask the students to give you another way of saying the same things. If they cannot, give them a hint and write *so* and *neither* on the board. If they still do not know, tell them to look at the Form box on page 101 to find the answer.

If at least one student can give you a sentence, write his sentence on the board. Do not correct any problems with *so* and *neither* at this time. Tell the students to look at the Form box on page 101 to check the sentence.

Ask them to tell you the important form difference between using *too* and *so* and *either* and *neither*. *(And so and and neither are inverted forms. The auxiliary comes before the subject.)*

Examining Meaning and Use: *But/And*

➡ The students should have their books closed. Use ridiculous statements to introduce the concepts of *too/either/so/neither* as rejoinders. Go up to a student and say *I hate long, boring movies.* Ask her to respond. If she says *I hate long, boring movies too,* ask someone to give you a shorter way of saying that. Someone will probably say *I do too.* If they do, write it on the board. If they do not, write it on the board as an example.

Go up to another student and make a similar comment. (For example: *I don't like fish with chocolate sauce.*) Go through the same procedure as the above.

Make two more ridiculous statements to elicit *So do I* and *Neither do I.* (For example: *I love getting good marks. I don't like painful visits to the dentist.*)

Tell the students to look at the Meaning and Use box on pages 102–103 in the Student Book to find the rejoinders used in informal conversations.

Note that points 1–3 of the Meaning and Use box were covered in the presentation of form that immediately precedes this section.

Additional Activities

1. Writing a conversation. Working in small groups, the students should imagine that a group of several eighteen-year-olds are spending an evening together talking about their futures. Have the students write the conversation. Ask them to include at least one example of each of the four forms of the future they have just studied. Circulate to help students correct their own errors. Collect the conversations when the students are finished and give the best one as a dictation.

2. Writing about life in the future. Ask the students to write a short essay that describes life in the year 2050.

3. Advertisement search. Have the students bring to class newspapers and magazines. Ask them to look for examples of the four forms of the future, and have them decide if any of the other three forms could replace the one being used.

4. Dictation. Use the conversation between *You* and *Friend* in the Preview on page 75 of the Student Book.

CHAPTER 5

Complex Sentences: Past Time Clauses, Future Time Clauses, and Real *If* Sentences

Most students will probably not have too much trouble with these structures. However, if you can afford the time, do not work through the material too quickly. It can serve as a consolidation and review of the tenses the students have just worked on. In addition, students who find grammatical concepts difficult to grasp will probably welcome a break before moving on to the present perfect and present perfect continuous.

The chapter contains some grammatical terms that will help students to understand the material. Use the Preview in the Student Book or another activity to introduce this terminology before you begin the chapter. Note that all these terms can be found in the Glossary at the back of the Student Book.

Using the Preview

➡ Introduce the students to the Glossary with this activity. Tell them to read over the Preview. Meanwhile, write these terms on the board:

complex sentence   independent clause

dependent clause   time clause (future/past)

if clause

Give the students ten minutes to look up the terms and find an example of each one in the Preview. Circulate as they are working to make sure that they understand the activity. Then go over their answers.

Past Time Clauses

Examining Form

➡ The students should have their books closed. Review the past continuous from Chapter 3. Ask a student *What were you doing last night at eight o'clock?* (Possible answer: *I was watching television.*)

Ask another student to tell you about the first student. *(Ali was watching television at eight o'clock last night.)* Write this sentence on the board.

Elicit a time clause with the past continuous by asking other questions. Find a student who has an alarm clock at home. Ask him this question: *What were you doing when the alarm rang?* (Possible answer: *I was sleeping.)* Ask another student to tell you about what the first student said. *(Clara was sleeping when the alarm rang.)* Write this sentence on the board.

Elicit a time clause with the past tense by asking other questions. Ask a student this question: *What did you do before you came to class today?* (Possible answer: *I did my homework.)* Ask another student to tell you about the first one. *(Miguel did his homework before he came to class.)* Write this sentence on the board.

Ask the students to identify the past time clauses in the sentences on the board. (For example: …*when the alarm rang…before he came to class.)* Underline them. Circle the words *when* and *before.* Tell the students that these are time words and they begin a past time clause. Ask them to tell you any other time words they can think of. (For example: *while, after,* etc.) Write all of their answers on the board.

Choose one of the sentences on the board and switch the clauses. (For example: *When the alarm rang Clara was sleeping.)* Ask the students if this sentence is correct (*No. It needs a comma after the time clause.)* and whether it has the same or a different meaning as the other sentence. *(The same meaning.)*

Tell the students to look at the Form box on page 110 to check the time words on the board and their answers to the questions in the step above.

> **Troubleshooting:** Do not belabor this activity. It must move quickly or students will get bored. If students ask you the difference between *when* and *while*, tell them to wait. It is dealt with in the very next box.

Examining Meaning and Use

➡ The students should have their books closed. Use student-generated sentences to check their understanding of the order of events. Divide the class into pairs. Ask each pair to write sentences with past time clauses under these time word headings: *before, after, when,* and *while.* Some of their sentences should begin with the time clause and some should begin with the main clause. Just for now, tell them that the time clause with *while* must use the past continuous. Do not get into an extensive discussion of *while.*

Then write four columns on the board, spaced two and two. The column headingss should read:

   1st action   2nd action   2nd action   1st action

Call on different students to write their sentences on the board. They should write each clause in the correct column. If they seem confused, do one together as an example.

Continue until you have examples of all the time words and the different configurations. Analyze each sentence with the class. Write a question mark next to any sentences that students seem unsure about. Then ask them to open their books to pages 111–112 and use points 1–4 to check on the order of events.

Give them three or four minutes to read the information. Go back to the sentences on the board and make any corrections that are necessary.

➡ Tell the students to close their books. Drop a heavy book on the floor. Ask a student *What were you doing when I dropped my book on the floor?* (Possible answer: *I was listening to you.)* On the board, write *Tom was listening to the teacher when she dropped a book on the floor.* Then ask the students if they know how to say this using *while.* (For example: *While Tom was listening to the teacher, she dropped a book on the floor.)* If they do not know, tell them. Write the sentence on the board.

Write the following two sentences on the board. Check comprehension by calling on extroverted students to act them out. (Change the verbs if you prefer, but keep the forms):

   Bill and Mary were arguing while Tina was dancing with Mike.

   While Bill and Mary were arguing, Tina and Mike left.

Ask the students to study the sentences and tell you the difference in meaning of the use of the past continuous and simple past. Write the word *when* underneath *while* in each sentence and ask the students if that is correct. *(Yes.)*

Then tell them to open their books to page 112 to check their answers.

Future Time Clauses

Examining Form

➡ The students should have their books closed. Write this sentence on the board:

   Before you leave, I will give you some homework.

Ask the students which parts of the sentence refer to the future. *(Both.)* Ask them which verb is marked for the future *(Only **give**.)* Tell them to look at the Form box on page 118 in the Student Book to find out why.

Examining Meaning and Use

➠ The students should have their books closed. Use the same technique as with past time clauses to have students analyze the order of events.

Working in pairs, the students should write sentences with time clauses under the headings *before, after,* and *when.* Some of their sentences should begin with the time clause and some should begin with the main clause.

Write four columns on the board spaced two and two. The column headings should read:

   1st action   2nd action   2nd action   1st action

Call on different students to write their sentences on the board. They should write each clause under the correct column. If they seem confused, do one together as an example.

Continue until you have examples of all the time words and the different configurations. Analyze each sentence with the class. Write a question mark next to any sentences that students seem unsure about. Ask them to open their books to page 120 to use points 2 and 3 to check the order of events.

Give them two to three minutes to read the information. Go back to the sentences on the board and make any corrections that are necessary.

Real *If* Sentences

Examining Form

➠ The students should have their books closed. Call on students to give you an example of a sentence with *if*. If they give examples of unreal *if*, just tell them that you want a real situation. Write one or two correct examples on the board.

Ask them if the clauses can be interchanged without changing the meaning. *(Yes.)* Write at least one of the sentences on the board, switching the order of the clauses. Then have the class look at the Form box on page 122 in the Student Book to check their answers.

Examining Meaning and Use

➠ The students should have their books closed. Have them examine the different uses of *if*. Write the following *if* clauses on the board and ask the students to complete them in their notebooks:

   If you save your money, _____

   If you work hard today, _____

   If you buy this top-of-the-line music system, _____

   If you buy this cheaper music system, _____

   If you don't study hard, _____

   If you walk out of here now, _____

Give the students two minutes to complete the sentences any way they wish. Call on different students to read aloud their completed sentences. Write one or two possibilities for each clause on the board.

Tell the students to look at the Meaning and Use box on pages 123–124 to find the use of each sentence. Tell them to note any uses that have no example sentence, as well as any sentences that do not match the uses given.

Additional Activities

1. Advertisement and advice-column search. Have the students look for sentences using future time clauses and real *if* clauses in both print and broadcast advertisements and newspaper advice columns.

2. Writing advertisements. Ask the students to write advertisements for different products, using future time clauses and real *if* clauses. (For example: *If you use Skin Smoother Beauty Cream, your wrinkles will vanish.)*

3. Talking about cultural behavior. Have the students write questions about cultural behavior and/or expectations in their countries using *will.* For example: *If a child in your country interrupts an adult, will the adult get angry? In your country, if a woman likes a man, will she ask him out on a date?* Then have the students move around the room and ask each other their questions.

4. Writing a conversation. Working in small groups, ask the students to imagine the following situation:

A young man is talking to the parents of the woman he wants to marry. Both the young man and his girlfriend are still studying and neither one has a job. The young woman's parents want to know the young man's plans for the future.

The parents ask him many questions using time clauses with *before*, *after*, and *when*. Have the students write the conversation. Collect their work and use the best conversation as a dictation.

5. Using the Preview. Ask the students to look at the conversation between *Parent* and *Teen* in the Preview on page 109. Have them finish the conversation using as many time clauses and real *if* sentences as possible.

6. Dictation. Use Exercise 5 (Student Book page 116).

Songs
"Hush Little Baby" (traditional folk song)
"When I'm Sixty-Four" by John Lennon and Paul McCartney

CHAPTER 6

Connecting the Past and the Present: The Present Perfect and the Present Perfect Continuous

Most intermediate-level students should be able to master the form of the present perfect and the present perfect continuous. Some students, however, may still have problems sustaining accuracy. While they should be expected to have a general idea of meaning and use once they complete this chapter, full understanding may require greater exposure to everyday English.

Using the Preview

➤ Write the numbers 1, 2, 3 across the board to make three columns. Instruct the students to open their books to the Preview on page 133. Tell them that there are three different ways to talk about the past in these examples. As you read the examples aloud together, ask the students to look for the three different past forms. Write the verb forms (for example: *have reached*) on the board as the students tell you. Have them tell you which column to write their example under. You may need to guide them by asking, for example, *Is **announced** the same form as **have learned**?* Then ask the students if they know what each of the three forms are called, and write *present perfect*, *present perfect continuous*, and *simple past* over the appropriate columns.

More able classes can read the information following the sample language and answer this question: *What is the main difference between the present perfect and the simple past tense?* More able students may even be able to suggest some differences first and then confirm their suggestions by reading the information.

The Present Perfect

Examining Form

➤ Use the topic of job interviews to elicit examples of the present perfect. Have the students look at the job interview conversation in the Preview on page 133.

Ask them if they can think of other job interview questions that begin with *Have you ever...?* (For example: *Have you ever used a fax machine?*) Write the questions students give you on the board.

Call on a student to answer the questions on the board. Try to elicit short answers. (For example: *Yes, I have./No, I haven't.*) Then call on a second student to ask and answer questions about the first: *Has Ana ever used a fax machine?* Try to elicit short answers. (*Yes, she has./No, she hasn't.*) Write the answer on the board.

Ask a third student who has used a computer how long he has known how to use it. Make sure he answers in a complete sentence. Write his answer on the board.

To elicit a negative statement, ask a student who has not used a fax machine if she has sent a fax recently. Again make sure she answers in a complete sentence. Write this sentence on the board too.

➡ Check the students' familiarity with the form of the present perfect. Ask them to identify the auxiliary and main verbs in the questions and statements on the board. Either have a volunteer come to the board to underline auxiliary verbs and double-underline main verbs, or ask the students to copy the sentences from the board and identify auxiliary and main verbs while working individually or in groups. Give the students a few minutes to work, then ask them what form the sentences have in common *(has or have + the past participle)*. Explain that this is the form for the present perfect.

Ask two students to change two of the sentences on the board into information questions, one using *who*, the other using *what*. Then tell the students to look at the end of the Form box on page 135 to check the sentences. Make corrections if necessary.

Troubleshooting: If many students seem unfamiliar with the past participle form of the verbs, refer them to the Appendix on irregular verbs at the back of their Student Books.

Using the Conversation Notes (page 135)
Students may have problems with the contractions of *has* and *have* in the present perfect with nouns, pronouns, and *wh-* words. They may confuse the contraction of *has* in the present perfect with *is*. For example, they may write the *'s* in *Mary's gone* as *is*, and the *'ve* in *They've gone* as *of*. Point out the problem. Then have the students read the sentences with the contracted forms. To practice, do the following dictation. Tell the students that you will pronounce contractions, but ask them to write the long forms:

She's won the race.
She's one of the winners.
The people've gone.
Who's read this book?
Whose book is this?
What've we learned?

Examining Meaning and Use: Indefinite Time

➡ Ask the students to write sentences similar to the answers they gave to the questions in the previous section about office experience. Write some of their sentences on the board. For example:

Joaquín has worked in an office.
Michel has never used a postage meter.
Trahn has written many memos.
Boris hasn't done word processing.

Point to one of the sentences. (For example: *Joaquín has worked in an office.*) Tell the students to change it to both the simple present and the simple past tense. (For example: *Joaquín works in an office* and *Joaquín worked in an office.*) Then ask how *Joaquín has worked in an office* differs in meaning from the other two sentences. Allow students to offer several different possibilities if they can. Make notes of their ideas on the board.

➡ Use personal questions to elicit more present perfect sentences. Prepare the questions carefully to ensure that they refer to an indefinite time in the past. (For example: *Have you ever read a novel in English? Have you ever eaten dinner at The Golden Lamb? Have you ever been a guest in an American home?*) Write the students' answers on the board. If they make mistakes, do not correct them at this time. Ask the students to give you full sentences. (For example: *No, I have never read a novel in English. Yes, I've eaten at The Golden Lamb many times.*)

Then tell the students to read the information in the Meaning and Use box on pages 137–138 to check if the answers they gave are correct or not. Ask them to correct the wrong answers. Conclude by asking the students this question: *Do any of the sentences tell you exactly when in the past the sentence happened? (No.)*

Examining Meaning and Use: Recent Time

➡ Use personal questions to elicit the present perfect. Prepare questions that refer to recent time. (For example: *Have you made a long distance phone call lately? Have you gone to a movie recently? In the last two days, have you had an argument with anyone?)* Write the questions on the board. Ask the students if they can tell what words in the sentences refer to recent past time *(lately, recently, In the last two days).* Call on different students to answer the questions. Write their answers on the board.

Now tell the students to look at the Meaning and Use box on page 142. Working in pairs, the students should write sentences to illustrate points 1 and 2. Call on individual students to read aloud their sentences. Go over the students' sentences one by one and ask the class if they are correct. If not, ask the students what corrections need to be made.

Examining Meaning and Use: Continuing Time up to Now

➡ Use personal questions to elicit the present perfect. Prepare the questions carefully to ensure that they refer to continuing time up to now. (For example: *For how many years have you worn glasses? How long has it been since you had a haircut? How long have you been in this room?)* Write the students' answers on the board.

Point to one of the sentences. (For example: *Yuki has worn glasses for twelve years.)* Ask the students to change it to the simple past tense. (*Yuki wore glasses for twelve years.*) Write this sentence on the board. Ask the students if the meaning of the two sentences is the same or different *(different).* See if they can tell you what the difference in meaning is. *(In the first sentence, Yuki still wears glasses, while in the second one she no longer wears them.)*

To illustrate the difference between the two sentences, draw a simple timeline on the board. Draw a horizontal line. Shade a section on the left to represent a twelve-year period in the past (for example, 1960–1972). Mark the timeline past the middle and label the mark with a date twelve years in the past. Mark the timeline near the right-hand end and label it *now.* Shade the section from the point *12 years ago* to *now* in order to represent the last twelve years. It should be clear that the past action began and ended in the past, and that the present perfect began in the past and continues up to now.

| 1960 | 1972 | 12 years ago | now |

Then tell the students to read the Meaning and Use box on page 146. Pairs should write three more sentences to illustrate the usage of *for* and *since* with the present perfect. Call on several different students to read aloud their sentences.

Examining Meaning and Use: The Present Perfect versus the Simple Past

➡ Make the students aware of how much they know about the use of the present perfect versus the simple past by having them analyze incorrect sentences. Write these incorrect sentences on the board. Mark them with an asterisk. Do not write the information in parentheses.

Columbus has sailed from Spain to North America. *(#2)*

I have seen her last week. *(#3)*

He has worked there two years ago. *(#5)*

She and I have gone to Disney World two times before she died. *(#1)*

A: When has the plane arrived? *(#4)*
B: At 3:05.

Tell the students that these sentences use the wrong form of the verb. Ask what form each sentence should use *(the simple past).* Ask the students if they can tell you why the present perfect forms are wrong. In some cases, students will probably not be able to give very precise answers. The point is to make them really think about the difference in meaning between the simple past and the present perfect. Make short notes of their answers on the board.

Now tell the students to look at the Meaning and Use box on pages 147–148. Give them five minutes to read the information. As a class, compare these explanations with the sentences and the students' notes on the board. Make any necessary changes. (Points 1–5 are covered, as indicated in the parentheses above.)

Together, look at the information in points 6 and 7. As a homework assignment, ask the students to look in the newspaper for examples of point 6, and to listen to conversations for any examples of point 7.

The Present Perfect Continuous

Examining Form

➡ Use the Preview on page 133 to elicit examples of the present perfect continuous with *he.* Have the students look at the telephone conversation. Tell them to assume that Alex has been lying and ask them to imagine what he has really been doing. Require that they answer in complete sentences. Write their answers on the board. (For example: *Alex has been playing soccer with his friends.)*

Working in groups, the students should copy the sentences from the board. Ask them to identify the main and auxiliary verbs. This task will probably cause some debate among students, as they may be confused by the fact that each sentence has two auxiliary verbs. Allow them to discuss this among themselves for a while before checking their answers.

Using one of the sentences on the board, call on a student to make a *yes/no* question and write it on the board. (For example: *Has Alex been playing soccer with his friends?*) Elicit short-answer responses. Write them on the board. (*Yes, he has./No, he hasn't.*) Then to elicit a negative statement, require that the students answer the question in a full sentence. (For example: *Alex hasn't been playing soccer with his friends.*) Write this sentence on the board too.

➡ Ask personal questions to elicit further examples of the present perfect continuous with *I*. Ask the students what they have been doing since the class began. (For example: *I've been reading. I've been sitting in my chair. I've been listening to you. I've been daydreaming.*) Make sure that they describe activities that were either unfinished or just being finished when you asked the question.

Write their correct answers on the board and approve them. Put an asterisk next to their incorrect answers. Ask the students to look at the incorrect sentences and correct any errors of form. Make corrections on the board. (If any of the sentences are incorrect because of meaning, erase them from the list, and write them somewhere else on the board. Come back and correct these sentences with the students after examining meaning and use.)

Ask the students to work in pairs to change two of the sentences on the board into information questions. Have two students write their questions on the board. Ask the students to look at the Form box on page 151 to check their answers and the sentences on the board.

Examining Meaning and Use

➡ Have the students familiarize themselves with the Meaning and Use box on pages 153–154 by matching the examples below with the points in the box. Divide the students into groups and assign one of the examples to each group. Ask each group to find the point in the box that best describes their example (shown in parentheses):

1. I've been having trouble sleeping lately, but last night I slept well. *(# 2)*

2. A: I've been taking a writing class. It's great.
   B: You're lucky. I've taken several writing classes, but I've never found a good one. *(# 5)*

3. Look at that mattress and those clothes. It looks as if someone has been living here. *(# 3)*

4. She's owned that old car for eight years. *(# 8)*

5. A: I've been studying English for two years and I'm not very good.
   B: Don't feel bad. I've studied Spanish for five years and I can hardly speak it. *(# 4)*

6. I've been standing here in the rain waiting for you for an hour! *(# 6)*

7. She's been cleaning her room for three hours. *(# 1)*

8. A: What have you been doing?
   B: I've been watching the weather forecast.
   A: How many times have you watched the weather forecast today?
   B: I've watched it four times so far. *(#7)*

If the examples are not yet on the board, write them there while the students work. Then call on a student from each group to tell the class their answer. Have the class read each Meaning and Use point to make sure that they agree. If they do not agree, mark the example with a question mark. Then go back and consider it again when you have finished with the other examples.

Additional Activities

1. Newspaper search. Ask the students to bring to class a copy of their daily newspaper. Working in small groups, the students should find and copy sentences with the present perfect. Tell them to label each sentence either *indefinite past, recent past,* or *continuing time up to now.*

2. *Have you ever...?* game. Ask the students to come up with questions starting with *Have you ever...?* that they would like to ask their classmates. Write the questions on the board. Have the students move around the classroom and ask the questions of different classmates. Ask the students about their classmates' answers. For example: *Paulo, who in this class has ever climbed a mountain?*

Note: Do not ask them to report their classmates' answers because that could require the past perfect (for example: *He said that he had never skied.*)

3. Dictation. Use Exercise 15 from Student Book page 155. Read *have* and *has* as contractions, but ask the students to write the long forms.

4. Writing about photographs. Bring in photographs from newspapers and magazines. Choose pictures that will allow the students to make several different guesses about what has been happening. Put the students in groups and ask them to write sentences about what the people in the photographs have been doing. The group that thinks of the greatest number of plausible answers is the winner.

5. Writing conversations with lies. Tell the class that they are going to practice telling lies using the present perfect and present perfect continuous. Put students in four groups and give each group one of these situations:

> A man is trying to impress a woman he finds attractive.

> A young woman is at a job interview for a well-paying job that she is not really qualified for.

> A teacher is talking to a student who has come to class half an hour late without his homework because he went to a party the night before.

> A mother wants to know how her teenaged daughter has been doing in school. The daughter has been failing all her classes and has gotten in trouble for her behavior in class. But she wants her mother to believe that she has been getting excellent grades and has pleased all her teachers.

Tell each group to write a conversation in which one of the characters tells several lies. Circulate around the classroom as the students are working and correct any errors in their conversations.

Then have two people in each group read their conversation aloud. Ask the rest of the class to guess who the characters are.

Songs

"Never Been to Spain" by Hoyt Axton
"The Battle Hymn of the Republic" (archaic language, but many examples of the present perfect)
"I've Been Loving You Too Long" by Otis Redding

CHAPTER 7

Social Modals: Requests, Permission, Suggestions, Advice, Opinions, Obligations, Necessity, Lack of Necessity, and Prohibition

Most intermediate-level students are probably already familiar with the most common modals. They may not, however, have realized that each modal can have more than one meaning or use. Another potential problem is the confusion between *must not* and *don't have to*. Even students who have studied these forms before may continue to confuse them. Do not deal with *must not* and *don't have to* until they are covered in the Meaning and Use box on page 191 of the Student Book.

Using the Preview

➡ Introduce the concept of modals. The students should have their books closed. Ask the students if they have ever heard of the term *modals* and if they can name a few. If they have not heard the term, explain that modals are words like *can* or *should*. Write these words on the board. Ask the students what other words they know that are grammatically similar to *can* and *should*. Write them on the board. If they say *have to, ought to*, and other items that are not true modals, write them on a different part of the board.

Tell the students to look at the language samples in the Preview on page 163. Ask them to tell you what true modals they will be studying in this chapter *(can, could, would, should, must, may)*. Check these modals on the list on the board, or add them if they are not there.

Ask the students in what way modals change the meaning of a statement. Write their ideas on the board. Then give them four or five minutes to read the information in the Preview and check their answers.

Ask the students to look at the Preview again and tell you what items they will be studying in this chapter that are not true modals *(have to, have got to, ought to, had better)*.

Social Modals

Examining Form

➡ To focus on the forms of modals, have the students analyze language samples in order to try to construct the rules themselves. The students should have their books closed. Write the following incorrect sentences on the board. Do not write the rules in parentheses that follow each sentence:

You can to borrow my car.
*(Rule: no **to** between the modal and the main verb.)*

You don't can borrow my car.
*(Rule: no **do**; negation comes after the modal.)*

Can she uses your car tomorrow?
(Rule: no -s on main verb.)

When do I can return your car tomorrow?
*(Rule: no **do**; question begins with **wh-** word followed by modal.)*

Ask the students what these sentences have in common. *(They're all incorrect.)* Mark each one with an asterisk. Ask the students to tell you the correct form of each sentence and the rules. Write the students' corrected versions and the rules on the board exactly as they tell you. If they make mistakes in their corrections and the rules, do not correct them at this time.

Now tell the students to look at the Form box on pages 164–165 to check their corrections and the rules. Ask them to tell you what further corrections, if any, need to be made to the information on the board.

Examining Meaning and Use: Requests

➡ Ask the students to judge the levels of formality of modals by analyzing situations. Books should be closed. Read these statements to the class. Then write them on the board:

Mother to son: Will you turn down that music?

Employee to boss: Could you sign these forms before the meeting?

Bus driver to passenger: Would you please sit down, sir?

Teacher to student: Can you close the door?

Husband to wife: Will you pick up some milk while you're out?

Two strangers: Could you open the door, please?

Tell the students to look at the statements and decide which are formal and which are informal. Mark their decisions on the board.

Now tell them to read the information in the Meaning and Use box on page 166 to check their answers.

> **Troubleshooting:** It is very important that the students realize that many of the rules regarding the use of modals are rules of thumb, rather than hard and fast dictums. The students should understand that some modals are generally used in more formal situations and others in less formal situations, but that formality and politeness can also be conveyed by tone of voice and gesture.

Examining Meaning and Use: Permission

➡ The Meaning and Use box on pages 171–172 examines the levels of formality when asking for permission. Students should have their books closed. Write the word *permission* on the board. Ask a student for permission to do something. (For example: *Can I borrow your pen?*)

Ask another student what modal you used to ask for permission *(can)*. Write *can* on the board. Ask the students to tell you any other ways they know of to ask for permission. Write *may* and *could* on the board. (If they mention *would*, point out that it asks the listener to do something, not for permission for the speaker to do something.)

Tell the students to look at the Meaning and Use box on pages 171–172 to check their list of permission modals.

Then tell the students to look at point 7. Divide the students into pairs. Assign each pair a modal — *can, may,* or *could*. Ask them to write a short conversation in which someone asks for permission. They should also incorporate at least one of the answers in point 7. They should also look at the other points in the box to help them write their conversations.

Give the students five minutes to write their conversations. Then ask different students to perform for the class. Ask the rest of the class to give their opinions about the acceptability of the modal in the chosen situation.

Examining Meaning and Use: Suggestions, Advice, Warnings, Instructions

➡ Let the students find out what they know about these modals by asking the class to order them according to how strongly the speaker feels about what is being said. Students should have their books closed. Write the following on the board:

	had better	
	should	
	might	
You	must	ask the teacher.
	ought to	
	could	
	have got to	

Working in groups of three or four, have the students order the modals from the one where the speaker does not feel very strongly about the message to the one where the speaker feels very adamant about the message. Tell the students that you do not expect them to decide on exactly the same order. They should start by finding the strongest and the weakest. They should mark the modals that they are unsure of with question marks.

Give the groups five minutes to discuss it among themselves. Call on several groups to write their order on the board. With the whole class, note the similarities and differences among the lists.

Now tell the students to look at points 1 and 2 in the Meaning and Use box on page 176 and compare their list with the one in the book.

Assign these pairs of points to different groups of students: 3 and 9; 4 and 8; 6 and 7; 3 and 7; 4 and 9; 6 and 8. (This pairing means that each group will work with different types of modals. Notice that point 5 has been omitted for the moment.) Tell the groups to think of two very short conversations that illustrate the points they were assigned. Tell the students to make sure that their conversations have to do with suggestions, advice, warnings, or instructions.

Give them five minutes to work. Ask different groups to perform their conversations. Before each group performs, give the class one minute to read the relevant point in the box. Make sure that points 3, 4, and 6–9 are covered by the groups who perform.

Now tell the students to look at point 5. Read it aloud. In addition, you can say that Americans sometimes use *shall* as in *Shall we dance?* to be amusingly formal.

Using the Conversation Notes (page 177)
Encourage the students to use conversational pronunciation. As they follow along in their books, read the spoken forms in point 1 so that the class will be able to hear the correct pronunciation. Then go over points 2 and 3 together.

Examining Meaning and Use: Opinions, Obligations, Necessity, Requirements, Rules, Laws

➡ The students should have their books closed. Write the word *opinion* on the board. Elicit *should* for giving opinions by asking the students what they think about chewing gum in the classroom. Keep asking until someone says *Students should/shouldn't chew gum in the classroom.* Write the sentence on the board.

Write these sentences on the board: *I have to study tonight. I should study tonight.* Ask the students to tell you which is stronger *(have to)*. Write the word *obligation* next to the sentence with *should* and *necessity* next to the sentence with *have to*.

Write the word *requirement* on the board. Ask the students to tell you one of the requirements for passing your course. (For example: *You must get a C.*) If they use *have to,* ask them to give you another alternative. Write the statement on the board.

Write the word *rule* on the board. Ask the students to tell you one of the rules of the school. (For example: *Students must not chew gum in the classroom.*) If they give you this example, contrast it with the opinion above with *should*. (If the students do not use *must not* in their answers, give them an example that uses it.)

Write the word *law* on the board. Ask the students to give you an example of a law. If they are confused about the difference between *rule* and *law,* tell them that laws come from the government, which can punish people for disobeying them. A rule is made by a nongovernment organization. (For example: *Taxpayers must send in their tax returns by April 15. [law]/ Students must get a C to pass a course. [rule]*)

Tell the class to look at the Meaning and Use box on pages 184–185. Assign pairs one point from 2 to 9. Ask the pairs to explain the point by preparing a short conversation, or by giving examples. Assign the easier points (3, 5, 8, 9) to weaker pairs, and the more complex ones (2, 4, 6, 7) to more able pairs.

Circulate to help as needed. Call on different pairs to present their conversations or examples to the class. Make sure that all the points are covered.

Troubleshooting: If some students confuse *don't have to* with *must not,* try not to get into a long discussion at this point. Simply correct it and tell them that this will be discussed in the next Meaning and Use box.

Using the Conversation Notes (page 186)
Read the two points aloud with the students. Encourage them to use contractions when they are doing the exercises on *have/has got to* in the Student Book.

Examining Meaning and Use: Lack of Necessity and Prohibition

➥ Write these two sentences on the board:

You don't have to drive over the speed limit.

You must not drive over the speed limit.

Ask the students if the sentences have the same or different meanings *(different)*. If the students think the sentences have different meanings, ask them to explain the difference *(**don't have to** is lack of necessity, **must not** is prohibition)*. If the students cannot explain the difference in meaning, help them by providing a context for each sentence. (For example: first sentence — *We have plenty of time to get to the party. You don't have to drive over the speed limit*; second sentence — *The sign says "Speed limit 45 mph in the construction area." You must not drive over the speed limit*.) For additional practice, ask the students to give more examples. Write their examples on the board.

Now tell the students to look at the Meaning and Use box on page 191 to check their examples.

Additional Activities

1. Writing advice for a new grandmother. Tell the students to write suggestions for Betty, who just had her first grandchild. She wants to help her son and daughter-in-law by giving advice about parenting, but she does not want them to think she is meddling. Tell the students to advise Betty when she should give her opinion, when she should not, and how she can make suggestions tactfully.

2. Examining modals in parenting advice. Bring to class magazines and/or books that give advice about parenting. Ask the students to find different modals and explain why particular modals are being used.

3. Examining modals in newspaper advice columns. Make copies of an advice column from your local paper. Ask the students to identify modals and explain their use. Then have them write alternative responses to the letters.

4. Writing advice to a friend. Ask the students to write a letter to a friend who is about to visit the United States. Tell them to give advice using as many different modals as possible.

8 CHAPTER

Modals of Ability and Belief; Past Modals

This chapter continues the analysis of modals. Some of the concepts may seem confusing to students. Do not belabor the information in the Meaning and Use boxes. Move on to the exercises where more examples in context are found. Do one or two exercises and then come back to the appropriate Meaning and Use box and relate the exercises to the explanations.

Past modals are also introduced in this chapter. Many students may not have seen them before and may have problems with their form, as well as their meaning and use.

Using the Preview

➥ Call on different students to read aloud the conversations in the Preview on page 199 of the Student Book. As the students read the sentences, ask them to underline any words or phrases that are new to them. Ask what words or phrases they underlined. Do not explain any of the words in bold. Simply note who may be coming new to this material. Briefly explain any other problems that they may have.

Tell the students to read the information at the bottom of page 199. Again, tell them to underline any parts that they do not understand. Ask the students what, if any, words or phrases they underlined. Tell them that you are not going to explain at this time, but that they will get the answers as they work through the chapter.

Modals of Ability

Examining Form: Present Ability

➥ The students should have no problem with the form of this structure. Go over the Conversation Note on Student Book page 201 and have the students do Exercise 1. If the students have a problem with the structure, go back and review the material in the Form box on page 200.

Using the Conversation Note (page 201)

The students should have their books closed. Very often it is difficult for students to hear the difference between *can* and *can't*. Using an informal, conversational style, read several sentences aloud, choosing *can* or *can't* at random. (For example: *He can't come. She can go with us. Can't you hear her? You can leave. I can't hear you.*) Ask the students to tell you what you said. Call on different students to write the sentences on the board.

Now tell the students to look at the Conversation Note. Point out that most students listen for the *t* when trying to differentiate between *can* and *can't*. This causes a problem because the *t* is often barely audible. The real difference is the quality and length of the vowel. The vowel in *can't* is much longer than the vowel in *can* in its unstressed position. (For example: *She can't go* vs. *She can go*.)

Examining Form: Past Ability

➡ Have the students do Exercise 2 in the Student Book on page 202. Go back to the Form box on pages 201–202 only if students have problems with the structure of sentences with *could*.

Examining Meaning and Use: Present, Past, and Future Ability

➡ The students should have their books closed. Find out what the students know about ways to express present, past, and future ability by writing this chart on one side of the board:

Past	Present	Future
	I can swim.	

Working in groups of three, the students should think of ways to say the sentence on the board in the past and future. Give them three to five minutes to come up with ideas. Then call on different students to go to the board and write their sentences in the chart. Go over the sentences and see how much consensus there is among the students. Put question marks next to the ones students seem unsure of. Tell them to look at the Meaning and Use box on pages 203–204 in the Student Book to check their answers. Go over the answers. Do not focus on the difference between *was able to* and *could* at this time.

➡ Tell the students to close their books. Check their understanding of the difference between *could* and *was able to* by writing the following sentences on the board. Tell them that one of the sentences is incorrect. Have them work in pairs to decide which one *(the second sentence)*:

I was able to swim five miles yesterday.

I could swim five miles yesterday.

I wasn't able to swim five miles yesterday.

I couldn't swim five miles yesterday.

I could hear the birds when I swam yesterday.

I was able to hear the birds when I swam yesterday.

Go over the students' guesses. Tell them to look at the Meaning and Use box on pages 203–204 to check their answers. Mark the incorrect sentence with an asterisk. Then have the students tell you why the other sentences are correct, using the information in the Meaning and Use box.

Modals of Belief

Examining Form

➡ The students should be very familiar with the form of statements with modals. Tell them to look at the Form box on pages 209–210 to familiarize themselves with the modals they are going to study next.

Examining Meaning and Use: Certainty About the Present

➡ With their books closed, the students should order sentences according to degrees of certainty. Write the following on the board:

	must	
	might	
	should	
That woman	has to	be his mother.
	could	
	has got to	
	may	

Divide the class into pairs. Tell them to decide which modals show that the speaker is more sure of the statement and which show that the speaker is less sure of the statement. Tell them that some of the modals are equal. Give them five minutes to come up with an order.

Call on several students to write their orders on the board. Ask them to look at the Meaning and Use box on pages 211–212 to check their answers.

Divide the class into groups. Assign points 5, 6, 7, and 9, one to each group. Ask them to write a short conversation illustrating their point. Call on different groups to read their conversations. Ask each group to explain their point to the class. Make sure that all the different points are covered.

Examining Meaning and Use: Certainty About the Present (Negative)

➧ Use imaginary situations to illustrate the meaning of the negative belief modals. Make a statement that the students will know is impossible. (For example: *I'm engaged!* [impossible because you are already married].) Ask them to respond to your statement with a modal. (For example: *You can't be!*) Write their ideas on the board. Make another statement that is not outrageous, but that may or may not be true. (For example: *I'm going out tonight.*) Ask them to respond with a negative belief modal. (For example: *You might not be going out because your favorite television show is on tonight.*) Finally, give them a situation that is not outrageous, but that is probably not true. (For example: *I'm sick today./You must not be sick. You look fine.*)

Tell the students to look at the sentences on the board and put them in order of certainty. Ask them to look at the Meaning and Use box on page 218 to check their answers.

Examining Meaning and Use: Certainty About the Future

➧ The students should have their books closed. Do the following as a class activity. Find out what students know about modals of belief in the future by writing this on the board:

I _____ pass the test tomorrow.

Ask the students to complete the statement with as many different modals as they can think of. Then ask them to order the modals according to levels of certainty. Write their ideas on the board.

Tell the students to look at the Meaning and Use box on pages 221–222 to check their answers.

➧ Divide the class into groups of three or four. Ask the groups to write conversations where people are discussing the possible outcomes of something in the future. Some possibilities are: a sports contest, an election, the weather, and so on.

Past Modals

Examining Form

➧ Try to elicit some past modals from the students. Give them the following situation and ask them to respond with a modal. Write down all their responses, correct or incorrect:

Mary was absent yesterday. Where was she?

Possible responses: *(She may have been at home. She might have gone shopping with her mother. She could have gone to a movie because it was raining.)*

If someone comes up with the correct form of a past modal, work with that one and have the students transform it to a negative, a *yes/no* question, and an information question. Then ask the students to look at the Form box on page 224 to check their answers.

If no one comes up with the form, give the students three minutes to look at the Form box on page 224. Then ask them to close their books again and try to give answers.

> **Troubleshooting:** Students might confuse the past form of modals with the present perfect studied in Chapter 6 because the form of the main verb is the same (*have* + past participle of the main verb). If this comes up, tell the students that *have* + past participle of the main verb here does not have the same meaning as the present perfect. It just indicates past time.

Using the Conversation Notes (page 225)
To check the student's aural comprehension of past modals, use this short dictation. The students should have their books closed. Make sure that you read the sentences in an informal, conversational style without emphasizing *have*:

He should have won.

They may not have believed you.

It might have worked.

She couldn't have done it.

We must have had the books.

Examining Meaning and Use: Ability and Belief Modals

➧ Lead into an examination of the meaning and use of the past modals by asking the students to compare the meaning of these sentences:

When she was ninety   she could walk five miles.
                       she could have walked
                                       five miles.

(In the first sentence, she did walk five miles. In the second, it was possible, but we do not know if it happened.)

You   could win   that prize.
        could have won

(The first sentence refers to ability/opportunity in the future. The second means that you had an opportunity but you did not win; perhaps you did not even try.)

Make notes of the students' ideas on the board. Then let them look at the Meaning and Use box on pages 226–227 in the Student Book to check their ideas.

Examining Meaning and Use: Past Modals as Social Modals

➡ Have the students analyze the meaning of the social modals in the past by comparing them to the social modals in the present/future.

Ask the students to use *should* in a sentence giving advice. (For example: *You should exercise every day.*) Write this sentence on the board. Then ask them to transform it to the past. *(You should have exercised every day.)* Ask them if the two sentences mean the same thing. *(No.)* If they think they do not, ask them to explain why. Note their answers on the board.

Tell the students that your back hurts. Ask them to give you a suggestion with *could*. (For example: *You could buy a hard bed.*) Write this sentence on the board. Then ask them to transform it to the past. (For example: *You could have bought a hard bed.*) Ask them if the two sentences mean the same thing. *(No.)* If they think they do not, ask them to explain why. Note their answers on the board.

Ask the students to tell you something that they are allowed to do in school with *may*. (For example: *Students may ask for an incomplete.*) Write this sentence on the board. Ask them to transform it to the past. If they say *Students may have asked for an incomplete,* write it on the board. Tell the students that although this sentence is grammatically correct, the meaning is incorrect. Put an asterisk next to the sentence. Write the correct sentence on the board. *(Students were permitted to ask for an incomplete.)*

Using the same method, ask the students to tell you of an obligation with *must*. (For example: *Students must pay their fees by the first week of class.*) Ask them to transform this sentence to the past. (For example: *Students had to pay their fees by the first week of class.*)

Ask the students to examine the Meaning and Use box on pages 229–230 to check the sentences on the board.

Additional Activities

1. Writing about present and past ability. Ask the students to write a short essay about things they could do when they were in their countries but they cannot do now; and things they can do in the United States that they could not do when they were in their countries.

2. Writing with modals of belief using TV commercials. Tape two or three television commercials. Play them in class with the sound turned off. Tell the students to write sentences that make assumptions about the products being advertised and the people in the commercials. (For example: *That must be a beauty cream. He could have a headache,* and so on.)

3. Writing with modals of belief using magazine photographs. Cut several full-page photographs out of magazines and bring them to class. Ask the students to work in pairs. Give each pair one photograph. Have the students write sentences that make assumptions about the people in the photographs. Then put all the photographs in a place where the whole class can see them. Have each pair read aloud their sentences. Ask the other students to identify the photograph.

4. Writing with past modals using a short story. Ask the students to all read the same short story. Then ask them to write about what *could have happened* differently, what characters *should have done* that they did not do, and what *must have happened* after the story ended.

5. Newspaper search. Ask the students to bring to class a copy of their local paper. Tell them to circle examples of modals of ability, modals of belief, and past modals.

Song
"I Should Have Known Better" by John Lennon and Paul McCartney

CHAPTER 9

Relative Clauses

Even students who have not studied relative clauses before should be able to understand most statements that contain them, especially relative clauses with subject relative pronouns. Reassure the students that the grammatical terms may sound more difficult than they are. Generally, elicit as much information as you can from the students. At the beginning, aim at identifying relative clauses and figuring out what they do in the sentence by examining a few basic patterns.

Using the Preview

➡ Use the examples in the Preview on page 239 in the Student Book to introduce the students to important grammatical terms found in the chapter. Read the sentences in the sample language as the students follow in their books. Write the following terms on the board. (Do not write the information in parentheses). Tell the students to read the information on the bottom half of page 239 to find out about these terms:

relative clause *(clause that begins with a relative pronoun)*

relative pronoun *(who, whom, that, which, whose)*

restrictive relative clause *(identifies the noun)*

nonrestrictive relative clause *(adds extra information)*

Give the students a few minutes to read the information. Then ask them to look at the *Summary* example at the top of the page, and have them explain why the examples in boldface are relative clauses.

Ask four students to each write one of the relative clauses from the *Summary* on the board. Tell them to underline the relative clauses and circle the relative pronouns. Call on another four students to draw an arrow from the relative clause to the noun they think it modifies. Ask them if they know what kind of relative clause the first sentence contains (*restrictive*) and discuss why. Tell the students the second relative clause is nonrestrictive. See if anyone can tell the class why. If

students are unable to answer these questions, go back to the text and find the answers with them.

If students seem worried by the grammatical terms, reassure them that this is only the introduction and that the concepts will become clearer as they work through the chapter.

Restrictive Relative Clauses

Examining Form

Troubleshooting: The purpose of the Form box on page 240 is to give a general introduction to all types of restrictive relative clauses (those with relative pronoun subjects, objects, objects of prepositions, and possessive pronouns). Do not expect the students to be able to form all of these relative clause types at this point. Instead, concentrate on identifying the different types of relative pronouns that restrictive relative clauses may contain, and the other general features listed in the Form box.

➡ Write this sentence on the board:

The man   that made all the noise   is over there.

Ask the students what other pronoun could replace *that*. (Write **who** over **that**.)

Now write *The machine* under *The man*. Ask the students to complete the sentence with the appropriate relative pronouns. Write these on the board *(that, which)*.

Finally, write *The animal* under *The machine* and ask the students to complete the sentence with the appropriate relative pronouns. Write these on the board *(that, which)*. If the students give you answers using *whom* or *whose*, explain that these are used in different types of restrictive relative clauses, and the class will examine them in a few minutes.

Change the singular subjects, *The man, The machine,* and *The animal*, to plural form. Ask the students if there should be any changes in the relative pronouns. *(No.)* Then ask them if there are any other changes that need to be made in the sentences. *(Yes. Is needs to be changed to are.)*

Have the students look at the Form box on page 240. Ask them to tell you which relative pronouns have not been discussed yet *(whom, whose)*.

➠ Now write this sentence on the board:

The man   whom we saw   is over there.

Ask the students what other pronouns could replace *whom*. Write these on the board *(who/that)*.

Now write the phrase *The machine* under *The man*. Ask the students to complete the sentence by using the appropriate relative pronouns. Write these on the board *(that, which)*.

Finally, write *The animal* under *The machine* and ask the students to complete the sentence with the appropriate relative pronouns. Write these on the board *(that, which)*.

Change the singular subjects, *The man, The machine,* and *The animal,* to plural form. Ask the students if there should be any changes in the relative pronouns. *(No.)* Then ask them if there are any other changes that need to be made in the sentences. *(Yes. Is needs to be changed to are.)*

➠ Now write this sentence on the board:

The man   whose car we saw   is over there.

Ask the students if this is the only relative pronoun they can use. *(Yes.)* Tell them that this is the possessive relative pronoun.

Change the singular subject to plural form. Ask the students what changes need to be made. *(The possessive relative pronoun does not change, only the verb needs to be changed from is to are.)*

Examining Meaning and Use

➠ Bring to class newspapers, magazines, or use any books that the students have. (The books should not have a lot of dialogue.) Working in pairs and with the Student Books closed, the students should look for at least five examples of restrictive relative clauses. (You may have to remind them what these are.)

When they have found their examples, tell the students to look at the uses of relative clauses given in the Meaning and Use box on pages 241–242. Ask them to relate the clauses they found to one or more of the points in the box.

When they have finished, call on different students to read aloud their sentences. Write the relative clauses on the board as they read. With the entire class, look at the point(s) in the text that they think are related to each relative clause.

Subject Relative Pronouns

Examining Form and Use

➠ The students will already have experience forming relative clauses with subject relative pronouns if they have done Exercises 2–5 on the meaning and use of restrictive relative clauses. To introduce the concept of subject relative pronouns, return to some of the examples given in Exercise 3. Call on different students to combine the sentences using a relative pronoun. For example:

We walked down the steps. They led to the basement.
(We walked down the steps that led to the basement.)

The professor called me. He speaks Russian.
(The professor who speaks Russian called me.)

My friend went on a diet. She was overweight.
(My friend who was overweight went on a diet.)

Ask the students to identify the subject relative pronouns. Underline them. Ask them if they can guess why they are called that. *(Because they act as the subject of the verb.)*

Then tell the students to look at the Form and Use box on page 246 to check their guesses. (You can also point out to the students how each subject relative pronoun replaces the subject of the second sentence in the combined example sentences.)

Object Relative Pronouns

Examining Form and Use

➠ Introduce the students to the concept of object relative pronouns by asking them to identify the sentences in which they appear. Write these sentences on the board. Do not write the words in parentheses:

The man whom Tom arrested is my brother. *(object)*

The man who arrested Tom is my uncle. *(subject)*

The cars that he owned were old. *(object)*

The cars that went down the road were old. *(subject)*

The dog which was howling was a poodle. *(subject)*

The dog which he carried was a poodle. *(object)*

Ask the students to tell you which sentences contain subject relative pronouns and which have object relative pronouns. Ask them what the difference in structure is. *(When the pronoun is a subject, it immediately precedes* the verb. *When it is an object, the subject comes between the relative pronoun and the verb.)*

Then tell them to look at the Form and Use box on page 250 to check their answers.

➠ Ask the students to close their books. Write the sentences below on the board. Divide the students into pairs and ask them to decide which of the sentences are incorrect and why. *(The first and the last are incorrect.)*

The boat that I sailed it was big.

The student you failed was me!

The people who you met liked you.

The doctor took care of him was young.

Go over their answers together. Mark the incorrect sentences with an asterisk. Then ask the students to open their books to page 250 and look at the Form and Use box again to confirm their answers.

Object Relative Pronouns with Prepositions

Examining Form and Use

➠ Try to elicit object relative pronouns with prepositions by asking the students to combine the following sentences into one sentence. Write them on the board:

The girl was blind. I spoke to the girl.

Tell them to try to combine the sentences beginning with *The girl: (The girl who/whom I spoke to was blind.* OR *The girl to whom I spoke was blind.)* Write all of their ideas on the board. Then tell them to look at the Form and Use box on page 254 to check their guesses.

If the students were not able to combine the sentences correctly, ask them to try once more as they look again at the box on page 254. Ask the students to give you both possibilities and tell you the difference between them. *(The second is more formal.)*

Possessive Relative Pronouns

Examining Form and Use

➠ Try to elicit possessive relative pronouns with prepositions by asking the students to combine these sentences:

The man's daughter left. The man called me.

Tell them to try to combine these sentences beginning with *The man.* Write all of their ideas on the board. Then ask them to look at the Form and Use box on page 258 to check their guesses.

If the students were not able to combine the sentences correctly, ask them to try once more as they refer again to the Form and Use box on page 258.

Nonrestrictive Relative Clauses

Examining Form

➠ Write these questions on the board. Tell the students to look at the Form box on pages 260–261 to find the answers:

How are nonrestrictive relative clauses punctuated? *(With a comma before and after the clause.)*

Which relative pronoun is never used in a nonrestrictive relative clause? *(That.)*

Can you omit a relative pronoun in a nonrestrictive relative clause? *(No.)*

Give the students three or four minutes to find the answers. Then go over their answers together as a class.

Examining Meaning and Use

➠ Tell the students to look back at the Preview on page 239. Ask them to find the two nonrestrictive relative clauses. Call on a student to read aloud the sentences that contain the relative clauses. Call on another student to read each sentence without the relative clause. Ask the students if the sentences seem complete without the relative clauses. *(Yes.)*

Ask a student to find and read a sentence with a restrictive relative clause. Ask another student to read the sentence without the relative clause. Ask the students if the sentence seems complete without the clause. *(No.)*

Ask the students to tell you the main difference in use between restrictive and nonrestrictive relative clauses. *(Nonrestrictive relative clauses can be omitted, restrictive relative clauses cannot be omitted.)*

Tell the students to turn to the Meaning and Use box on page 263. Together, go over points 2 and 3.

Using the Conversation Note (page 263)
Read over the note together. Tell the students to listen for this type of statement while they are watching television. Tell them to note a few examples. Ask them in one or two days if anyone has heard any examples.

Additional Activities

1. Newspaper search. Ask the students to bring to class a copy of your local paper. Tell them to look for relative clauses. Have them label the clauses they find as restrictive or nonrestrictive. Also have them identify clauses that could be written differently without changing the meaning.

2. Writing with relative clauses. Ask the students to read the poem listed below. Then have the students make up their own storyline that follows the same format.

3. Using relative clauses to describe photographs. Cut out of a magazine several photographs that have crowd scenes. Ask the students to describe the people in the photographs with sentences using relative clauses.

Poem
"The House That Jack Built" (traditional; available from Dial Books for Young Readers.)

Song
"The Riddle Song" *(I gave my love a cherry…;* traditional folk song.)

CHAPTER 10

Count and Noncount Nouns

Most students will have already been introduced to the concept of count and noncount nouns. Therefore, as you go through the chapter, let them give you as much information as they can.

Using the Preview

➡ Review some grammar terminology. Read with the students the examples on the top of page 269 *(Signs* and *An ad).* Write the terms *proper noun, common noun, count noun,* and *noncount noun* on the board as column headings.

Tell the students that the Preview examples contain these four kinds of nouns. Ask them to find examples of each term. Encourage them to guess. Do not correct. Write all their ideas on the board under the heading they tell you.

Then ask them to read the rest of the Preview on page 269 to check their answers. Go over each column on the board and make corrections as necessary.

Then write the word *determiner* on the board and ask the students which words are determiners in the signs and in the ad.

Count Nouns

Examining Form

➡ The students should have their books closed. Elicit singular/plural pairs of count nouns. If the students do not give you any that end in *-es,* ask them for the plural of *dish (dishes).* Then ask them to think of others that end in *-es.*

If the students give you only regular pairs, ask them for an irregular pair. If they are unable to think of one, give them an example (for example: *child — children).*

Then write the following chart on the board. Ask the students to complete the singular/plural pairs where appropriate:

Singular	Plural
	clothes
	feet
fish	
	glasses
	groceries
	jeans
ox	
	police
series	

Call on different students to write their guesses on the board. Then ask them to look at the Form box on pages 270–272 to correct their answers.

Noncount Nouns

Examining Form

⟹ Bring to class magazines and newspapers, or use the books that the students have. Divide the students into pairs and have them look for noncount nouns. Ask them to tell you how they can tell if a word is a noncount noun. *(If it is a subject, the verb in the sentence will be singular. Noncount nouns do not have a plural form. Noncount nouns will not be preceded by a or an, or a number. They can occur alone without any determiner, or with certain expressions of quantity.)*

Give the students five minutes to look through the material. Call on different pairs to tell you some of the words that they have found. Write the words on the board. Ask the students if they agree with the list. Write a question mark next to any words that the class does not agree on.

Then tell the students to look at the Form box on page 273. Tell them to look for information that will show that the words on the board are correct or incorrect. If students still seem unsure, have them look at the list on page 275. As a last resort, you can tell them the answer.

Focus on Vocabulary:
Common Noncount Nouns

⟹ Tell the students to look at the list of words on page 275. Students should work in groups of three. Assign each group a type of noncount noun from the

list. Do not assign *Weather* or *Gerunds*. Tell the students to look at the groups of noncount nouns and add as many nouns as they can think of to each group. Some possibilities are:

Solids: wood, plastic, metal

Liquids: soda, wine, soup

Gases: water vapor

Grains and Powders: oats, barley

Category Names: glassware, silverware (cutlery), electronics, lumber

Abstract Nouns: democracy, justice, kindness

Fields of Study and Languages: literature, French

Call on a representative from each group to write their list on the board.

Go over the lists on the board with the students. If they disagree on whether the words are count or noncount, help them out. (You may want to suggest that they consult an ESL dictionary if one is available.)

Examining Meaning and Use:
Count and Noncount Nouns

⟹ The students should have their books closed. Write this sentence on the board: *Chicken cooks quickly.* Ask the students if it is a correct sentence. *(Yes.)* Then ask them if the word *chicken* is a count or noncount noun and how they know. *(It is noncount because the verb is singular and it has no determiner.)* Write *noncount* under the word *chicken*. Then write this sentence on the board: *The chickens cook quickly.* Ask the students if it is a correct sentence. *(Yes.)* Then ask them if the word *chickens* is a count or noncount noun and how they know. *(It is count because it is plural.)*

Ask the students to tell you how the word *chicken* can be both count and noncount. (Do not expect them to word their answer exactly as suggested here: *(The meanings are different. The noncount meaning of **chicken** in the first sentence refers to chicken as a substance in general. **Chickens** in the second sentence refer to particular examples of chickens.)*

Make notes of any ideas that the students have. Tell them to look at points 1–4 in the Meaning and Use box on pages 277–278 to check their ideas.

Then read point 5 together as a class.

Additional Activities

1. Newspaper search. Ask the students to bring to class a copy of a local newspaper. Working in small groups, they should choose an article and classify all the nouns they find in it as either count or noncount.

2. Classifying objects in the classroom. Ask the students to compile lists of all the count and noncount nouns that are present in their classroom. (For example, *chalk, electricity,* and *air* are noncount nouns; *desks, tables,* and *chairs* are count nouns.)

3. Using noncount abstract nouns to describe the ideal friend. Tell the students to make lists of qualities that they would like in an ideal friend. (For example: *honesty, patience, generosity,* etc.)

4. Sign search. For homework, have the students copy signs and billboards that they see in their communities. First ask them to identify all the nouns. Then tell them to classify each noun as count or noncount.

CHAPTER 11

Quantity Expressions and Articles

This chapter expands on the subject of count and noncount nouns studied in Chapter 10. Some of the quantity expressions will be familiar to students, but some will be new.

Most students will have seen definite and indefinite articles before, but are probably not very clear about their use. The question of when to use definite articles is particularly complex. Do not let students get discouraged. Remind them that this is one of the most difficult areas of English grammar.

Using the Preview

➡ The Preview contains a number of grammatical terms. Some of these will be familiar to many students, some will not be. Do not let the class become embroiled in a lengthy discussion of terminology; the students need only to identify examples of these forms in context. Write these terms on the board as column headings:

   general   specific

Have the students follow along in their books and circle the boldfaced words as you read the first language sample in the Preview on page 285. Ask them what these expressions have in common. *(They all describe a quantity of something.)* See if they can tell you under which heading these expressions should be listed *(a few is general, the rest are specific).*

Next have the students look at the rest of the Preview language samples. Write these terms on the board:

   definite article   indefinite article

Tell the students to look for some examples of each type of article along with its associated nouns. List them on the board in the appropriate column. See if the students know why the indefinite and definite articles are used in the various examples. Make notes of their ideas on the board. Do not correct them at this time.

Then tell the students to read the last two paragraphs at the bottom of the Preview page to see if their ideas are discussed.

General Quantity Expressions

Examining Form

➡ Before you go to class, make a list of objects in your classroom that represent count and noncount nouns. For example, noncount nouns include *furniture, chalk, wood, plastic, light, paper,* and *ink.* You can also use some abstract nouns such as *talking, trouble, information, knowledge,* and so on. Count nouns may include *pencils, books, notebooks,* and *rulers.*

Read the words on your list to the students one at a time, mixing count and noncount nous. Pause after each word and ask the students to identify the nouns as count or noncount. Ask them to raise their hands for noncount nouns. In this way, you can quickly see if students are identifying the nouns correctly or not.

Then divide the students into groups of three or four. Ask them to make a list of at least five count nouns and five noncount nouns. Remind the students that they can use abstract nouns as well. Give the students three minutes to come up with a list. Ask them to write the nouns on the board, with one half of the board for count nouns and the other half for noncount nouns. Go over the lists to make sure that they are correct.

➡ Assign each group one noncount expression, one count expression, and one expression that applies to either from the Form box on page 286. Ask the students to come up with true statements using nouns from the list on the board and the expressions you have given them. Allow them five minutes to work. Then call on different students to read aloud their sentences. The class should decide if the sentence is true or not. If any sentence has a grammatical error in the quantity expression, write the sentence on the board without correcting the problem.

Erase the nouns from the board (but leave the incorrect sentences). Ask the students to use their work and their classmates' work to help construct a chart showing how the different quantity expressions are used.

Create the chart on the board by writing the column headings as shown in the Form box on page 286. Complete the chart as the students call out suggestions. When they are finished, give them six or seven minutes to read the box and compare their chart with the Form box on page 286. Finally, have them look at the incorrect sentences on the board. Ask the students to correct the errors.

Examining Meaning and Use

➡ Write these pairs of sentences on the board:
  I have little money. I have a little money.
  She has few friends. She has a few friends.

Ask the students if the sentences mean the same thing. *(No.)* It might be helpful to tell the students that the difference between *a little/little* and *a few/few* is a matter of opinion or perspective, and not of quantity. The expressions *a few* and *a little* reflect positive ideas, and *few* and *little* reflect negative ideas.

Then ask the students to write a sentence that would precede or follow each sentence clarifying the meaning. (For example: *I have little money. I can't even pay my rent./I have a little money. Do you need to borrow some?//She's very lonely, I think. She has few friends./She seems quite happy. She has a few friends.*)

If the students seem unsure about the activity, let them work in pairs. Then call on different students to read aloud their sentences. Write some examples on the board. Then tell the students to check the sentences by looking at the Meaning and Use box on page 288.

Focus on Vocabulary: General Quantity Expressions

➡ Write these sentences on the board:
  There were _____ problems.
  There was _____ confusion.

Write the words *large quantities, small quantities,* and *none* on the board as column headings. Ask the students to tell you as many quantity expressions as they can think of that come under each heading. Tell them to use the skeleton sentences on the board to help them come up with more examples. Write their examples on the board. Then tell the students to look at the Focus on Vocabulary section on page 290 to check their answers. Correct and add to the list on the board as necessary.

Specific Quantity Expressions

Examining Form

➡ Tell the students you are going shopping and you are going to buy *a pound of meat* and *a loaf of bread.* Write these two specific quantity expressions on the board. Then ask the students for other examples of specific quantity expressions.

Divide the class into teams. Tell them to brainstorm as many different specific quantity expressions as they can, along with an example of a noun that it goes with (For example: *a piece of paper, a jar of mustard, a box of candy,* etc.) Tell them that the team with the most expressions wins.

Give the teams five minutes to work. When they are finished, call on different teams to read their expressions. Write the expressions on the board.

To check the information on the board, ask the students to look at the Form box on page 292 in the Student book.

Examining Meaning and Use

➡ Write the following nouns on the board. Tell the students that you need these items. Ask them to tell you what quantity expressions to use with each noun:

bread	soap
lettuce	wood
grapes	advice

Write their ideas on the board. Then ask them to check their answers by reading the information in the Meaning and Use box on pages 293–294.

Indefinite and Definite Articles

Examining Form

➡ Write the articles *a, an,* and *the* in a vertical column on the left side of the board. Then write the following nouns below in a vertical column on the right side of the articles:

a	hospital
	books
an	object
	information
the	lamp

First ask the students to identify the indefinite versus the definite articles *(indefinite = **a/an**; definite = **the**)*. If no one remembers, ask the class to look back at the Preview on page 285 in their books.

Then ask the students to look at the nouns and tell you which articles can go with which nouns. If they seem unsure, give them a couple of minutes to talk to a partner. Then have them draw lines between the articles and the nouns they can accompany.

Tell the students to look at the Form box on page 296 to check their answers.

Examining Meaning and Use: Introducing and Identifying Nouns

➡ Have the students guess the meaning and use of indefinite articles that they find in their Student Books. Tell them to look at the first paragraph of the To the Teacher section in the front of the Student Book. Tell them to circle all the noun phrases with indefinite articles. (For example: *a package, a bill,* etc.) Ask them to try to explain why the indefinite article is used. *(Because the noun is not specific. It can be any package, bill, and so on.)*

Then tell the students to look at the information under points 1 and 2 under the heading *Indefinite Articles* in the Meaning and Use box on page 297. Ask them to decide which point describes the use of the indefinite articles in the paragraph under discussion *(point 2)*.

> **Troubleshooting:** Tell the students that the use of the definite article is quite complex and that they will learn it gradually as they go through the exercises. The purpose right now is to introduce the ideas. It will be helpful to refer back to individual points in the Meaning and Use box on pages 297–299 when they are working on the exercises.

➡ Write the following sentences on the board:

I need a pencil.

I need the pencil.

Ask the students if the two sentences have the same meaning. *(No.)* See if they can explain the difference. Then read point 1 with the students and tell them that the meaning of the second sentence depends on what information the speaker and the listener share about the pencil. Assure them that if this is unclear, it will become clearer as they work through the box and the exercises.

Divide the class into pairs. Secretly assign each pair one of the nine points under the heading *Definite Articles.* Weaker pairs should be assigned points 2, 4, 6, 7, and 8. More able pairs can be assigned points 3, 5, and 9. Tell the students that they must write a sentence that is a good example of their point. Give them three to four minutes to work.

Then call on different pairs to read aloud their sentences. Ask the class to guess which point it illustrates. Continue calling on students until all the points have been covered.

Examining Meaning and Use:
General Statements

➡ Write on the board the following word list and incomplete sentences (do not write the italic answers in parentheses):

architect   criminal
bald eagle   rabbit
clarinet   telephone

_____ are mammals. *(Rabbits)*

_____ are a danger to society. *(Criminals)*

_____ is a person who designs buildings.
(An architect)

Alexander Graham Bell invented _____.
(the telephone).

She plays _____ very well. *(the clarinet)*

_____ is the national symbol of the United States.
(The bald eagle)

Let the students compare the use of definite and indefinite articles by asking them to complete the sentences with the correct nouns. Tell them that they can use the noun alone or an article plus the noun. They should also change the noun to plural if necessary.

Give the students five minutes to complete the sentences. Then call on different students to write their answers on the board.

Tell the students to look at the Meaning and Use box on pages 306–307 to check their answers.

Then write this next sentence on the board. Tell the students to choose from the items in the word list above to complete it:

_____ he bought were very inexpensive.
(The clarinets/rabbits/telephones)

Ask the class which point this sentence relates to in the Meaning and Use box *(point 8).*

Additional Activities

1. Articles exercise. Take one paragraph from a newspaper article or short story. Retype it and omit all the articles. Have the students add all the missing articles.

2. Newspaper search for expressions of quantity. Clip a restaurant review from your local newspaper. Hand it out to the students and ask them to circle expressions of quantity.

3. Writing about an ideal place to take a vacation. After students do Exercise 4 on page 290 in the Student Book, have them write a description of what they believe is the ideal place to take a vacation. Instruct them to use the general quantity expressions on page 290.

4. Writing a review of the school cafeteria. Ask the students to write a critique of the campus cafeteria or a local restaurant. Tell them to use as many quantity expressions as possible.

CHAPTER 12

Expressing Differences and Similarities: Comparatives, Superlatives, As...As, The Same...As

The material in this chapter reviews and expands on the different forms of comparisons. Most intermediate-level students have already been introduced to simple comparisons of adjectives and adverbs. Therefore, try to elicit as much information from the students as possible.

Using the Preview

➡ Use the examples in the Preview on page 313 to familiarize the students with different ways of comparing things in English. Write the words *comparative, superlative, as...as,* and *the same...as* across the board as column headings. Ask the students to find the different forms used for comparisons in the examples. Write their ideas on the board under the column heading they tell you.

Then give the students five minutes to read the information in the second half of the Preview. When they are finished, go over each example on the board and make corrections as necessary.

Comparative Adjectives and Adverbs

Examining Form

➡ To familiarize the students with additional information on comparative and superlative forms of adjectives and adverbs, tell them to refer to the corresponding Appendix at the back of their Student Books. If your students seem uncertain about this topic, or the diagnostic quiz reveals that they do not know the rules of forming these structures, encourage them to read through this material. Tell them to use this information as reference as they are doing the exercises in the Student Book.

➡ Write these sentences on the board:

Frank is short.   Paul is very short.
Carol dances gracefully. Patricia dances
                          very gracefully.

Pair the students and have them write comparative sentences. Remind them of the Appendix information on the spelling rules, irregular forms, and usage with comparative forms.

Call on different students to read aloud their sentences. Write their sentences on the board. Do not correct at this time.

Next erase *Frank is* and replace it with *I am.* Ask the students to write comparative sentences. Call on different students to write their sentences on the board.

Now tell the students to turn to the Form box on page 314 and read the information. Tell them to check their sentences based on the information in the box. If they have fewer possibilities than those listed, ask them to add to their list. Write these additional sentences on the board as the students tell you. Together, make corrections as necessary.

Examining Meaning and Use

➡ Have the students explore the different uses of comparative adjectives and adverbs by asking them to write comparative sentences that state a preference, state an opinion, or give a compliment.

Ask the students to tell you their sentences. Write any that seem problematic on the board. Ask the writer and then the class to find the problem. If the form is the problem, refer the student back to the Form box on page 314 or to the information in the Appendix.

➡ Write these sentences on the board:

Mike is less fat than Tim.

She's more intelligent than me.

She's more intelligent than I.

She's more intelligent than I am.

Ask the students if the first sentence is correct. *(No.)* Ask them why not. Working in pairs or groups, the students should give the correct form for the first sentence and the reason for their correction. *(Mike isn't as fat as Tim.)* Then ask them to rank the other three sentences on the board according to levels of formality.

Give the students five minutes to work. Then discuss their answers. Refer the students to the Meaning and Use box on page 316 to check their work.

Superlative Adjectives and Adverbs

Examining Form

➡ Write three names on the board (for example: three famous people, three house pets, three foods, etc.). Elicit superlative sentences from the class using the information on the board. The students should work in pairs. Ask them to write as many different kinds of superlative sentences as they can. Remind them to try to use the superlative form of *less* and as many irregular superlatives as they can think of.

Give the class five minutes to work. Then call on different students to read aloud their sentences. Write on the board as many different kinds of sentences and different irregulars as they provide you with. Then ask them to check their answers in the Form box on pages 318–319. (Note: Emphasize to the students that the article *the* must be part of the superlative.)

Examining Meaning and Use

➡ Let the students work alone or in pairs. Ask them to use the following phrases in sentences that also contain a superlative adjective or adverb:

of the year	at the dance
in my class	on my block
of all	one of the

Give the students five minutes to work. Then ask them to read aloud their sentences. As each student reads his sentence, ask him to tell the class which point in the Meaning and Use box on pages 320–321 relates to that sentence.

As...As

Examining Form

➡ Demonstrate the meaning of *as...as* by writing a few sentences on the board such as *Maria is as tall as I am. Joe speaks English as well as Marcy does.* Discuss the examples with the students.

Then as a reinforcement, ask the students to compare two people or things in the classroom to elicit the same structures as in the examples you gave them. Tell them to write as many possible forms as they can think of.

Give them two to three minutes to work. Then call on different students to read aloud their sentences. Write the sentences on the board as the students tell you. Then ask them to look at the Form box on page 323 to check their answers. Correct the sentences on the board as necessary.

Examining Meaning and Use

➡ Write these sentences on the board. (Do not write the information in parentheses.) Ask paired students to rewrite these sentences using *not as...as*. Remind them that the asterisk means that the sentence is incorrect:

Chemistry is more boring than history.
(*History is not as boring as chemistry.*)

My children are happier than hers.
(*Her children are not as happy as mine.*)

*Turtles are less fast than rabbits.
(*Turtles are not as fast as rabbits.*)

Give the pairs five minutes to work. Then call on students to write their sentences on the board. Ask the class if they agree with the sentences. Write a question mark next to any that are controversial. To check their answers, ask your students to look at points 2, 3, and 4 of the Meaning and Use box on page 324.

Comparative Nouns, Superlative Nouns, *The Same...As*

Examining Form

➡ Ask the students to write sentences with comparative and superlative nouns for the two situations below. (For example: *Diego has more money than Mohammed. Diego has less money than Hans. Hans has the most money.*) They should write as many possibilities as they can think of. Remind them of *less*, and that they may also want to use a form of *few*. Give them five minutes to work:

Mohammed has $5.

Diego has $10.

Hans has $20.

My soup has 50 calories

Her soup has 150 calories.

His soup has 300 calories.

Ask the students to write sentences with *the same...as* for the next two situations. Tell them that the word that goes in the blank must be a noun, but do not tell them that the noun for *tall* is *height*. (For example: *Pablo is the same height as Carl.*):

Pablo is six feet tall.

Carl is six feet tall.

I go to Acme Language School.

Marta goes to Acme Language School.

Go over all four situations with the students by asking them to write their sentences on the board. Do not correct for errors in the target structures. Tell them to look at the Form box on pages 325–326 to check their work.

Examining Meaning and Use

➠ Divide the class into groups. Tell them that they are advertising executives. They should choose a product to advertise (for example: a breakfast cereal, a computer, etc.) and then write as many sentences with comparative and superlative nouns as they can think of. Tell them to use a variety of phrases including, *more, fewer, less, the most, the fewest, the least*. In addition, tell the students that they must write at least one sentence with *the same...as* about their product.

Give them five to seven minutes to work. Then call on different students to talk about their products. Write any sentences that contain problems with the target structure on the board.

Tell the students to look at page 328 and correct the sentences with problems.

So...That/Such (a)...That

Examining Form

➠ Have the students analyze sentences with the target structures to decide which are incorrect. Write these sentences on the board:

She was so sick she couldn't walk.

She was such a sick that she couldn't walk.

They were so bad doctors that they couldn't help her.

She was so sick that she couldn't walk.

It was such a bad hospital that we made her leave.

Ask the students to work in pairs and decide which sentences are incorrect *(the second and third)*. Give them five minutes to work. Then go over their answers. Write question marks after sentences that students do not agree on. Put an asterisk next to the

sentence(s) they think are incorrect. Tell them to look at the Form box on page 332 to check their answers.

Examining Meaning and Use

➠ Have the students complete sentences containing *so* and *such(a)...that*. Divide students into pairs. Ask them to write one clause beginning with *that* (for example: *...that I failed the course*) and one containing *so* or *such(a)* and ending with *that* (for example: *He was so nasty that...*). Tell them to write on a separate piece of paper. Collect the papers and redistribute them to other pairs. Ask the pairs to complete the sentences.

Call on students to read aloud their sentences. Write any illogical sentences on the board. Ask the students to look at the Meaning and Use box on page 333 to find out more information and to correct the sentences on the board.

Additional Activities

1. Comparing food. Bring to class two types of food that have some similarities and some differences. (For example: bagels and doughnuts; cookies and crackers; chocolates with nuts and chocolates without nuts; pretzels and potato chips. You might collect a quarter from each student ahead of time in order to pay for the food.) Display these groups of food items in a central location in the class and invite students to sample each group. While they are eating, write several adjectives on the board. (For example: *expensive, cheap, sweet, salty, nutritious, chewy, crunchy, greasy,* etc.) Explain the meaning of any words students do not know. Then ask them to write comparative sentences using the adjectives. Have the students write their sentences on the board. Ask the class to correct the errors.

2. Comparing objects. Bring to class two objects that serve the same function but are different ages or of different designs. For example: a rotary-dial telephone and a touch-tone phone; a CD and a record album; a large floppy diskette and a small floppy diskette; a printed bilingual dictionary and a computer bilingual dictionary; a mug and a plastic cup; a hardcover and paperback version of the same book; a stapler and a box of paper clips.

For a presentation of superlatives, a third item can be added. For example: a rotary-dial telephone, a desktop touch-tone phone, and a cordless phone; a notebook, a large floppy diskette, and a small floppy diskette; a mug, a plastic cup, and a paper cup. Then ask the students to write comparative and superlative sentences.

Ask several different students to write their sentences on the board. Ask the class to correct the errors.

3. Comparing languages. Ask the students to compare features of their own language with those of English. (For example: *Spelling in Spanish is easier than spelling in English. There are more letters in Japanese than in English. There are fewer verb endings in English than there are in my language.*)

4. Comparing characters in a story. Have the students all read the same short story with two main characters and write comparative sentences about them. They can then compare themselves with one of the characters.

Song

"My Dog's Bigger Than Your Dog" by Tom Paxton

CHAPTER 13

Expressing Unreal Situations:
***Wish* Sentences and**
Imaginary *If* Sentences

Some students will have seen unreal *if* and *wish* sentences in previous courses. These students should have little trouble with this chapter. The biggest problem will be to make sure that the students do not slip into past unreal conditions, which will be discussed in Chapter 15.

The most difficult issue for students coming new to these sentence structures is to understand that the past is used even though the situation is not past. They should have little difficulty with the sentence structures, especially if you relate them to the real *if* sentences that they may have studied in Chapter 5.

Using the Preview

➡ Tell the students to open their books to the Preview on page 339. Ask them to look for examples of *wish* sentences and imaginary *if* sentences in the language samples. Give them three minutes to find the examples. Then ask them to read aloud the sentences.

Ask the students to tell you the answers to these questions: *Does Mark have room for his books?(No.) Can Pat buy the jacket? (No.)*

Let them give you their ideas, then tell them to read the information in the first paragraph under the language samples to check their answers.

Tell the students to look at the two sentences with *if* in the text *(If I take the job,…).* Ask them to try to explain the difference between them. Then tell them to read the rest of the information to check their answers.

Wish Sentences

Examining Form

➡ Check the students' grasp of the form of *wish* sentences by asking them to make four wishes about the present or the future. One wish must contain a form of *can*, one wish must contain a form of *be*, one must use a form of *will*, and the other can be anything that they like.

Give them five minutes to write down their ideas. Then call on different students to write their sentences on the board. Let the class evaluate the sentences. Underline places that the students seem to think are incorrect or they are unsure of. Then tell them to look at the Form box on page 340 to check the sentences.

Briefly point out the Conversation Note on page 340 to the students. Make sure the students understand that this is for informal conversation only.

Examining Meaning and Use

➡ Tell the students to look at point 1 in the Meaning and Use box on page 341. Go over the point with the entire class. Elicit wishes from individuals. Write some of the wishes on the board. Make sure that all of their wishes express a desire for something that is not real now.

Divide the students into pairs. Assign each pair a point from 2 to 5. Tell them to write a short conversation incorporating a wish of the type presented in the point assigned to them.

Give the pairs five minutes to work. Then call on different students to read their conversations and the point that they were assigned. Ask the class to decide if their conversation illustrates that point.

Imaginary *If* Sentences

Examining Form

➡ Let the students analyze the form of imaginary *if* sentences by having them compare imaginary *if* sentences to real *if* sentences. They should have their books closed. Write this sentence on the board:

    If I go to Cleveland, _____.

Ask the class to finish the sentence. (For example: …*I'll visit her.*) Then write this sentence on the board:

    If I went to Cleveland, _____.

See if the students can finish the sentence for you. (For example: …*I would/could visit her.*) Write down all their ideas. If most of the class seems familiar with the structure, then continue on. If they do not, then have them look at the Form box on page 346. After the students read the information, have them close their

books again and ask them to give you a correct final clause for the sentence above.

Write these clauses on the board and ask the class to finish the sentences:

    She'd be happy if _____.
    She'll be happy if _____.
    If they knew you, _____.
    If they know you, _____.

Give them three minutes to work. Then ask them to read their sentences. Write some on the board, especially those that have incorrect verb forms. Tell the students to look at the Form box on page 346 and check the sentences on the board.

Point out the Conversation Note on page 347, making sure the students understand that this is for informal conversation only.

Examining Meaning and Use

➡ Help the students to discuss the difference in meaning of the real and imaginary *if* sentences. If the sentences from Examining Form above are still on the board, use those as a basis for discussion. If they are no longer on the board, write two more pairs of real and imaginary *if* sentences:

    She'd be happy if he arrived today.
    She'll be happy if he arrives today.
    You could leave if you were finished.
    You can leave if you are finished.

Write the students' ideas on the board. (Get them to notice that in the imaginary sentences, the speaker feels that it is impossible or very unlikely that the action or state in the *if* clause is or will be true. In the real sentences, the speaker feels that it is possible that the action or state in the *if* clause is or will be true.) Then tell them to look at points 1–3 in the Meaning and Use box on page 347. Check their understanding by asking them to write imaginary *if* sentences such as the following that have no parallel *if* sentences. (For example: *If I were you, I'd leave. If I were ten years younger, I'd join the navy.*)

➡ The students should have their books closed. Write these pairs of sentences on the board:

1. A: _____.
   B: If I were you, I'd tell him.

2. A: Would you mind if I took my vacation next month?
   B: _____.

3. A: Would it bother you if I closed the door?
   B: _____.

4. A: Would it be OK if I listened to the radio?
   B: _____.

Working in pairs, the students should complete the conversations. Give them five minutes to work, then call on different pairs to read aloud their sentences. Write a couple on the board. If some students write *Yes* as a positive answer to items 2 and 3, do not tell them yet that it is incorrect. Simply write it as a possible answer.

Now ask the students to go back to the conversations and give you an alternative for the sentences with *if*. (For example: *1B. I think you should tell him. 2A. Can I take my vacation next month? 3A. Could I close the door? 4A. Could I listen to the radio?*)

Write their alternatives on the board. Then ask them to look at the Meaning and Use box on pages 347–348 and check their conversations and the alternative sentences.

Additional Activities

1. Writing a conversation about wishes. Working in small groups, the students should write a conversation among three friends who are complaining about their boyfriends/girlfriends or bosses. Tell them to use as many *wish* sentences as possible.

2. Writing about being the opposite gender. Have the students write a composition about how their lives would be different if they were the opposite gender.

3. Discussion about cultural customs. Lead a class discussion about what customs in the United States the students wish were different.

4. Newspaper search. Ask the students to look for examples of *wish* sentences and imaginary *if* sentences in the newspaper. Interviews are particularly good places to look.

Songs
"If I Had a Hammer" by Pete Seeger
"If I Were a Rich Man" by Jerry Bock and
   Sheldon Harick

CHAPTER 14

Gerunds and Infinitives

Most students have probably studied the most common gerund and infinitive structures. (For example: *I like working. He wants to leave.*) However, they may not be familiar with the terms *infinitive* and *gerund*.

The most difficult part of learning gerunds and infinitives is remembering which verbs occur with each of them. You may want to consider planning two or three quizzes on gerunds and infinitives during the time you are working on the chapter just to motivate the students to memorize some of the material. The chapter offers a great deal of practice to reinforce their efforts. Reassure them that this is a slow process.

Using the Preview

➡ Use the Preview on page 355 to introduce the students to the terms *gerund* and *infinitive*. Read the sentences in the sample language as the students follow in their books. Have the students circle examples of gerunds and underline examples of infinitives. If the students cannot identify gerunds or infinitives, help them by supplying an example for each term. Write what they tell you on the board under the headings *gerund* or *infinitive*.

Ask the class to give you further examples of gerunds that could be added to a summer recreation program guide (*diving, running*). You can also ask the students for examples of gerunds describing activities that could be included in a winter recreation program guide (*skiing, figure skating, etc.*).

Tell the students that the gerunds and infinitives in the two language samples have various uses and that they will learn what they are as they go through the chapter.

Ask the students to read the information at the bottom of the page in the Preview as a follow-up.

Overview of Gerunds

Examining Form and Meaning

➡ The students should have their books closed. Write the following sentences on the board exactly as they are here:

1. Having your own room is important.
2. Skiing are very expensive.
3. She enjoys no getting up early.
4. I thought about leaving.

Ask the students to identify the gerunds in the sentences. Ask them to tell you what a gerund is. *(A gerund is a simple form of a verb + -ing.)* Then ask the students to decide if these are all correct sentences. *(No.)* Place an asterisk next to sentences 2 and 3. See if they can correct them. Make the corrections as they tell you.

Tell the students to check their corrections by looking at the Form and Meaning box on page 356. Make any additional changes as needed.

Troubleshooting: Some students might be hesitant to use the *-ing* form of stative verbs since they should have learned previously that these do not have a continuous form. Point out to them that all verbs, including stative verbs, can be used as gerunds. To emphasize your point, give them a few examples. *(Knowing you is a pleasure. I am looking forward to having my own car.)*

➡ Have more advanced students analyze the corrected sentences above to identify subjects, objects, and objects of prepositions. See if they can tell you in which sentences the gerund is the subject of the sentence *(1 and 2)*, in which sentence it is the object of a verb *(3)*, and finally, in which it is the object of a preposition *(4)*.

Tell them to check their answers by looking at the Form and Meaning box on page 356.

Subject Gerunds

Examining Form and Use

➡ Use these sentences to check your students' understanding of what the subject of a sentence is. Write them on the board:

1. Sending a fax can be frustrating.
2. They delayed calling the ambulance.

3. Playing tennis is a good way to exercise.
4. Do you enjoy managing a big firm?
5. The patient insisted on consulting a specialist.
6. Buying a house is stressful.

First ask the students to underline the gerunds. Then ask them to tell you in which sentences the gerund functions as the subject of the sentence *(1, 3, 6)*. If they do not have problems with this concept, then ask them to come up with three additional examples using gerunds as subjects. Give them three minutes to work. Then call on different students to write their sentences on the board.

Tell the class to look at the Form and Use box on page 357 to check the sentences on the board.

Troubleshooting: If students seem very confused by the concept of subject and object, back up and let them look at sentences without gerund subjects and objects. (For example: *I like candy. The boys took the money. I sent a fax. They called the ambulance.*)

Object Gerunds

Examining Form

➡ Write these sentences on the board:

1. I enjoy my work.
2. I've considered moving to New York City.
3. Mary finished writing her essay.
4. I enjoy my life in a big city.
5. Do you enjoy managing a big firm?

Ask a student to come to the board and underline the gerunds that are objects *(moving to New York City/writing her essay/managing a big firm)*. Then call on a second student to come to the board and underline the objects in the other sentences. Tell the students to transform these latter sentences *(1 and 4)* using gerunds as objects. *(I enjoy working./I enjoy living in a big city.)* Then ask the students to write three more sentences using gerunds as objects. Give them three minutes to complete the task. Then call on different students to write their sentences on the board.

Tell the class to look at the Form box on page 359 to check their answers and the sentences on the board.

Focus on Vocabulary: Common Object Gerunds

> **Troubleshooting:** Tell the students that eventually they will need to know which verbs take a gerund and which take an infinitive. However, it will take some time to learn them. Reassure them that they will become much more familiar with these verbs plus gerunds through practice as they work through the exercises.

➡ Have the students look over the list on Student Book pages 360–361 and look up the meaning of any verbs or phrases that are new to them. If they do not have dictionaries, provide definitions yourself if the students ask.

Give the class another five minutes to look over the list. Then have a "gerund bee." Call on the students one by one to make a sentence with an object gerund with the verb you give them (for example: *deny* — *He denied cheating on the test.*) Give them a time limit of thirty seconds.

Tell the students that their sentences must be logical and grammatically correct.

For a more complete list refer the students to the Verb + Gerund Appendix at the back of the Student Book.

Examining Meaning and Use

➡ Tell the students to use the list of verbs on pages 360–361 to find the verbs that express likes, dislikes, and feelings. (For example: *appreciate, dislike, enjoy, mind, miss, regret.*) Ask them to write three sentences using some of these verbs. Also have them think of a verb that is often used when people talk about recreational activities and shopping (*go*). Again ask them to write three sentences using this verb. Call on different students to read aloud their sentences.

Then ask the students to turn to page 362 and look at the Meaning and Use box to check their sentences.

➡ Write this conversation on the board. Ask the students to complete it:

    A: Would you mind opening the window?
    B: _____.

Write some of the students' responses on the board. Tell the students to write one more conversation similar to the one on the board.

Then ask the students to look at point 4 in the Meaning and Use box on page 363 to check their conversations.

Preposition + Object Gerunds

Examining Form and Use

➡ Do not belabor this point, but do make sure that students are familiar with prepositions. Ask them to name some. If they cannot, supply examples to get them started. Write their ideas on the board. Write only the words that really are prepositions. After writing each one on the board, ask a student to make a sentence using the word as a preposition. This is important because some words (for example: *to*) function as prepositions in some structures and not in others.

Write two or three sentences on the board incorporating different prepositional phrases, but leave the phrases incomplete:

    Before _____, he turned out the light.
    She's not afraid of _____.
    I get good grades by _____.

Ask the students to complete the phrases with gerunds.

Give them two minutes to work. Call on different students to read their sentences to the class. Write two or three different answers on the board. Tell the class to check the answers by looking at the Form and Use box on page 365.

Focus on Vocabulary: Common Preposition + Object Gerunds

➡ Ask the students to compare the list on Student Book pages 360–361 with the list on pages 366–367. Ask them to tell you the difference. (*Every item on the second list is a verb or phrase + preposition.*)

Tell the students to go over the second list and underline phrases that they do not understand. They can ask you or look them up in a dictionary.

Divide the class into groups of three or four. Tell them to write a conversation incorporating as many of the items on this list as they can. The group that uses the most items wins.

Give the groups ten to fifteen minutes to work. Then call on the groups to perform their conversations.

Overview of Infinitives

Examining Form and Meaning

➠ Have the students analyze correct and incorrect sentences. They should have their books closed. Write these sentences on the board. Ask them to decide which are incorrect *(the first and the last)*:

I need to leave in order to getting there on time.

It's important to drive carefully.

They like to swim.

She promised no to tell him.

Put an asterisk next to the sentences that the students are sure are incorrect. Write a question mark next to the ones that they are unsure of.

Tell the class to check their answers by looking at the Form and Meaning box on pages 369–370.

Verb + Infinitive

Examining Form

➠ Write the following conversations and sentences on the board and ask the students to complete them:

1. A: Do you want _____ (read) or _____ (watch TV)?
    B: _____ (read).

2. A: I hope my secret is safe with you.
    B: Don't worry. I promise _____ (tell/not) anyone.

3. A: Will she go with you?
    B: Yes, she _____ (hope).

4. They don't want to help but they _____ (need).

5. I want to leave tonight and I _____ (plan).

Give them five to seven minutes to work. Then call on different students to read aloud their completed sentences.

Tell them to check their work by looking at the Form box on page 371.

Focus on Vocabulary: Common Verbs + Infinitives

➠ The list on page 373 presents only a partial list of verbs followed by infinitives. Encourage the students to become familiar with these verbs. As with gerunds, emphasize that the process for learning these verbs is a combination of memorization and practice. For additional verbs followed by an infinitive, refer the students to the Verb + Infinitive Appendix in the back of the Student Book.

To promote familiarity with the list on page 373, do short activities as you go through the exercises. For example:

Give a five-minute quiz at the end of class. Ask the students to write sentences with certain verbs, some of which take gerunds and others that take infinitives.

Have a "gerund and infinitive bee." Divide the class into two teams. Have the teams stand on opposite sides of the room. The students must make logical and grammatically correct sentences with the verbs you give them. When a student makes a mistake, she must sit down. The team with the most members standing at the end wins.

Examining Meaning and Use

➠ Have the students decide on the correctness of sentences to check their understanding of the meaning and use of verb + infinitive constructions. Write the sentences below on the board:

1. He likes to shop.
2. She likes shopping.
3. We look forward to dancing.
4. We look forward to dance.
5. A: Would you like to dance?
   B: Yes, I like it. It's good exercise.

Ask the students to tell you which are incorrect *(4 and 5)*. Give the students two or three minutes to work. Then ask them to tell you their guesses. Put an asterisk next to the sentences they think are incorrect, and a question mark next to any they are unsure of. Then tell the students to look at the Meaning and Use box on page 374 to check their answers.

Verb + Infinitive or Gerund

Examining Form

➠ Ask the students if they know any verbs that can take both an infinitive or a gerund. They should know *like* because they saw it in the previous box. Write their ideas on the board. Ask them if the infinitive and gerund constructions always have the same meaning. *(Sometimes they do and sometimes they do not.)* Note their answers on the board. Do not try to explain differences in meaning now. Tell them to look at the Form box on page 375 to compare their verbs with those in the box and to check their answer to your question.

Examining Meaning

➠ Tell the students to look at the Form box on page 375 again. Tell them that the verbs in this box are grouped according to whether or not their infinitive and gerund forms are the same, similar, or very different in meaning. Ask the students to look at each group and decide if the gerund and infinitive constructions have the same meaning.

Have the students work in pairs for five minutes. Ask them their decisions and note them on the board. Then tell them to look at the Meaning box on pages 376–377 to check their guesses. Give them five to seven minutes to read the information. Then ask them to correct the answers on the board. As you correct the answers, go over the points in the box. If students seem confused or worried by all the information, remind them that this box is for reference and that they will learn the information by using it in the exercises. Reassure them that knowing which verbs have different meanings when followed by gerunds or infinitives, even if they do not yet understand the differences, is an important first step.

It...+ Infinitive

Examining Form

➠ Ask the students to analyze the form of an *It*...+ infinitive construction. Write this sentence on the board:

It is easy to get rich.

Ask the students what the subject of the sentence is. *(It.)* Tell them that pronouns almost always substitute

for something (there are exceptions). Ask them what *It* substitutes for here. Note their ideas on the board. Then tell them to look at the Form box on page 380 to check their answers.

Examining Meaning and Use

➠ Ask the students to transform sentences with gerunds as subjects into sentences with an *It*...+ infinitive construction. Write these sentences on the board:

Studying self-defense is useful.

Learning a language takes a long time.

Paying for lessons costs a lot.

Going alone seems impossible.

Working with the entire class, ask them to transform the sentences. If students come up with different constructions, write the alternatives on the board. Then tell the class to look at the Meaning and Use box on page 381 to check their answers.

In Order + Infinitive

Examining Form

➠ Write *in order to* on the board. Ask the students if anyone can give you a sentence with it. Choose a few correct sentences and write them on the board. Call on a student to come to the board and underline the infinitives in each sentence.

Now write this sentence on the board:

I'm studying hard in order to pass.

Change the word *pass* to *fail*. Ask the students if this sentence makes sense. *(No.)* Ask them to change the sentence to make it logical. Tell them that they cannot change the beginning. *(I'm studying hard in order not to fail.)* Write their ideas on the board.

Now ask them to look at the Form box on page 383 to check their answers.

Examining Meaning and Use

➠ Write these sentences with *in order* + infinitive on the board:

I borrowed a car in order to pick you up.

You should buy an alarm clock in order to get up on time.

Ask the students if they can shorten the sentence and keep the meaning the same. *(Delete in order.)* Note their ideas on the board.

Then tell them to look at the Meaning and Use box on page 384 to check their answers.

CHAPTER 15

Additional Activities

1. Newspaper headline and advertisement search. Have the students look for examples of gerunds and infinitives in the headlines and advertisements of your local newspaper.

2. Bookstore search. For homework, tell your students to go to a bookstore and see how many book titles they can find that contain gerunds and infinitives.

3. Creating book titles. Ask the students to work in small groups. Have them use gerunds to create book titles of books that they would definitely want to read and books that they would never want to read.

The Past Perfect and the Past Perfect Continuous, Past *Wish* Sentences, and Past Imaginary *If* Sentences

It may seem that there is a lot of material in this chapter. However, you will probably find that students will not have difficulty with any of the structures. These structures relate easily to forms the students have studied before.

Using the Preview

➡ Read the first language sample *(News report)* on page 389 as the students follow along in their books. Ask the students to underline the two past actions in each sentence. See if they can figure out which action took place first in each sentence and circle it. Then have the students read paragraph two to check their guesses.

Conclude by asking them this question: *In a sentence with past perfect and simple past, which form indicates the earlier activity? (The past perfect.)* Explain to the students that the past perfect continuous works in a similar way.

➡ Read the second language sample with the students. Ask them if Eva was the person who had the problem. *(No.)* Ask them if Eva was in the restaurant. *(No.)* Then ask them to circle the forms that give the answers to these questions. They can check their answers in the third paragraph.

The Past Perfect

Examining Form

➡ Work with the entire class to complete the following sentence with the past perfect. (For example: ...*had taken a walk/had eaten supper/had gone outside*, etc.):

| By ten o'clock last night, | I
my friends and I
my neighbor
my dog
you | _____. |

Do not correct their answers. Then ask them to transform one of the sentences into a negative and one into a *yes/no* question. Finally, ask them to transform two sentences into information sentences — one with a *wh-* word as nonsubject, and one with *who* or *what* as subject.

Tell them to look at the Form box on page 390 to check their answers.

Using the Conversation Note (page 391)

Read aloud the sentences in the spoken form column to let your students hear how they sound. Then give a short dictation to check your students' aural comprehension of the contraction *'d* in informal speech. Read the following sentences in an informal, conversational style:

He'd left early.

He stopped the car.

We'd read the book before.

Carol'd needed a lot of help.

Martha bought a book.

Examining Meaning and Use

➡ Ask the students to analyze sentences containing the past perfect and simple past or just the simple past in order to explore the chronological relationship between events. Write these sentences on the board:

She had left by the time he arrived.

When the telephone rang, I had just stepped out of the shower.

He had never eaten a mango before he went to Mexico.

They had lived with us ever since they were children.

After you graduated, you paid back your student loan.

Then write four column headings that say:

1st event   2nd event   2nd event   1st event

Pair the students and have them decide which event is first and second in each sentence. Give them five minutes to do this task. Then call on different students to write their sentences under the proper column heads. Do not correct. Tell the students to look at the Meaning and Use box on pages 393–394. Ask them to check their answers.

If the students have not already noticed that the last sentence uses only the simple past, tell them to look at it and note what is different about it. Then tell them to look at the Meaning and Use box and find the point

that explains the use of the simple past in this sentence *(point 7)*.

To compare the past perfect with the present perfect, ask the students to read points 8 and 9 and then look at the following sentences on the board:

The bus had crashed at noon.

The bus has crashed at noon.

Tell the students that one of these sentences is wrong *(the second one)*. Ask them to find the point that explains why *(point 8)*.

The Past Perfect Continuous

Examining Form

➡ Write on the board this example from the Preview on Student Book page 389:

He had been staying at the most expensive hotel in town....

Ask the students to give you other sentences with the past perfect continuous. Ask them for a positive sentence, a negative sentence, a *yes/no* question, and two types of information questions. If they seem unsure, let them work in pairs. Give them five minutes, then call on different students to write their sentences on the board. Write question marks next to the sentences that students are not sure are correct in form.

Tell them to look at the Form box on page 398 to check their answers.

Troubleshooting: If students make sentences with stative verbs (for example: *He had been owning that car...*, etc.), remind them that stative verbs do not usually occur in the continuous.

Examining Meaning and Use

➡ Ask the students to compare sentences with the past perfect continuous and the past perfect in order to discover some of the differences between them. Write these clauses on the board:

She'd been exercising, _____.

She'd exercised _____.

Ask them which sentence is more likely to be followed by:

...the sweat was still pouring down her face. *(The first.)*

Note their guesses on the board. Then write these two clauses on the board:

> We'd been waiting for them _____.
>
> We'd waited for them _____.

Ask the class which clause is more likely to be followed by:

> ...many times in the past. *(The second.)*
>
> ...for three hours. *(The first.)*

Write these two clauses on the board:

> She'd been having _____.
>
> She'd had_____.

Ask the class which clause is more likely to be followed by:

> ...the car for three years. *(The second.)*
>
> ...lunch. *(The first.)*

Note their guesses on the board. Then ask them to look at the Meaning and Use box on page 400 to check their answers. Have them make any corrections necessary to the work on the board.

Past *Wish* Sentences

Examining Form

➡ Remind the students of the form of wishes in the present by asking them to give you examples of things they wish now. Write them on the board.

Then ask the class if anyone knows how to change the present *wish* sentences to the past. Write their ideas on the board.

Tell them to look at the Form box on page 403 to check their answers.

Examining Meaning and Use

➡ Tell the students to give you a present *wish* sentence and a parallel past *wish* sentence. Write them on the board. Ask the class to tell you the difference between them. Note their ideas on the board.

Then tell them to look at the Meaning and Use box on page 404 to check their answers.

Past Imaginary *If* Sentences

Examining Form

➡ Remind the students of the form of imaginary *if* sentences by giving them an example: *If I had the day off, I'd meet my best friend for lunch.* Ask them to make up a few more present imaginary *if* sentences. If they have trouble with the form, tell them to look at Chapter 13.

Write one or two sentences on the board. Ask the students to change them to the past. Write their ideas on the board.

Tell them to check their answers in the Form box on page 406.

Examining Meaning and Use

➡ Check the students' comprehension of the relationship between the *if* clause and the result clause in past imaginary *if* sentences by having the students complete these sentences. Write these clauses on the board:

> If you had been here, _____.
>
> We would never have arrived if _____.
>
> I could have telephoned if _____.
>
> If I had been you, _____.

Give the students five minutes to work. Then call on several students to read their completed sentences. Write their ideas on the board. Ask the class to comment on the form and the meaning. Ask the students to correct any problems with form.

Tell them to look at the Meaning and Use box on pages 407–408 to check any questions that they may have about meaning.

> **Troubleshooting:** Mixed conditionals with the cause in the past and the result clause in the present or future, such as *If you'd been more careful, you wouldn't be in trouble today,* are not dealt with here. If the students ask about sentences such as these, simply say that they are correct, but that, at the moment, they are learning about sentences where both the cause and the result are in the past.

Additional Activities

1. Newspaper search. Ask the students to bring to class a copy of their local newspaper. Have them look for examples of past perfect, past perfect continuous, past *wish* sentences, and past imaginary *if* sentences. Interviews in the sports section may be especially fruitful, particularly if coaches and players being interviewed have recently lost an important game.

2. Using a short story to practice the structures. Have the students all read the same short story. Then ask them what various characters *had been doing* before certain events in the story; and what *would have happened* if the characters *had* or *had not taken* various actions.

3. Dictation. Use the conversation in the Preview on page 389 between Tina and Eva. Pronounce the auxiliary verb *have* with the contractions and reduced stress that you would in normal speech.

CHAPTER 16

Passive Sentences

Many intermediate-level students will be somewhat familiar with the passive voice, particularly the simple present and simple past passives. They should be able to understand these sentences, but they probably know more about forming the passive than they know about why it is used. The first step in teaching students about how to use the passive is to get them to notice it. Encourage them to bring in examples of passive sentences that they find outside of class. You might even start a "passive wall" where students can hang the examples that they have collected.

The teaching suggestions for this chapter are somewhat different from previous chapters. The first two boxes that serve as an introduction to the passive voice have fairly long presentations. Most classes will probably not require a presentation for the last few boxes and can simply use them for reference. As always, adjust the presentations to the level of your class.

Using the Preview

➠ Use the Preview on page 415 to show the relationship between active and passive sentences. Read the language samples with the students. See if they can think of appropriate active sentences that express the same meanings. If they need help, give them the first word (the subject) of each equivalent active sentence and let them complete the rest of each sentence. *(We/They serve dinner from 5:00 to 9:00 P.M. A tornado injured five people. We will prosecute violators.)* Ask the students to tell you the difference between the active and passive sentences. Write their ideas on the board.

Then ask the students to find the answer in the information following the language samples. (They do not need to read the last paragraph at this time.) Call on different students to read aloud the answers from the text. Correct the information on the board, if necessary. (You may want to follow up by having them read the final paragraph and asking them to find the sentence that explains why the news report is in the passive.)

Overview of Passive Sentences

Examining Form

➡ One of the first concepts that students need to learn is the relationship between the form of the active and passive voices. Point this out by having them transform passive sentences into active ones. Tell the students to look at the passive voice sentences at the top of the Form box on page 416.

Working as a class, ask the students to change the simple present passive sentence into an active sentence. Do not tell them that they need to add a subject. Let them discover it for themselves. Write what they tell you on the board. If they do not give you a subject, write an *X* in the subject position. Ask the class what some possible subjects might be. (For example: *The school, The teacher,* etc.) Decide on a subject and put that in place of the *X*. Then ask the students to look at the information in the box and see how they can add that subject to the passive sentence (*by* + noun). Rewrite the simple present passive sentence on the board with the *by* phrase.

Give the students three minutes to write active sentences for all the passive sentences listed in the Form box. Then call on different students to read aloud their sentences. Write any problematic sentences on the board. Ask the student who wrote the sentence to correct it. If he cannot, ask the class to help. Do not spend a lot of time on correcting the active voice, however.

➡ The students should have their books closed. To introduce the concept of *transitive* and *intransitive* verbs, write these sentences on the board:

> She cried for him.
> It rained for three days.
> We should walk the dog.
> I ran three blocks.
> They go with Marty.

Ask the students to work in pairs. Tell them that only one of these sentences can be changed to the passive voice *(the third one).* See if they can identify the sentence and explain why. Give them a few minutes to discuss this. Put a check next to the sentence(s) that they tell you. (They may disagree.) Then tell them to look at the information in the Form box on page 416 again to check their guesses. Mark, if necessary, the one sentence on the board that can be changed.

Ask the students to tell you which verbs in the example sentences on the board are transitive and which are intransitive. If they do not notice themselves, point out

that *walk* is listed as an intransitive verb when you are simply talking about the action of walking. The meaning of *walk* in this sentence is different, however. It means "to take someone/something for a walk," and it is transitive. Point out that some intransitive verbs have related transitive meanings. You may want to remind the students of some other examples. (For example: *taste good vs. taste the cookie/smell awful vs. smell the fumes,* etc.)

Examining Meaning and Use

Troubleshooting: The information in the Meaning and Use box on Student Book pages 417–418 is important and will be referred to throughout the chapter. Therefore, the activity that follows is quite extensive and will probably take almost an entire class period. If you do not feel that you can or want to spend that much time on it, you can instead have the students do the related Student Book exercises first and use the box for reference.

➡ To sensitize the students to the passive voice, let them conduct a "passive voice scavenger hunt." Bring to class newspapers and magazines if students do not usually have enough different kinds of reading material with them.

Divide the class into small groups. Distribute the reading material. Tell the students to look through the texts and try to find about ten examples of the passive voice. Tell them to mark their examples in some way so that they can find them again. Give the groups ten to fifteen minutes to do this task.

Now ask the students to turn to the Meaning and Use box on pages 417–418. Together, read the first paragraph. Tell the students to try to relate the examples of the passive voice that they found in their hunt to the uses listed in the box. To do this, they should first read through the information in the box. The point of this activity is to have the students begin thinking about why some sentences are written in the passive voice. Tell them that you do not expect them to be certain about all of the uses.

Go over their answers by looking at all the points in order and asking the class if anyone has found an example of that use. It is unlikely that they will have found examples of all the uses.

Finally, challenge the students to keep their eye out for passive voice sentences outside the classroom. Ask them every day if anyone has found any interesting uses of the passive.

Simple Present and Simple Past Passives

Examining Form

➠ One of the best ways to learn the form of the passive construction is to transform sentences from active to passive. Make this activity more exciting by turning it into a competition. Write these sentences on the board:

Our office recycles paper.

Scientists study insects.

The class elected her.

Michael ate the cake.

Divide the class into pairs. One student from each pair should work with the simple present tense sentences and the other the simple past tense sentences. Tell the pairs to transform their sentences into the passive voice and then change each one into a negative, a *yes/no* question, and an information question. Tell them to work as fast as they can. The first pair to finish all their sentences correctly is the winner.

Note the finishing order of the pairs, but do not stop the activity until most of the class is done. Then, starting with the first pair to finish, call on them to write their sentences on the board. If they make any mistakes, tell them to sit down and call on the next pair to continue.

Finally, have all the students look at the Form box on pages 420–421.

Examining Meaning and Use

➠ Tell the students to look at the information in the Meaning and Use box on page 423. Ask them to give you other examples that they have noticed of the uses given in point 2. If they cannot think of any, tell them to bring to class the next day as many different examples as they can.

Ask the students to state why the passive is used for each of the examples in point 2 (in signs, definitions, etc.). If they have difficulty answering, do the following activity: Divide the class into groups of two or three and assign each group one of the uses of the passive on page 423. Ask them to turn back to the Meaning and Use box on pages 417–418 and find the reason that best explains the use of the passive that they were assigned.

All Other Forms of the Passive

Examining Form

The following applies to the Form boxes of the Simple Future Passives (page 429), the Continuous and Perfect Passives (pages 431–432), and the Modal Passives (page 438).

➠ Since the form of the passive should be familiar to the students by now, have then do the exercises in the Student Book before they look at the box. Let the students use the appropriate box for reference. If you feel that your students do need a presentation first, do it as a transformation activity.

Examining Meaning and Use

The following applies to the Meaning and Use boxes of the Future, Continuous, and Perfect Passives (page 434), and the Modal Passives (page 440).

➠ Give the students three to five minutes to read through each box. Then let them do the exercises, using the appropriate box and the one on pages 417–418 for reference as necessary.

Additional Activities

1. Newspaper search. Have the students find examples of the passive voice in your local newspaper. As an additional task, have them find headlines in the passive and rewrite them as active sentences.

2. Sign search. As a homework assignment, ask the students to be on the lookout for examples of passive voice that they see in signs as they come to school, go to work, or go about their everyday activities.

3. Encyclopedia search. Ask the students to look up topics that interest them in the encyclopedia. Have them copy examples of the passive voice. Ask them to decide why they think the passive was used in their examples.

4. Writing about a process. Ask the students to write about some type of process. (For example: how something is made, how something is done, etc.) Instruct them to include some sentences in the passive voice.

Song
"When Will I Be Loved?" by Phil Everly

CHAPTER 17

Noun Clauses and Reported Speech

Some intermediate-level students will have already seen many of these structures and they should be able to understand the sentences in which they are used. However, students may know these structures by different terms (for example: *indirect questions*). Students still need to work toward more accuracy in forming these structures, particularly in relation to word order. It should be noted that errors related to tenses, pronouns, and adverbs are best treated as questions of meaning and use from the perspective of the reporter.

Using the Preview

➡ Read the language samples in the Preview on page 447 with the students to introduce them to the different kinds of noun clauses. Write these phrases on the board as column headings:

wh- clause   *if/whether* clause   *that* clause

Ask the students to underline the boldfaced parts of the sample sentences in the Preview. Tell them that the sentences contain three different kinds of noun clauses. See if they can tell you examples of each. Write all their ideas on the board under the heading they indicate.

Then ask the students to read the information in the first paragraph following the language samples to check their answers. Make corrections as necessary on the board. Ask the class to give further examples by substituting their own noun clauses for the boldfaced parts of the sentences in the sample language. (For example: *Do you believe that we need a final exam at the end of the semester? Do you think that people should be allowed to drive at age sixteen? The president said last night that he was not going to veto the proposed budget.*)

Wh- Clauses

Examining Form

➡ Have the students analyze incorrect sentences in order to describe *wh-* clauses. Write these incorrect sentences on the board. Mark them with an asterisk:

I wonder what was she doing.

Do you know where the phone?

I don't know when they arrived?

Can you remember, who left?

Divide the class into small groups. Tell the groups to correct each sentence and discuss why it is wrong. If they need help, tell them to think about word order and punctuation.

Give them five minutes to work. Then call on different students to come to the board to correct each sentence and state why it is wrong. Write their ideas on the board. Then tell the students to look at the Form box on page 448 to check their work. Correct the students' answers on the board if necessary.

Examining Meaning and Use

➡ Write the sentence below on the board:

I know why she is angry.

Ask the students to give you verbs or phrases about knowing or mental activity that can replace *know* (*remember, forget, wonder, am not sure, understand, am certain*). Tell them that the meaning of the sentence will change, but it will still make sense and be grammatically correct.

Write their ideas on the board. Ask them to look at point 1 in the Meaning and Use box on page 450 to check their answers.

➡ Tell the students to close their books. Go up to one student and ask him a direct question. Make sure that it can be transformed into a *wh-* clause. (For example: *Where's the post office? What time is it?*) Ask in a slightly aggressive or gruff manner. Then ask another student the same question in indirect question form (*Can you tell me...? Do you know...?*). Ask in a more polite manner to emphasize the difference. See if the class can tell you which one sounded more polite. Tell them to look at point 2 in the Meaning and Use box on page 450 to check their answer. Point out that your manner and tone of voice were for demonstration purposes. However, it is easier to sound polite when you use an indirect question rather than a direct question.

If/Whether Clauses

Examining Form

➡ Try to elicit *if/whether* clauses by asking students to change a direct *yes/no* question into an indirect one. Write two *yes/no* questions on the board. (For example: *Is there a good movie on tonight? Did Frank arrive by plane?*) Ask the students to change these into indirect questions and answers beginning with *I don't know...* or *Can you tell me...?*

Write the students' ideas on the board. Do not correct any mistakes at this time. Tell the students to look at the Form box on pages 452–453 to check and correct their answers.

Examining Meaning and Use

➡ Ask the students if they think there is any difference between the two statements below. *(The meaning is the same but **whether** is more common in formal situations.):*

> I don't know   if   he has arrived.
>   whether

Then ask the class to check the Meaning and Use box on page 454 to verify their answer.

That Clauses

Examining Form

➡ The students should be familiar enough with noun clause formation to do Exercise 10 on page 457. Use the Form box above it as a reference if necessary.

Examining Meaning and Use

> **Troubleshooting:** There is a wealth of information in this box. Neither the teacher nor the students should expect the class to learn it all right off. They should become familiar with the box and then use it for reference as they work through the exercises.

➡ Tell the students to open their books to point 1 in the Meaning and Use box on page 458. Tell them to look at the list of verbs and circle or underline any that they do not understand. If they have dictionaries, they can look up the meaning. If they do not, let them ask their classmates for the meanings or example sen-

tences that will help them understand the meaning. Circulate as they are talking to help sort out the problems. At the end, go over any words that students are still unsure of. As the students work through the exercises, encourage them to refer to this list and try to use as many of these verbs as they can.

➡ Tell the students to close their books. Write these pairs of sentences on the board. (Do not include the italic information in parentheses.):

1. a. I think he can stay.
   b. I think that he can stay. *(#2)*
2. a. He thought you are driving too fast.
   b. He thought you were driving too fast. *(#3 and 4)*
3. a. She imagined you would pass.
   b. She imagined you were going to pass. *(#6)*
4. a. Galileo proved that the earth revolves around the sun.
   b. Galileo proved that the earth revolved around the sun. *(#7)*
5. (Is John here?)
   a. I think not.
   b. I don't think so. *(#10)*

Divide the students into pairs or small groups. Ask them to decide which of these sentences are correct *(all except item 2a):*

Mark the ones that they tell you are incorrect with an asterisk or a question mark if they are unsure. Let the class tell you their ideas. Have them read point 4 on page 458 to find out why item 2a is incorrect.

Then ask the students to look at sentence pairs 1, 3, 4, and 5 (written on the board) and decide which pairs mean the same thing. *(They all mean the same thing.)*

Finally, tell the students to look at the Meaning and Use box on pages 458–459 to check which points relate to each sentence pair shown above.

Overview of Reported Speech

Examining Form

➡ Ask the students to think about reported speech in order to make them aware of what they already know about this type of structure. Write these four sentences on the board and ask the students to listen to you read the news report from the Preview on page 447:

> "Please raise taxes this year."

> "I will not raise taxes this year."

"When will you raise taxes?"

"Will you raise taxes this year?"

Ask the students if they can tell which of these sentences the president said last night. Point out that the correct sentence is a statement. Then, one at a time, read the reported sentences in the Form box on page 461. Ask the students to identify the original sentence as a statement, a *yes/no* question, an information question, or an imperative. Write their ideas on the board. Then tell them to check the Form box on page 461 to verify their answers.

Examining Form: Quoted Speech versus Reported Speech

➡ Have the students analyze quoted speech/reported speech pairs in order to find some of the basic differences. Write these pairs on the board:

"Go home."	He told me to go home.
"Did you give me this?"	He asked if I had given him that.
"I'm happy."	She said that she was happy.
	She says that she is happy.
"They may quit."	He said that they might quit.
"I can go."	She said that she could go.

Divide the students into groups. Ask them to write down any differences that they notice between quoted speech and reported speech. Tell them to pay special attention to punctuation, pronouns, verb forms, and modals.

Give the groups five to seven minutes to work. Write their ideas on the board. Tell them to look at the Form box on pages 462–463 to check their answers. Correct the information on the board if necessary.

Ask the students to look for other differences in the Form box that were not in their example sentences. (For example: *other modals: **must** changes to **had to,*** etc.)

Examining Meaning and Use: Reported Speech

Troubleshooting: The Meaning and Use box on pages 465–468 has much more information than the students can be expected to digest at once. The material will need to be revisited as the students go through the exercises in their books. In addition, the Meaning and Use box focuses on instances where English speakers do not have to backshift tenses. If students cannot make these distinctions, then teach them to backshift, since this is always correct. Most important, students need to know that they must be consistent once they have made their choice in a particular context.

➡ Have the students familiarize themselves with at least part of the information on pages 465–468 by assigning them points to teach the rest of the class. Divide the students into groups of three or four. Assign each group some information to present to the rest of the class. Divide the information up into sections as follows: Tense Changes; Pronoun Changes; Adverb Changes; Reporting Verbs, points 1–4; Reporting Verbs, points 5–8.

Tell the students that they are responsible for learning their section very well and deciding how best to present it to the rest of the class. They can simply talk about it, write a conversation, or do an activity that demonstrates the meaning of their information.

Give the groups at least fifteen minutes to work. Circulate to help and give ideas when necessary. Call on the different groups to present their work. If some students seem very interested in presenting a topic (even if another group has already presented the same information), let them do it on a different day. The review will benefit everyone.

Additional Activities

1. Changing a conversation to reported speech. Ask the students to work in small groups. Have them write a conversation between two people. You can suggest different conversation topics to different groups. Then ask the groups to rewrite the conversation as a story. Instruct them to change all quoted speech to reported speech.

2. Writing indirect questions. Have the students write what they would like to know about their classmates' countries. (For example: *I would like to know when Mexico became an independent country. I don't know what kind of food people eat in Norway.*) Then have the students from these countries answer the questions.

3. Newspaper search. Tell the students to find examples of noun clauses and reported speech in their local newspaper.

Song
"I Feel Fine" by John Lennon and Paul McCartney

DIAGNOSTIC AND
ACHIEVEMENT QUIZZES

The Simple Present

Four of the following 12 items are correct. The rest each have one error.
Find and correct each error.

1. My family live in Boston.

2. Paul don't like football.

3. What means the title of this book? I don't understand it.

4. Kate doesn't smoke. Her brother does.

5. Everyone helps with the housework. Pam cooks, George does the laundry, and Van washs the dishes.

6. What happen at a typical American wedding?

7. A: What do birds eat?
   B: They are eating worms and insects.

8. Most elderly people don't listen to rock music.

9. A: What does your sister do?
   B: She's an engineer. She works downtown.

10. A: Does this map show the three schools in the neighborhood?
    B: Yes. The elementary school is on Main Street, the junior high school was on Riverside Avenue, and the high school is on Broadway.

11. Classes at the elementary school begin at 9:00 A.M. At the junior high and high schools, classes start at 8:15 A.M.

12. Here are the results of our survey. In general, adults want to be younger and children wanted to be older.

Intermediate Grammar: From Form to Meaning and Use
© 1996 Oxford University Press. Permission granted to reproduce for classroom use.

The Present Continuous

One of the following 10 items is correct. The rest each have one error.
Find and correct each error.

1. Right now Paul is talking on the telephone and Betsy working in the garden.

2. It's a beautiful day outside. Many people is sitting in the park.

3. Where is studying your son?

4. A: What classes are you taking this term?
   B: I'm take biology, English, and calculus.

5. At this moment Jenny is playing with the cat.

6. It's raining right now, so the boys don't playing baseball.

7. A: Is your band playing at a lot of weddings these days?
   B: Yes, it does.

8. A: Who's making that loud noise?
   B: Tommy. He plays with pots and pans in the kitchen.

9. A: Is Joselin singing in the chorus today?
   B: No. Most Sundays she is singing in the chorus, but today she's studying for an important exam.

10. Everyone's staring at Suzie. She's wearing a silk dress and white gloves.
    Normally she's wearing dirty jeans.

CHAPTER 1 Diagnostic Quiz

Stative Verbs

Three of the following 10 items are correct. The rest each have one error.
Find and correct each error.

1. A: Which are you liking better, oranges or lemons?
   B: Oranges. Lemons taste too sour.

2. Lucille is having green eyes and blonde hair.

3. Now I understand the first and second math problems. But I'm not knowing the answer to the third one.

4. Parent: Your sister is wearing your new sweater.
   Child: I know. I'm not minding.

5. Polly is being very funny today. It's strange. Most of the time she's being very serious.

6. June has three sons. She's having trouble with the oldest one.

7. A: Do you see anyone outside right now?
   B: I see a tall man with a dog.

8. Brenda weighs 190 pounds now. She's appearing upset about it.

9. At this moment I feel terrible. My shoulder aches and my knees hurt too.

10. This is my favorite cookbook. It's containing many recipes for chocolate desserts.

The Simple Present, the Present Continuous, and Stative Verbs

A. Complete the sentences using the appropriate simple present or present continuous forms of the verbs in parentheses.

1. The average person in the United States _____ (eat) too much junk food.

   But these days nutritionists _____ (try) to change this situation.

   They _____ (want) people to eat less junk food and more fruits and vegetables.

2. This week Dan _____ (work) extra hours because one of his co-workers

   _____ (be) on vacation.

3. Lilly _____ (have) a job as a baby-sitter for two little girls. Usually the girls

   _____ (behave) very well. But this week the girls _____ (act)

   like devils. They _____ (drive) Lilly crazy. Lilly _____(know/not)

   the reason for the sudden change in their behavior.

B. Two of the following 10 items are correct. The rest have one error each. Find and correct each error.

1. Coreen usually shops at Mike's Market. But today that store isn't being open, so right now she's shopping at GrandRite.

2. A: How many pets do you and your husband own?
   B: Right now we're owning one dog and one cat.

3. Cassie's an accountant. She doesn't likes her job very much, but she earns a lot of money.

4. A: What you are doing?
   B: I'm writing a list of guests for my party.

5. Look at that man. He wearing a T-shirt in the middle of winter!

6. At this moment Julie is cooking dinner and Benny is tasting everything in the pots on the stove.

7. A: What do you think about this dress?
   B: It's seeming a little small on you.

8. The accident is very serious. We need to call Dr. James. Are you knowing his telephone number?

9. Cars cause air pollution. Bicycles don't.

10. These cookies are containing milk, butter, eggs, and sugar. They have a lot of calories, but they taste delicious.

Adverbs of Frequency

A. Five of the following 12 items are correct. The rest each have one error.
Find and correct each error.

1. Always Tom eats eggs for breakfast.

2. Rob often stays at work after 5:00 P.M.

3. A: Who usually cooks breakfast in your family?
   B: My sister. Occasionally I help her.

4. Ever are you late?

5. Stephanie takes never public transportation.

6. Sometimes I eat eggs for breakfast. Never I eat cold cereal.

7. A: Do you ever skip breakfast?
   B: Yes, I often do.

8. Paul doesn't never go to the opera.

9. Kathleen and Craig don't rarely eat in restaurants.

10. I don't often tell Harry my opinions. He seldom agrees with me, and I don't like arguments.

11. George is constantly borrowing money from me. It's very annoying.

12. A: Do you go to church on Sundays?
    B: Yes, I never do.

B. Match the adverb of frequency on the left with the phrase on the right that best
describes it.

Answers to the question:
How often do you watch the evening news?

Phrases that describe the adverbs of frequency

1. sometimes   a. 100% of the time

2. almost never   b. about 99% of the time

3. always   c. about 90% of the time

4. almost always   d. about 50% of the time

5. never   e. about 20% of the time

6. frequently   f. about 2% of the time

7. rarely   g. 0% of the time

There Is and *There Are*

Four of the following 12 items are correct. The rest each have one error.
Find and correct each error.

1. There are many divorced people in the United States.

2. Receptionist: Milltown Limited. One moment please. Ms. Drake, is a call for you on line 1.

3. There aren't no swimming pools in my neighborhood.

4. There a lot of interesting programs on television tonight.

5. A: Please take out the apples.
   B: There aren't some apples in the refrigerator.

6. Is there a rock in your pocketbook? It's very heavy!

7. A: Are there any bills in the mail?
   B: Yes, there are one. It's from the telephone company.

8. A: Is anything you can do to help me?
   B: No, I'm sorry, but there's nothing I can do.

9. A: Is that book interesting?
   B: Yes. It's a wonderful story.

10. It's a pile of dirty dishes in the sink and bread crumbs all over the floor!
    You said you had a clean apartment! Obviously that wasn't true!

11. There are two nickels in a dime and there are ten dimes in a dollar.
    So how many nickels are there in a dollar?

12. A: Can you recommend a good Japanese restaurant?
    B: Yes. It's one on Third Street. It's opposite the movie theater.

Imperatives

Three of the following 8 items are correct. The rest each have one error.
Find and correct each error.

1. Don't park there. It's a bus stop.

2. No walk on the kitchen floor, please. I just washed it.

3. Pay you attention to what I tell you. I'm not going to repeat it.

4. Tell please me your address and telephone number.

5. A: How do I get to Joe's Supermarket?
   B: Walk five blocks. Then turn right and go another two blocks.

6. I need everyone's help. Here, you carry the blue suitcase, you carry the red one,
   and you take the green one. I'll take the rest.

7. *A recipe in a cookbook:* Combine the first four ingredients. You mix at medium speed.
   Add the dry ingredients. Mix again until smooth.

8. The pot is very hot. Please you are careful.

Intermediate Grammar: From Form to Meaning and Use

CHAPTER 2 Achievement Quiz

Adverbs of Frequency, *There Is* and *There Are*, and Imperatives

Six of the following 20 items are correct. The rest each have one error.
Find and correct each error.

1. This apartment is good for someone who likes to cook. There's a large kitchen with new appliances.

2. There two children in the average American family. In your country, are there many families with more than two children?

3. Go to the store and buy some apples. Don't buy anything else.

4. Ursula doesn't never wear jeans to school. She always wears a skirt or a dress.

5. Open please the door.

6. Betty and Jim are always criticizing other people. This bothers me a lot.

7. Valerie is talking always on the telephone. So I always get a busy signal when I try to call her.

8. Never Susan comes to school on time. Every day her teacher gets angry at her.

9. I'm bored. It's nothing to do.

10. I never shop at that supermarket because there are always long lines and the cashiers rarely smile.

11. A: How many senators there are in Congress?
    B: One hundred. But usually they're not all present at the same time.

12. Bill rarely visits his grandmother. He's making up always some excuse about his busy schedule.

13. A: Jane attends class every day. She has perfect attendance.
    B: That means she is usually absent.

14. Please don't ask my father about his job. There are always a problem at work. So he doesn't like to talk about his work at all.

15. There two coats on the sofa. Please put them in the closet.

16. A: Do usually you eat breakfast?
    B: It depends. I always do on Saturday and Sunday. Sometimes I don't have time on workdays.

17. Don't always ask me for help! Try to figure out the answer yourself first.

18. A: Do you have good neighbors?
    B: Yes and no. There's a very friendly young man in the apartment on the right. But in the apartment on the left, there's a family with two young children. They sometimes make a lot of noise.

19. There aren't some movie theaters in my neighborhood. But there are a lot of video stores.

20. A: Is a problem with unemployment in your country?
    B: Yes, there are many people without jobs.

The Simple Past

One of the following 16 items is correct. The rest each have one error.
Find and correct each error.

1. Did you made that chocolate cake?

2. Why Mike and Joe got home late last night?

3. Andrea and Carla was at the party, but I didn't see them.

4. I bought a new stereo on November. It broke immediately. What a waste of money!

5. Did Andy be sick yesterday? I didn't see him in my chemistry class.

6. Did Veronica went to the dance with Pete?

7. Tony hurted his foot two weeks ago.

8. Was you in the library earlier today?

9. Horace participated in the bowling tournament last month, but he didn't won.
   His best friend, Tyrone, did.

10. A: What did Rose and Frank buy their niece for her birthday?
    B: They didn't buy anything. They builded her a treehouse.

11. Several days ago, Helen fall off her bicycle and broke her leg.

12. A: Did Rachel catch the ball?
    B: Yes, she does. But then she dropped it.

13. A: Please help me. Did I forget anything?
    B: Do you bring your passport?

14. A: Were you a high school student in 1970?
    B: No. I was only two years old then.

15. Two months ago I took a trip to Barbados. I had a great time. I go to the beach
    every day and I ate a lot of seafood.

16. A: Why are you late?
    B: I miss the bus, so I walked to work.

Used to

Three of the following 10 items are correct. The rest each have one error.
Find and correct each error.

1. I didn't used to like vegetables, but now I eat more vegetables than meat.

2. Rick use to be very short. Today he isn't tall, but his height is about average.

3. Mr. and Mrs. Brickman used to loved each other, but now they are planning to get a divorce.

4. Irene used to has a job she hated. Fortunately, she now has a job she loves.

5. Today Esther lives in California, but she used to living in Arizona.

6. When Sally was in high school, she never used to study. But now that she's in college, she studies all the time.

7. Yesterday I used to see a very good movie.

8. I used to be jealous of my brother. But that changed a few years ago.

9. Marianne used to speak to Jeff every day. She would call him at night and they would talk for at least thirty minutes.

10. Two days ago I used to have a very difficult exam in my accounting class.

The Past Continuous

Two of the following 10 items are correct. The rest each have one error.
Find and correct each error.

1. A: What was you doing at five o'clock yesterday afternoon?
   B: I was cooking dinner.

2. A: Where your parents were living twenty years ago?
   B: They were living in New Mexico.

3. A: Why was Louisa crying last night?
   B: She was thinking about her fight with her husband.

4. A: Who was dancing with Maria at the party?
   B: Doug did.

5. A: Did you talking on the telephone about an hour ago?
   B: Yes, I was.

6. A: What was wearing Judy yesterday?
   B: She was wearing a blue skirt and a white blouse.

7. A: How many children were not paying attention to the teacher?
   B: Six. Two were look out the window, three were drawing pictures, and one was sleeping.

8. All the humans in the house were sleeping, but the animals were having fun. The cat was playing with a ball of string, the parrot is trying to fly out of her cage, and the fish were swimming in their tank.

9. Everyone was watching the football game on television. Then suddenly the electricity was going out.

10. Naomi and Joel were playing the guitar. Tammy was singing. Bart was listening and trying to understand the words of the song.

The Simple Past, *Used to*, and the Past Continuous

Seven of the following 20 items are correct. The rest each have one error.
Find and correct each error.

1. Theodore Roosevelt didn't ran for president during the 1930s. Franklin Roosevelt did.

2. Kim used to be afraid of the water. But now she loves to swim.

3. A: The food at that restaurant was wonderful.
   B: Yes, it was. The service was also very good.

4. The nightclub was crowded. The band was playing a romantic song. Some couples are dancing.
   The waiters were taking orders.

5. A: Were you watching television last night at nine o'clock?
   B: No, I wasn't. Did I missed something interesting?

6. Abe used to smoked cigars. But he quit last year.

7. A: Those comedians were terrible!
   B: No, they wasn't. I laughed at most of their jokes.

8. Frieda was doing the crossword puzzle and Lenny was reading the financial news.
   Their daughter was looking at the comics. Suddenly, a mouse ran across the room.

9. A: Did you hear about Sue's accident?
   B: No, I didn't. What happened?

10. A: Did you forgot to lock the door?
    B: No, I didn't. Nancy left after me. She probably didn't lock it.

11. When I was a child, I used to be mean to my little sister. I would hide her dolls
    and steal her crayons. Then my mother would find out and I would get in trouble.

12. A: What you thought of the mayor's speech last night?
    B: It wasn't very interesting.

13. A: Who wrote *Cat on a Hot Tin Roof?*
    B: Tennesse Williams did.

14. A: Did you use to believe in Santa Claus when you were a child?
    B: No. I knew that my Christmas presents come from my parents.

15. Police officer: Where were you at nine o'clock last night?
    Thief: I was eat dinner at Arnie's Bar and Grill.

16. A: Did you pay all the bills?
    B: I payed the rent and the telephone bill. I didn't pay the gas bill.

17. Teacher: Why didn't you do your homework?
    Student: My grandfather's ghost visit me last night. He took me on a tour of heaven.
    I got back at midnight. By then it was very late and I was tired.

18. A: Did your grandmother use to has red hair?
    B: Yes, she did. It was just like mine.

19. A: Why wasn't your car working yesterday?
    B: Someone put sugar in the gas tank.

20. Yesterday I used to hear some interesting news.

Be Going to

Two of the following 6 items are correct. The rest each have one error.
Find and correct the errors.

1. A: When are you going to speak to your boss about a raise?
   B: Next month, right after his vacation. He going to be in a good mood then.

2. A: Are you going to vote in the election?
   B: Yes, I'm going to vote for Marge Peterson.

3. A: What you are going to do this afternoon?
   B: I'm going to relax and listen to my new CDs.

4. Yesterday I'm going to talk to my lawyer.

5. The lights are dimming. The show is going to begin in five minutes.

6. A: What are Tom's plans for tonight?
   B: First he studies for his exam. Then he's going to call me.

✂

Will

Four of the following 10 items are correct. The rest each have one error.
Find and correct the errors.

1. Alicia will knows the answer to your question. I'll ask her about it tomorrow.

2. Lisa don't will be in class next week.

3. A: Will you be there on Thursday?
   B: No, I don't.

4. Customer: What's today's special?
   Waitress: Pasta Primavera.
   Customer: I'll have that and a bowl of soup, please.

5. A: Will Gene win the contest?
   B: He probably doesn't, but I think he'll come close. Maybe he'll win second or third place.

6. Customer: When will you have summer clothing in the store?
   Salesclerk: I think we'll receive a big shipment of bathing suits and shorts in a few weeks, but you'll have to ask the manager exactly when.

7. I bring a blanket and some paper plates to the picnic tomorrow.
   Please tell Jane to bring a case of soda.

8. A: Will you be at the concert next week?
   B: No, unfortunately I won't. I'll be in Los Angeles at a sales conference.

9. A: Please answer the telephone. I'm washing the dog.
   B: Sure, just a second. I'll get it.

10. I promise I don't tell anyone your secret.

The Present Continuous as a Future Form

Three of the following 8 items are correct. The rest each have one error.
Find and correct the errors.

1. A: Do you have plans for Linda's baby shower?
   B: Yes. I'm have a party next Monday.

2. Marcy has a lot of homework. She doesn't coming to the movies tonight.

3. A: Have you heard the news? Peter and Marsha are getting a divorce!
   B: I'm sorry to hear that.

4. A: When are you leaving for your trip?
   B: Next Tuesday. I'm buying the plane tickets tomorrow.

5. I just heard the news. It's snowing tomorrow.

6. A: What are you doing after work?
   B: I'm going shopping with my brother and sister-in-law.

7. I think that the Jets are winning the game this weekend.

8. Tom always drives very fast. So he's probably getting a speeding ticket soon.

✂

The Simple Present as a Future Form

Three of the following 8 items are correct. The rest each have one error.
Find and correct the errors.

1. Registration for summer sessions starts next Tuesday.

2. When do Jane's train arrive tomorrow night?

3. Hurry up! Our bus leave in five minutes.

4. Classes begin next Tuesday. They end on December 7.

5. I promise I remember to bring you the photographs tomorrow.

6. Who do you think wins first prize in the science fair tomorrow?

7. My train leaves at 10:00 tomorrow morning. It arrives in Miami at 9:00 P.M. on Wednesday.

8. John isn't sure about next year. Maybe he works for his uncle.

Connecting Sentences

Three of the following 12 items are correct. The rest each have one error.
Find and correct the error.

1. Billie Holiday was a singer, and Bessie Smith did too.

2. Mary will have some free time next week, but Eliza won't.

3. Camilla often gets angry at Mrs. Sanders, and so I do.

4. Eve doesn't play tennis very well, and neither Jenny does.

5. I work for a large company, and my husband is too.

6. A: He isn't French.
   B: I neither.

7. A: Jack needs to go to the store today.
   B: So do Mary.

8. I won't speak to Josephine again, and either will Angie.

9. Gertrude never speaks in class, and Rita does too.

10. Kathy is unhappy with the situation, and I am too.

11. The newspaper came yesterday, but the mail didn't.

12. My stereo isn't working, and so is my computer.

Be Going to, Will, the Present Continuous, and the Simple Present; Connecting Sentences

Eight of the following 20 items are correct. The rest each have one error. Find and correct the errors.

1. A: I'm going to a boxing match tomorrow.
   B: What time does the match start?

2. A: Will we have good weather on Friday?
   B: No, we don't. It's going to rain.

3. My heart is broken. I never fall in love again!

4. The violin is a string instrument, and so does the viola.

5. A: I hope that you'll enjoy the trip.
   B: I'm sure that I do.

6. Pigs don't go to school, and neither do snakes.

7. A: Will you help Johnny with his math homework?
   B: No, I won't. I'm too busy, and he never listens to me.

8. Parent: I won't punish you. But promise me you'll never do it again.
   Child: I promise. I don't do it again.

9. Client: When does the plane leave?
   Travel Agent: It leaves at six o'clock in the morning and arrives at ten.

10. I don't have much patience, but my sister is. She's an elementary school teacher.

11. Unfortunately, Hannah and Colin don't will be at the awards ceremony next week. They have an important appointment at the bank on the same day.

12. Lance won't play in the basketball game tomorrow, and Eric doesn't either. They both have injuries.

13. A: Which horse is you going to bet on?
    B: Spanish Stallion. I think he'll win the race.

14. I love silent movies, and Denise does too. So we're going to a Charlie Chaplin festival this Saturday.

15. Lucinda hardly ever spends a lot of money, but her daughter does.

16. Store Manager: I'm starting a new job in two weeks.
    Employee: Then who going to be in charge of the store?

17. A: The baby's crying.
    B: I'll give him a bottle.

18. Actress: Will I have my own dressing room?
    Director: No, you won't, and either will anyone else. We don't have enough space.

19. A: How long is your sister going to stay with you?
    B: I think she stays for a week. She isn't sure yet.

20. A: I want to pay you for your help.
    B: I appreciate your offer, but I won't accept any money from you.

Past Time Clauses

A. Combine the two sentences in any order. Use the time words in parentheses to introduce the time clause. You may need to change the position of the names and the pronouns. Use proper punctuation.

> Example: Peter hurt his back. He was shoveling snow. (while)
> While Peter was shoveling snow, he hurt his back. OR
> Peter hurt his back while he was shoveling snow.

1. Kate got help from a tutor. Her grades improved. (after)

_____

2. Gretchen was shopping. Dan was cleaning the apartment. (while)

_____

3. Mr. Thomas had a perfect driving record. His car ran off the road. (before)

_____

4. The prisoner was planning his escape. A guard walked into his cell. (when)

_____

5. Mr. James bought a used car. He discovered a leak in the radiator. (after)

_____

B. Two of the following 5 sentences are correct. The rest each have one error. Find and correct each error.

1. While Beatrice was sleeping, her cat was chasing a mouse.

2. Al picked up his hat after he was dropping it.

3. Bill was repairing the roof when he fell off the ladder.

4. Before we were buying a cat, we had a problem with mice.

5. Toby was shopping while she lost her wallet.

C. Underline the event that happened or started first.

> Example: After <u>Lou came back from vacation</u>, he lost his job.

1. When I opened a can of tuna fish, the cat ran into the kitchen.

2. Before Jerry started school, his mother taught him how to read.

3. The hot water heater stopped working while Peg was washing her hair.

4. Rick spent $200 on new locks after thieves broke into his apartment.

5. I spoke Spanish very poorly before I enrolled in a language school in Madrid.

Future Time Clauses

A. Combine the two sentences into one using a time clause. Use the time word in parentheses to introduce the time clause. You will need to change the tense of one of the verbs to the future. Use proper punctuation.

> Example: Mitch and Claude perform on television. Their agent gets them a contract. (after)
>   Mitch and Claude will perform on television after their agent gets them a contract. OR
>   After their agent gets them a contract, Mitch and Claude will perform on television.

1. Brad finishes his book. He lends it to me. (after)

_____

2. We decide what kind of wedding to have. We talk about it with our parents. (before)

_____

3. She is surprised. She discovers the truth. (when)

_____

4. We show you around the city. You leave. (before)

_____

5. They go to Europe. They take their next vacation. (when)

_____

B. Two of the following 5 sentences are correct. The rest each have one error. Find and correct each error.

1. I call you when I know the answer.

2. Jill sells her house after her son finishes high school.

3. After this television program is over, I'll fix your bicycle.

4. When June's boss retires, she'll get his job.

5. Before my hair will turn gray, I'll climb Mount Everest.

Real *If* Sentences

Three of the following 10 sentences are correct. The rest each have one error.
Find and correct each error.

1. If you dye your hair, your old friends won't recognize you.

2. Callie won't enjoy the trip if we will stay in cheap hotels.

3. If you will come in late one more time, the boss is going to fire you.

4. Your throat feel better if you have some chicken soup now.

5. If you help me with my science project, I'll edit your essay for your English class.

6. I never speak to you again if you don't tell me the truth.

7. If the bus doesn't arrive soon, we going to walk.

8. Susan will get the job if she won't get nervous during the interview.

9. Will you cancel the picnic if it will rain tomorrow?

10. If I lose fifteen pounds, I'll be able to wear my favorite dress.

11. I'm warning you. If you don't leave now, you missed the show.

12. Don't be foolish. The police are everywhere. You're getting a ticket if you drive that way.

Intermediate Grammar: From Form to Meaning and Use

Past Time Clauses, Future Time Clauses, and Real *If* Sentences

A. Complete the sentences with the appropriate forms of the verbs in parentheses.

1. Last night, Beth _____ (go) up the stairs when the phone _____ (ring).

2. When my new boss _____ (come up) to me at the party yesterday,

   I _____ (introduce) her to my husband.

3. If Eileen _____ (win) the contest, she'll share her prize with me.

4. Keisha _____ (decide) which job to take after she talks to her career counselor.

5. Melissa _____ (meet) her husband before she finished the tenth grade.

6. After Craig's father _____ (die), his mother moved to Florida.

7. Astrid is going to be happy when she _____ (hear) the news.

8. Ruby _____ (plant) the roses in her garden tomorrow if we help her.

9. When the children came home, Jamal _____ (tell) them about their mother's accident.

10. If Rachel _____ (go) to the Caribbean in July, the airfare won't be very expensive.

B. Three of the following 8 sentences are correct. The rest each have one error.
Find and correct each error.

1. Pauline was thinking about her boyfriend when her math teacher asked her a question.

2. If Mary marries Abe, Abe's mother has a heart attack.

3. Annette gave me the message before she leaves.

4. Kim won't go to bed before the sun will set.

5. Joanie will call you back after she finishes her homework.

6. While Corey was playing the piano, Elizabeth reads a book.

7. My neighbors will complain if I'll have a noisy party.

8. Lionel will go to college if he gets enough financial aid.

The Present Perfect

Two of the following 16 items are correct. The rest each have one error.
Find and correct each error.

1. Have gone to any parties this month?

2. Sally has broke three records for women volleyball players this year.

3. Greg seen that movie five times.

4. Gloria have liked milk since she was a child.

5. You have ever taken a long train ride?

6. A: Has Elizabeth spoken to you about the party yet?
   B: Yes, she's. She called me last night.

7. Harry has worked in the same office since six years.

8. Yesterday I have written several letters.

9. I'm still in the same apartment. I lived there for six years.

10. I have known Maria for ten years. I was so sad when she died last year.

11. So far Tom hasn't met any women he likes.

12. Emma has been sick for several months when she was four years old.

13. I owned my car since 1991. It runs very well.

14. He has worked for the company for seven years. He is very happy with his job.

15. They have lived here from 1990 to 1995.

16. Thomas Edison has invented the electric light bulb.

Intermediate Grammar: From Form to Meaning and Use
© 1996 Oxford University Press. Permission granted to reproduce for classroom use.

The Present Perfect Continuous

Two of the following 12 items are correct. The rest each have one error.
Find and correct each error.

1. I have going out with John for six months, but we're not ready to get engaged.

2. Allen and Jenny have been painting their house all day.

3. Mimi has been live in Boston for six years.

4. Paul have been playing baseball since he was four years old.

5. Ricky hasn't been talked to his parents since his mother criticized his girlfriend.

6. You have standing here for twenty minutes.

7. Have you been owning your car for a long time?

8. I've already been listening to the news four times today.

9. Ruth has been dating Andy since she was in high school.

10. I've been waiting for your telephone call since an hour.

11. Priscilla has been knowing Jeff for twelve years.

12. A: You look happy.
    B: I am. I've just been finding my wallet in my car.

The Present Perfect and the Present Perfect Continuous

Two of the following 20 sentences are correct. The rest each have one error.
Find and correct each error.

1. Alex has been read that book since noon.

2. Has you ever seen him so interested in a book?

3. He has met his new neighbors yesterday.

4. Tim's face is red because he been working in a hot kitchen for the past two hours.

5. Last year George has gone on his first trip to California.

6. He has went to California three times since then.

7. Have Sally told you about her new boyfriend?

8. Since her mother's death, Margaret has never been having enough money to take her family on a vacation.

9. Eliza has been talking on the telephone since three hours.

10. What you have been doing since I spoke to you last week?

11. Patty hasn't feeling well recently.

12. Ted's brothers haven't spoke to him about the party yet.

13. I have been watching that program three times this week.

14. Mr. and Mrs. Robinson have just bought a new house.

15. Yesterday Lisa has changed her clothes four times.

16. Have you been being sick lately?

17. Why hasn't been Allen getting enough sleep lately?

18. So far, I haven't chose a dress for the party.

19. Maria hasn't seen her grandfather from 1992 to 1995.

20. I'm bored. I've been reading that book for two weeks and I'm only halfway done!

Intermediate Grammar: From Form to Meaning and Use
© 1996 Oxford University Press. Permission granted to reproduce for classroom use.

Social Modals

A. One of the following 10 sentences is correct. The rest each have one error.
Find and correct the errors.

1. Penny ought be home by now.

2. Children must to attend school until they are sixteen years old.

3. Do I should tell Kate the truth?

4. We could fly to Ohio, or we could drive.

5. Latoya might wants to meet some of your friends.

6. The report have to be ready on Friday.

7. Aretha got to be at the airport at six o'clock.

8. You don't should give your credit card number to strangers.

9. You have better not be late. If you are, there will be serious consequences.

10. Why he has to be home so early?

B. Circle the correct modal in parentheses.

1. A: I need your advice. What should I do?
   B: You really have no choice. You (must/could/may) call the doctor immediately.

2. I really (would/may/ought to) call my brother. He's all alone this weekend.

3. The instructions say that you (should/might/will) take two tablets every four hours.

4. I think it's a good idea to take a computer course, but you (must/must not/don't have to)
   if you don't want to. The course isn't required.

5. (May/Should/Can) you wait a minute, please?

6. (Could/May/Must) you please go to the store and get me some milk?

7. (May/Must/Can) you listen to the stereo so loudly? You are going to make me deaf!

8. The sign says "Don't Even Think About Parking Here." This means you (don't have to/must not/must)
   park on that block under any circumstances.

9. Daniel (should/may/must not) spend more time with his children. He usually gets home
   after they go to bed and he doesn't even know their teachers' names.

10. (Would/Should/Must) you please tell me what the sign says? It's too far away for me to read.

11. A: What should I do? My car won't start.
    B: Well, you have two choices. You (could/have to/must) take it to the repair shop now,
       or you might wait until later.

12. You (might/have got to/could) call me immediately. It's urgent.

Social Modals

A. Two of the following 10 sentences are correct. The rest each have one error.
Find and correct the errors.

1. You must to get a passport if you want to travel outside your country.

2. Why I should go to the store? You're not doing anything right now!

3. Brenda may decides to get a new job.

4. Claire have got to finish her report. Otherwise she'll fail her history class.

5. I don't think that children should watch a lot of television.

6. People don't should drive after they drink alcohol.

7. Lillian doesn't better bother George today. He's in a very bad mood.

8. Ailene has got to wake up at 5:30 every morning in order to get to work on time.

9. Leonard ought buy that house. The price is very reasonable and the neighborhood is great.

10. Why does Pauline has to do all the work? Other people should help her.

B. Circle the correct modal in parentheses.

1. Child: I'm ready for dessert.
   Parent: No, you're not. You (couldn't/can't/don't have to) eat dessert until you eat all your vegetables.

2. Student: I forgot my I.D. card.
   Librarian: I'm sorry. Students (cannot/don't have to/might not) use the library unless they have valid I.D. cards.

3. (Must/Might/Can) you wear that shirt again? You've worn it every day this week! I'm tired of looking at it!

4. You (may not/don't have to/had better) park in a No Parking Zone. If you do, you'll get a ticket.

5. You (don't have to/had better/would) clean up your room right now or I won't cook dinner for you!

6. Sally (doesn't have to/must not/cannot) study a foreign language in order to graduate from her high school. But she wants to travel to South America, so she has decided to take a Spanish course.

7. Kathleen is having trouble finding a job. She (must not/would/ought to) talk to an employment counselor.

8. (Will/Should/May) you please stop interrupting me!

9. I don't know the answer to your question, but you (might/would/don't have to) ask Debby or maybe Alan. It's possible that they know the answer.

10. Adult supervision is required. Children under 10 (might not/would not/may not) enter unless they are accompanied by an adult.

Modals of Ability and Belief

Circle the correct modal in parentheses.

1. I just started running every day. Two months from now I (can/will be able to/could) run three miles.

2. Yesterday I (can/could/was able to) call home at noon. Today I can't.

3. The dog (might not/can't/must) be somewhere in the house. There are dirty paw prints all over the kitchen.

4. It's five o'clock, but Patty isn't here yet. She (might/must/should) be stuck in traffic, or she could still be at work. I really don't know.

5. Ian just got home. He was working for fourteen hours without a break, so he (could/must/may) be very tired.

6. Frieda is very worried because she hasn't heard from her son in two weeks. She is certain that he (should/might/must) be in serious trouble.

7. Wendy (can't/couldn't/shouldn't) afford to go to college when she graduated from high school. So she worked for three years, saved money, and then enrolled in Carlson College.

8. Kathy is staring out of a window with a smile on her face. She (could/should/must) be in love, or she might be happy because the sun is shining.

9. Margaret (could/must not/should) be able to help you with your math homework. She used to teach trigonometry and calculus at my high school.

10. I don't understand how my memory works. Right now I (could/can/should) remember the exact words of conversations that I had twelve years ago, but when I'm at the supermarket I never remember what I need to buy.

11. A: I didn't sleep all night.
    B: You poor thing. You (can/might/must) be exhausted!

12. A: Your grandmother is on the phone.
    B: That's impossible! It (may not/can't/might not) be her. She died several years ago.

13. The president has made a definite decision. He (could/may/will) raise taxes.

14. A: Do you have enough food for the party?
    B: Yes, I planned very carefully. There (ought to/could/might) be enough.

Past Modals

A. One of the following 7 sentences is correct. The rest each have one error.
Find and correct the errors.

1. Even though the sun is shining, there are puddles in the street. It must of rained earlier.

2. I should have took some food with me. I'm really hungry and there's no place nearby
   to get something to eat.

3. Trudi shouldn't have told Bobby about the fight.

4. Liz could worked as an actress when she was a young woman. When she was in high school,
   a director saw her in a school play and offered her a small part in a movie. But she wasn't interested.

5. I don't know where Leslie was yesterday. She might have went to the beach, or she
   could have been at her sister's house.

6. Jason could had been the person who answered the phone when you called.
   When I see him, I'll ask him if he spoke to you.

7. The package should have arrive yesterday, but the delivery truck had a flat tire.
   The package came today.

B. Circle the correct modal in parentheses.

1. I'm surprised to hear that Ariel is still attending college as an undergraduate.
   She started six years ago, so she (should have/may have/must have) graduated by now.

2. Marilyn (might not have/couldn't have/may not have) spoken to you last night.
   She's been in the hospital with a broken jaw for the past three days.

3. Jackie's finally getting divorced. She (must not have/shouldn't have/may not have) married
   that man in the first place.

4. Julian was very upset when he came home from work yesterday. He (may have/should have/must have)
   had an argument with his boss, or he might have spent the day with a difficult customer. I don't know
   exactly what happened. He didn't want to talk about it.

5. Heather (might have/can't have/must have) left for the airport already. I really don't know.
   She didn't tell me her plans.

6. The landlord told me that he was going to fix the leak in the ceiling while I was at work today.
   But he (shouldn't have/might not have/must not have) come. The ceiling has not been repaired,
   and the water is still dripping all over the kitchen.

7. My ancestors (should have/may have/must have) come to America in 1918. We're not sure.
   We're trying to locate old family records.

8. Zachary (should have/may have/must have) told Mrs. Grayson that he was allergic to shrimp.
   But he was too polite to tell her, so he ate the shrimp that she served him at the dinner party.
   An hour later he was really sick.

Modals of Ability and Belief; Past Modals

A. One of the following 10 items is correct. The rest each have one error.
Find and correct each error.

1. Fiona must of eaten a lot while she was on vacation. She gained twenty-five pounds.

2. Sydney shouldn't lied to the police. He's probably going to be in serious trouble when they find out the truth.

3. Right after I had my operation, I can't walk unless someone held my arm.

4. I should have wrote Sarah a letter, but I was too busy.

5. Charlie maybe on the golf course. Or he might be swimming in the pool.

6. The boy in that photograph might be Brian, but if you want to be sure you should ask his mother.

7. I just started ice-skating lessons. I'm not very good now, but I'm sure that by next month I can skate without falling down.

8. Peter can drives, but he doesn't own a car.

9. Tomorrow I be able to help you set up the computer.

10. Rodney will able to pay back his loans next month.

B. Circle the correct modal in parentheses.

1. Erin (may have/should have/must have) paid her credit card bills on time. But she didn't. She had enough money, but she forgot about the bills because she was busy at work. Now she has to pay 18 percent interest.

2. Gary (may/could/might) read when he was only four years old.

3. I'm very impressed with Harriet. She (could/may/can) speak three languages, she knows how to fly an airplane, and she has a terrific personality.

4. He (may/should/must) be out of town. His mailbox is full of mail, and his front step has four newspapers on it.

5. Denise is an accountant. So she (should/could/can) be able to explain that financial report to you.

6. Elliot (couldn't have/must have/may have) pleased his boss. His boss just fired him.

7. Gill (will not have/couldn't have/should not have) written that note. His handwriting is difficult to read, and the handwriting in the note is very clear.

8. I (must not/may not/could not) be able to attend the meeting. I'll try to make it, but I can't promise. It depends on how much work I get done this afternoon.

9. A few minutes ago Crystal (was able to/could/can) clear the paper jam in the photocopier.

10. Karen (could/must/should) be twenty-five years old, or she might be forty. It's impossible for me to tell.

Relative Clauses

Four of the following 18 items are correct. The rest each have one error.
Find and correct the errors.

1. Last night I met an interesting woman which has lived in China, Russia, and Brazil.

2. Carl is a painter who works mostly with watercolors.

3. I need to see a lawyer who know about immigration regulations.

4. A rose is a flower that it blooms all summer.

5. The path we took it was very pretty.

6. Kansas is the only state that I've never visited.

7. Let's make jewelry with the beads Aunt Julia gave us them.

8. I looked at the books what she was reading.

9. The young man I work with come from Mexico.

10. The lawyer to whom I am writing him has a very good reputation.

11. Did you read the article that I told you about?

12. The students who their grades were under 70 percent were allowed to take the test again.

13. Wendy lives in an old house whose roof leaks every time it rains.

14. There's the girl that her sister is on the swim team.

15. Mr. Plowright who used to work for a large company, now runs his own consulting business.

16. A: I understand that you have one son.
    B: Yes. Mario who is eighteen is a senior in high school.

17. Margie's husband, who is seven feet tall played basketball when he was in college.

18. Prattson University, which it has an excellent chemistry department, is going to spend several million dollars to improve its chemistry laboratory.

Relative Clauses

Six of the following 20 sentences are correct. The rest each have one error.
Find and correct each error.

1. The landlord doesn't rent to people who own dogs.

2. Belinda owns a car it uses diesel fuel.

3. A veterinarian is a doctor who treat animals.

4. Last night I saw a movie who made me cry.

5. Paula has a roommate who her mother is an actress.

6. Carnet Market is the store that have the best selection of fruits and vegetables.

7. The book that Phyllis and George gave me is very interesting.

8. Amy who is only seven years old is a very talented musician.

9. Melissa wrote the poem that won the prize.

10. Mary is the only person in the office whom the boss likes her.

11. The band in which my daughter plays in just got a record contract.

12. I don't know the names of the children Jenny takes care of.

13. Your father tells the best jokes, that I have ever heard.

14. I'd like to introduce you to Mr. and Mrs. Applethorp, which just moved into the house next door to mine.

15. Sharon doesn't like people who talk too much.

16. Kelly who is a fantastic cook, is opening her own restaurant.

17. This watch, which I bought it two days ago, stopped working this morning.

18. Albert and Karen are the people whose helped me when my car broke down.

19. These are the dishes what my grandmother gave me last year.

20. The restaurant we went to yesterday had good food but poor service.

Count and Noncount Nouns

One of the following 15 sentences is correct. The rest each have one error.
Find and correct the errors.

1. Our class has twelve men and fifteen woman.

2. The people in my country usually eats dinner after 8:00 P.M.

3. If you need an information about cultural activities, you should talk to Imogene.

4. Sarabeth is studying to be physical therapist.

5. I don't care about politics, but my sister is very interested in them.

6. Camilla needs an advice.

7. I like cake, fruit, and ice cream, but I don't like cookie.

8. It's crime if you don't report all of your income on your tax return.

9. Alex has interesting job. He helps companies reduce the amount of pollution their factories create.

10. When I take my daughter on a trip, I have to bring bottles, milk, and stroller.

11. The police doesn't patrol this neighborhood too often.

12. Mathematics are easy for some people.

13. If you have a homework, I'll help you.

14. Is crime a serious problem in your neighborhood?

15. He put his luggages down for a moment.

Intermediate Grammar: From Form to Meaning and Use
© 1996 Oxford University Press. Permission granted to reproduce for classroom use.

Count and Noncount Nouns

Three of the following 20 items are correct. The rest each have one error.
Find and correct each error.

1. There were three men and two woman at the dinner party.

2. Jenny's feet is very large. Her shoes are size 12.

3. It's hard to breathe in this disco. I'm going outside to get a fresh air.

4. The leafs on maple trees turn red in October.

5. Tammy just bought a lot of very expensive new furniture. She likes them a lot,
   but I think she wasted a great deal of money.

6. I can't believe that Coretta didn't tell you the news. She told them to all the other people in the office.

7. When you go to the drugstore, please get shampoo, suntan lotion, and toothbrush.

8. Carla is going to be lawyer when she gets older.

9. I'm going to donate a blood at the hospital.

10. There was serious crime in my neighborhood last night. At 8:00 P.M., a grocery store owner
    was killed during a robbery.

11. Peter is a wonderful teacher. He knows his subject and he has a great deal of patience.

12. Lucas is trying to decide between a job in Seattle and a job in San Diego. I think he should go to San Diego
    because it has a good weather. In Seattle there's a lot of rain.

13. Henrietta owns a beautiful jewelry.

14. Sarah works in an electronics store. If you want informations about computers or stereo systems,
    you should talk to her.

15. You can have either pancakes or cereal for breakfast.

16. Yvette left all her stuffs at her mother's house.

17. Noah thinks Amelia is beautiful. He especially likes her long, red hairs.

18. The waiter suggested a soup that I enjoyed very much, even though I don't normally like soup.

19. Mimi wants new bicycle for her birthday.

20. Is something burning? I see a smoke!

Quantity Expressions

Three of the following 14 items are correct. The rest each have one error.
Find and correct each error.

1. How many money do you have in the bank?

2. On Valentine's Day, Bert bought box of chocolates for his wife.

3. There's much orange juice in the refrigerator, so please help yourself.

4. There are too much people at the gym in the morning, so I always go in the afternoon.

5. Don't worry. We have enough meat for sandwiches. There are few slices left.

6. Benny has few hope that the situation will improve.

7. Kathy has a great deal of ambition.

8. Solomon gave me several idea for the show.

9. Few students wanted to study Latin, so the school stopped offering the course and the Latin teacher lost her job.

10. Please buy a tube toothpaste at the supermarket.

11. Let me give you piece of advice.

12. Rasheed bought two loaves of bread at the bakery.

13. Apples cost eighty-nine cents pound today.

14. How much does a head of bananas cost?

Intermediate Grammar: From Form to Meaning and Use
© 1996 Oxford University Press. Permission granted to reproduce for classroom use.

Articles

One of the following 14 items is correct. The rest each have one error.
Find and correct each error.

1. Botany is branch of biology.

2. A: What is margarine?
   B: Margarine is a substitute for the butter.

3. A: What's wrong with your car?
   B: When I turn a steering wheel, it squeaks very loudly.

4. A: Do you have a quarter?
   B: Let's see. I only have the dime. Do you want it?

5. A trapezoid is geometric shape.

6. A: What kind of music does April like?
   B: She doesn't like the country music.

7. A: What does Peter drink with his meals?
   B: He always drinks the water.

8. The cockroach is a insect that almost no one likes.

9. Tammy is scared of a dogs.

10. Gwen has to see the dentist tomorrow.

11. Sam needs new coat. He doesn't know what kind to buy.

12. Capital of England is London.

13. He's a very talented musician. He's been playing a piano since he was a very young child.

14. Scientists think sun will run out of energy some day.

Quantity Expressions and Articles

Five of the following 20 items are correct. The rest each have one error.
Find and correct each error.

1. Did Mrs. Burgos give you many information about Mexico?

2. A: Do you know anything about healthy snacks?
   B: Yes. The apples are healthy and are very good for snacks.

3. Lou Anne wants to buy a new dress for the party at Doug's house.

4. A: Is Ramona interested in sports?
   B: Well, she doesn't like the basketball, but she loves baseball.

5. There's very few traffic today because it's a holiday.

6. Marilyn ate two pieces of cakes for dessert.

7. Dinosaurs fascinate many people.

8. A cello is a large string instrument.

9. What happened to milk I put in the refrigerator yesterday? Did you drink all of it already?

10. When you open this jar, please don't dent a lid.

11. We have very few olive oil left. Could you go to the store and buy another bottle?

12. You can't buy lot of things for a nickel.

13. Celeste just moved to a new city. She has a few friends there, so she feels very lonely.

14. Marcus didn't like the pizza until he visited Renata's family. When he tasted the pizza
    that Renata's grandmother made, he changed his mind.

15. How much hours a week is your Italian class?

16. Ivy brought two bags of ice cube to the party.

17. I don't think that Mr. Morris is the right person for the job in the accounting department.

18. The basketball team has a very good players this year. I think they will win the state championship.

19. Eliza won a prize in a art contest for the portrait of her mother that she painted last year.

20. Could you tell me where the post office is? I just moved here and I don't know the town very well.

Intermediate Grammar: From Form to Meaning and Use
© 1996 Oxford University Press. Permission granted to reproduce for classroom use.

Comparative and Superlative Adjectives and Adverbs

Two of the following 14 items are correct. The rest each have one error.
Find and correct each error.

1. Joan's house has a more smaller kitchen than my house does.

2. Kay's Market has the most cheap prices in the city.

3. Who's the tallest person in your family?

4. I think that Bob's idea is more better than Aaron's.

5. Barbara is one of the best singer in the chorus.

6. Seth behaves badly, but his little brother's behavior is even more bad.

7. The Sears Tower in Chicago is the higher office building in the world.

8. A: How was the movie last night?
   B: It was the worse movie I've seen this year.

9. Of all the houses that we looked at, I liked the one on Elm Street the less.

10. The fruit store is expensiver than the supermarket.

11. He's stronger that I am.

12. Pat types more slowly than John does, but John's typing is less accurate than Pat's.

13. She's probably the richest woman than the world.

14. Last night was coldest night of the entire winter.

Comparative and Superlative Nouns, *As...As,* *The Same...As,* and *So...That/Such(a)...That*

Four of the following 16 sentences are correct. The rest each have one error.
Find and correct each error.

1. I'm not able to run fast as I could when I was in high school.

2. Eve has the same doctor as I do.

3. Of all the English classes in the school, my class has the least students.

4. Japan has few natural resources than Russia.

5. I have less pain today than I had yesterday.

6. It's very warm outside today that you don't need to wear a jacket.

7. Melissa slammed the door so hard than I could feel the vibrations.

8. Bobby isn't as strong as you are.

9. Strawberries have less calories than raisins.

10. Of all the men in his family, Arthur earns the less money.

11. Maureen used to wear most makeup than she does now.

12. Are you the same weigh as your sister?

13. Greta made such good impression at the interview that she was offered the job one day later.

14. Your face is as red a fire engine. Are you embarrassed about something?

15. Ralph had the least to say at the meeting. Everyone else couldn't stop talking. He hardly opened his mouth.

16. This shirt is same price as that one, but the quality is not as good.

Intermediate Grammar: From Form to Meaning and Use
© 1996 Oxford University Press. Permission granted to reproduce for classroom use.

Expressing Differences and Similarities

Four of the following 20 sentences are correct. The rest each have one error.
Find and correct each error.

1. California is more bigger than New Hampshire.

2. Audiocassettes cost less compact discs.

3. John is fastest runner on the team.

4. Sue has traveled less extensively that the other people in her family.

5. Hildegarde looks as unhappy as her mother does.

6. California is the more populous state in the United States.

7. Abigail works as many hours I do.

8. Ilana wants to move so badly that she's going to sell her house for less money than she paid for it.

9. Robert will call you as soon as he can.

10. The music was very loud that it gave me a headache.

11. Carol is the most tallest player on the women's basketball team.

12. Delaware has less people than New Jersey.

13. Gracie ate so much than she couldn't move.

14. Allie is not intelligent as Martiza.

15. The doctor says your condition is going to get worst unless you have an operation.

16. Kathleen is not prettier as Rachel.

17. Erin has the same physics teacher as Lyle.

18. Martha has more children as I do.

19. Candace is the same old as Jolene.

20. Everett is the less serious student in the class.

Wish Sentences and Imaginary *If* Sentences

Two of the following 15 items are correct. The rest each have one error. Find and correct each error.

1. Ella wishes that she lives in a quiet place, but she doesn't. She lives in an apartment right above a discotheque.

2. I wish I can go to the party, but I can't because I have to take care of my little brother.

3. My stereo broke and right now I don't have enough money to a buy new one. But I hope that I would be able to get a new one soon. I miss listening to music.

4. My sister always wears my clothes without asking me. I wish she will ask for my permission.

5. A: Look out the window. Is it snowing?
   B: No, but I wish it does. I love playing in the snow.

6. Annette earns very little money. I wish her boss gives her a raise soon.

7. Mr. Queenan is always in a hurry. He wishes had more time.

8. I can't lift this box. I wish I am stronger.

9. Sally and Bob are too young to understand the situation. If they are older, you could explain it to them.

10. I didn't decide what to do so quickly if I were you.

11. Would it be OK if we didn't go to a movie tonight?

12. What you would do if you won a million dollars in a lottery?

13. If I were president, I eliminate all taxes.

14. I'm really thankful that Sarah is helping me paint my apartment. If she weren't able to help me, I never be able to finish.

15. If Petra were here right now, she could answer your question. Unfortunately, she's away this week, and I don't know the answer.

Intermediate Grammar: From Form to Meaning and Use

Wish Sentences and Imaginary *If* Sentences

A. Put the verbs in parentheses in the correct form. In some cases you will need to add an auxiliary verb.

1. If Monica _____ (win) the lottery, she would quit her job.

2. Mr. and Mrs. Paulsen wish that their noisy neighbors _____ (move).

3. Would you mind if we _____ (see) a romantic movie?

4. I _____ (read) more if I had more free time.

5. Kristy wishes that she _____ (can) visit the moon.

6. Rachel hopes that she _____ (can) find a dress that she likes.

7. If Ruthie and George _____ (be) more careful with their money, they wouldn't be in debt.

8. Peggy wishes that she _____ (have/not) a little brother.

9. Would it bother you if I _____ (smoke)?

10. I wish that my parents _____ (worry/not) about me all the time.

B. Two of the following 10 items are correct. The rest each have one error. Find and correct each error.

1. If I were you, I don't tell the truth about what really happened.

2. A: Are you going to get Victor a present for his birthday?
   B: No. I wish I am able to, but I don't have any money.

3. Nancy lives in a bad neighborhood. I wish she will move.

4. Does Tara wish her brothers aren't so protective?

5. What you would do if you lost your wallet?

6. Peter won't be so depressed if his parents were healthy.

7. We'd take a walk if it weren't raining.

8. If I had six arms, I could carry all these suitcases.

9. Paulette would be shocked if she knows Julie's secret. But I'm certain she'll never find out about it.

10. If machines never break, mechanics wouldn't have any work.

Gerunds and Infinitives

Two of the following 20 items are correct. The rest each have one error.
Find and correct each error.

1. Eat chocolate makes Annabeth happy.

2. Trying to understand complicated grammar points give some students a headache.

3. Before move to Los Angeles, Lawrence lived in Nevada.

4. Penny went to the library for returning a book.

5. Would you mind to call me back in a few minutes? I can't talk right now.

6. When I was very young, I used to believing that animals could speak.

7. Richard and Jane look forward to visit their daughter next week.

8. It's difficult to get used to living in an apartment if you have always lived in a house.

9. Carl used to weigh 200 pounds until he stopped to eat junk food all the time. Now he only weighs 160 pounds.

10. Don't forget calling Aunt Jenny tonight. She expects to hear from you.

11. When Meredith finished to read the newspaper, she gave it to her husband.

12. Kate spent a lot of time to work on her project.

13. You can contact me by leave a message with my secretary.

14. Amber expects finding a new job within the next three months.

15. Please listen. I need tell you something.

16. Instead leaving work at five, she stayed late.

17. Read the manual in order operate the machine properly.

18. He regrets no attending the show. He forgot all about it.

19. Harold will never forget flying over the Alps last summer.

20. A: Let's go to the movies.
    B: I don't want. Let's do something else.

Intermediate Grammar: From Form to Meaning and Use

Gerunds and Infinitives

Four of the following 20 sentences are correct. The rest each have one error.
Find and correct each error.

1. By use electronic mail, people can communicate quickly and cheaply with friends in different parts of the world.

2. He promised no to drive so fast anymore.

3. Paul doesn't like talking on the telephone.

4. Georgina hasn't paid her rent. So she's trying avoid her landlord.

5. They talked about not go anywhere all weekend.

6. Instead of complain about your boss, you should get another job.

7. We were driving down the highway when we saw a beautiful view of the river. So we stopped taking some pictures, and then we continued our drive.

8. There's no point in clean this house. The children will make a mess of it in five minutes.

9. I can't remember telling Sally that story. But Sally is certain that I did tell her.

10. Wearing a suit and tie make Lou uncomfortable.

11. Fred enjoys to play basketball.

12. Carol stopped talking to Jim because she was angry at him. They haven't spoken for months.

13. Speak several languages can help you get a good job.

14. Cross-country skiing is more strenuous than downhill skiing.

15. It's important sleeping.

16. Leslie is not accustomed to eat a large breakfast.

17. Did you go to shopping last night?

18. Aaron dislikes to wait for other people. So we have to be on time.

19. Callie forgot to tells me about what happened yesterday.

20. Driving a car require a lot of concentration.

CHAPTER 15 Diagnostic Quiz

The Past Perfect and the Past Perfect Continuous

Choose the best answer to complete each sentence. Use the present perfect,
the present perfect continuous, the past perfect, or the past perfect continuous.

1. _____ the old project before he started a new one?
   a. Why Alvin hadn't finished
   b. Why Alvin hadn't finish
   c. Why hadn't Alvin finished

2. Gregory _____ his bicycle every day until he broke his leg.
   a. has been ride
   b. had been riding
   c. had riding

3. After Ursula _____ her dinner, she took a nap.
   a. had eaten
   b. had ate
   c. has eat

4. Could you please help me? I _____ to fix this photocopier for the past half hour, but it's still broken. You're good with your hands, so maybe you can fix it.
   a. have been trying
   b. had trying
   c. had been trying

5. _____ my car for two years when it first broke down.
   a. I'd been owning
   b. I've owned
   c. I'd owned

6. They were happy because they _____ all their basketball games.
   a. had been won
   b. had winning
   c. had been winning

7. Bill _____ a skyscraper before he visited New York.
   a. had never see
   b. had never saw
   c. had never seen

8. Agnes _____ the house before her parents arrived.
   a. has been cleaned
   b. had been cleaning
   c. had clean

9. Peter's accountant _____ Peter not to take illegal tax deductions, but Peter didn't take her advice.
   a. had warned
   b. had warn
   c. had warning

10. Before Alexis met Junko, she _____ Japanese food.
    a. has never eaten
    b. had never eaten
    c. was never eaten

11. Paul _____ Samantha for three years before they got married.
    a. had been knowing
    b. has known
    c. had known

12. When Lucille first met me in 1980, I _____ in England for six years.
    a. had been living
    b. have been living
    c. have lived

13. Carrie didn't go to the concert because she _____ her ticket earlier that day.
    a. has lost
    b. had been losing
    c. had lost

14. Before Emily was twenty years old, she _____ for three years.
    a. had already been working
    b. has already been working
    c. have already been working

15. Liz is worried because her husband _____ very strangely since this morning. Something unusual is going on today and she doesn't know what it is.
    a. had been acting
    b. has been acting
    c. has been

Intermediate Grammar: From Form to Meaning and Use

Past *Wish* Sentences and Past Imaginary *If* Sentences

Choose the best answer to complete each sentence. Use verb forms that are appropriate in present or past *wish* sentences and present or past imaginary *if* sentences.

1. I wish I _____ more movies last year.
   a. have seen
   b. had see
   c. had seen

2. Peter wishes he _____ more when he was a young man.
   a. could traveled
   b. could have traveled
   c. could of traveled

3. They didn't attend the concert, but they wish they _____.
   a. had
   b. have
   c. hadn't

4. Josie wishes that she _____ of school when she was seventeen years old.
   a. hadn't drop out
   b. hadn't dropping out
   c. hadn't dropped out

5. I am lonely. I wish you _____ come over later.
   a. had
   b. would
   c. have

6. Abigail wishes that her two boyfriends _____ about each other.
   a. haven't found out
   b. hadn't found out
   c. hadn't finding out

7. I don't understand these instructions. I wish I _____ how to use this computer program, but I don't.
   a. knew
   b. had known
   c. know

8. If my friends hadn't come to my house, I _____ my work last night.
   a. would have finished
   b. would had finished
   c. would finish

9. If we'd had more time, _____ more places.
   a. we'd have visited
   b. we've had visited
   c. we'd had visited

10. What _____ if Patty hadn't been home when you called?
    a. did you have done
    b. would you have done
    c. you would have done

11. Rita _____ to you right now if she weren't so busy.
    a. had spoken
    b. would have spoke
    c. would speak

12. Vernon _____ so upset if his son hadn't lied to him.
    a. would not have
    b. would not have been
    c. would not had been

13. The cheese is too expensive. If it were on sale, _____ more of it.
    a. I'd had bought
    b. I'd buy
    c. I'd bought

14. I _____ at George yesterday if I hadn't been tired and hungry.
    a. would haven't yelled
    b. wouldn't have yell
    c. wouldn't have yelled

15. If Bess had known the truth, she _____ the job.
    a. would never have taken
    b. would never of taken
    c. wouldn't never have taken

The Past Perfect and the Past Perfect Continuous, Past *Wish* Sentences, and Past Imaginary *If* Sentences

A. Choose the best answer to complete each sentence. Use the present perfect, the present perfect continuous, the past perfect, or the past perfect continuous.

1. Before Ian celebrated his twelfth birthday, he _____ shaving.

   a. has already started
   b. had already been starting
   c. had already started
   d. have already starting

2. I _____ Gayle all my life and we are still good friends. We meet for lunch every week.

   a. have known
   b. had been knowing
   c. have been knowing
   d. had known

3. When I looked at Betty's red eyes, I realized that she_____.

   a. had been cry
   b. had crying
   c. had been crying
   d. had been cried

4. Why _____ her problem with me before she decided what to do?

   a. Judy hadn't discussed
   b. hadn't Judy discuss
   c. hadn't Judy discussed
   d. Judy hadn't discuss

5. Rick _____ the newspaper when the telephone rang.

   a. has been reading
   b. has reading
   c. had been reading
   d. has read

6. Look at that lipstick on John's collar! I think that he _____ someone! What do you think?

   a. has been kissing
   b. had been kissing
   c. has been kissed
   d. had kissing

7. The last time I saw Maxine I was eighteen. I _____ from high school. That was twenty-one years ago!

   a. had recently graduated
   b. has recently graduated
   c. have recently graduated
   d. had recently graduate

8. Alexandra _____ as a waitress for three months. She likes it very much and she hopes to get a raise soon.

   a. had been working
   b. has work
   c. has been working
   d. had worked

B. One of the following 8 items is correct. The rest each have one error. Find and correct each error.

1. Look outside. It's raining. I wish it had been sunny right now.

2. The boys wish they could gone on the trip last year. But they couldn't.

3. Nick wishes he had been having a car. He doesn't like taking the bus anymore.

4. A: My fax machine isn't working. What should I do?
   B: If I had been you, I'd call the manufacturer's Help Line right now.

5. Zoey wishes that she hadn't said yes when Colin asked her to help him.

6. If it hadn't been raining yesterday, we would have went on a picnic.

7. Teresa would of won the contest if Jamie hadn't been playing also. Jamie is the best player, but Teresa is the second best.

8. If she had known about the delay, Clara hadn't have driven to the airport.

Passive Sentences

Two of the following 15 sentences are correct. The rest each have one error. Find and correct each error.

1. The omelette is being cook right now.

2. One hundred years ago, children were allowed to work in factories.

3. Pets are not allowing in my apartment building.

4. All students will expected to attend class regularly.

5. This shirt has being washed in hot water twice since last week. That's why the colors have faded.

6. While I was visiting June, her house was been painted.

7. Bills must pay by cash or money order. Checks are not accepted.

8. Eve should be permit to enter the discotheque. She's twenty-four, and you need to be twenty-one.

9. Five people injured in a fire at a warehouse yesterday.

10. The flight was arrived twenty minutes ago.

11. It was an emergency. The doctor should been called immediately, but the phone was broken.

12. All the children was weighed by the school nurse.

13. We had been told by our friends that this restaurant was wonderful.

14. Every day my mail delivers at noon. It is very regular.

15. My house has been robbed the same person two times.

Passive Sentences

Three of the following 20 sentences are correct. The rest each have one error.
Find and correct each error.

1. At the present time, French spoke in many African countries.

2. The rent must paid on the first day of the month.

3. This book written ten years ago.

4. If you go to the new Japanese restaurant, you will asked to take off your shoes.

5. Harry wasn't invite to the party.

6. Clothing, furniture, and cosmetics are all sold in a department store.

7. Your calculations should be check by another person so that you are certain there are no mistakes.

8. That fabric might had been manufactured in India.

9. Sugarcane cultivated in tropical countries.

10. Amy will be surprising by the news.

11. This house has been owned by someone in my family for three generations.

12. Christmas bonuses had been given to all the employees when Mr. Pringle still owned the store. But now, bonuses not given to anyone.

13. Last week, Alison hired to take care of three little girls.

14. The dog was took to the veterinarian this morning.

15. I bought this shirt on sale yesterday. It was cost twenty dollars.

16. Max has being promoted recently. Now he's a vice-president.

17. Nancy should be chose for the basketball team. She's a very good player.

18. That bus driver drove like a maniac! All the passengers could have killed in an accident!

19. I hope that I'm not asked to coordinate this project. It's too much work. But if I'm asked, it will be hard for me to say no.

20. The baby was weighed ten pounds.

Noun Clauses

Three of the following 15 items are correct. The rest each have one error.
Find and correct each error.

1. Frederica didn't understand what was saying the teacher.

2. Sheldon was wondering why Lisa hadn't called yet.

3. Jeremy believed, that his friends were going to help him.

4. Does Sandy know if or not the children will be home for dinner?

5. Faye couldn't remember why her sister wasn't coming to the meeting? So she called to ask her.

6. Kari knows how does a computer work.

7. A: Is Bertha coming with us tomorrow?
   B: Yes, I think.

8. Could you please tell me where is Amsterdam Avenue?

9. Julie wasn't certain if Colleen was planning to come with us.

10. I thought she will call me last week, but she didn't.

11. Do you understand what means this?

12. I need John's phone number, but I don't know where the phone book.

13. Can you please tell me whether if there are any seats left?

14. I wonder that she said.

15. I'm not sure when I first heard the news about Marilyn.

Reported Speech

Change the following sentences from direct speech to indirect speech. The first few words of the new sentence are given to you.

Assume that you are reporting sentences 1–11 *one week later*.

> Example: "I don't have any money now," Rita said.
> Rita said that she didn't have any money then.

1. "I lived in Ecuador a long time ago," Mark explained.

   Mark explained _____.

2. Rachel asked her husband, "Is Leona going to be home this afternoon?"

   Rachel asked her husband _____.

3. "Why are you smiling?" Gayle asked Harry.

   Gayle asked Harry _____

4. "When will the class be over?" Richard asked Danny.

   Richard asked Danny _____

5. "Manitoba is in Canada," the teacher told the class.

   The teacher told the class_____

6. "Go to the store and buy some milk," George said to Becky.

   George told Becky_____

7. "Don't forget your umbrella," Mrs. Gibson told her son.

   Mrs. Gibson told her son_____

8. "You should go to the beach," Clark told Andrea.

   Clark suggested that Andrea _____

9. "I haven't talked to Betty since yesterday," Tammy said.

   Tammy said that _____

10. "I couldn't speak French when I was in high school," Abigail said.

    Abigail said that _____

11. "You must hand in your homework tomorrow," the teacher said to Lucy.

    The teacher told Lucy that_____

Assume that you are reporting sentences 12–14 *five minutes later*.

12. "I've just started a new book," said John.

    John said that _____

13. "I'll be home in a couple of hours," Scott answered.

    Scott answered that_____

14. "This weather makes me feel depressed," Carolyn complained.

    Carolyn complained that _____

Noun Clauses and Reported Speech

A. One of the following 12 items is correct. The rest each have one error.
Find and correct each error.

1. Audrey said me that she had changed her plans.

2. Harold wants to know why did Patricia decide to sell her house.

3. A: Will you have enough money to take the trip?
   B: No, I don't think.

4. Ruth told me that where you had put the book.

5. Mimi said me if I would like to join the club.

6. A: What advice did Carl give you?
   B: He recommended that we bought a used car.

7. Barbara thought, the movie was very interesting.

8. Could you please tell me what Maureen did to her hair?

9. I need to know if or not you will be home for dinner.

10. Last night Laura asked me if she can take my notes home. I refused because I needed to study for the test.

11. We believed that the store will be open on Monday, but it wasn't. We were very disappointed.

12. I suggested that Nancy hires a new secretary.

B. Change the following sentences from direct speech to indirect speech.
Assume that you are reporting sentences 1–5 *two weeks later*.

1. "Take me with you," Kate told Allen. _____

2. "Why aren't you ready?" Vicky asked her sister. _____

3. "Did you like Jerry's new girlfriend?" Susan asked Paul. _____

4. "I haven't seen Tim this morning," Alice remarked. _____

5. "I probably can help you with your math homework," Amy told Bob. _____

_____

Assume that you are reporting sentences 6–8 *a few minutes later*.

6. "Don't answer the telephone," Craig said to James. _____

7. "Kay won't be at work tomorrow," Jeff explained to Arthur. _____

8. "I'm taking a very difficult physics class this semester," Debbie said. _____

_____

QUIZ ANSWER KEY

The Simple Present

FORM

1. My family lives in Boston.

2. Paul doesn't like football.

3. What does the title of this book mean?

4. Correct

5. Pam cooks, George does the laundry, and Van washes the dishes.

6. What happens at a typical American wedding?

MEANING AND USE

7. B: They eat worms and insects.

8. Correct

9. Correct

10. B: Yes. The elementary school is on Main Street, the junior high school is on Riverside Avenue, and the high school is on Broadway.

11. Correct

12. In general, adults want to be younger and children want to be older.

The Present Continuous

FORM

1. Right now Paul is talking on the telephone and Betsy is working in the garden.

2. Many people are sitting in the park.

3. Where is your son studying?

4. B. I'm taking biology, English, and calculus.

5. Correct

6. It's raining right now, so the boys aren't playing baseball.

7. B: Yes, it is.

MEANING AND USE

8. B: He's playing with pots and pans in the kitchen.

9. B: Most Sundays she sings in the chorus, but today she's studying for an important exam.

10. Normally she wears dirty jeans.

Stative Verbs

MEANING AND USE

1. A: Which do you like better, oranges or lemons?

2. Lucille has green eyes and blonde hair.

3. But I don't know the answer to the third one.

4. Child: I don't mind.

5. Most of the time she's very serious.

6. Correct

7. Correct

8. She appears upset about it.

9. Correct

10. It contains many recipes for chocolate desserts.

The Simple Present, the Present Continuous, and Stative Verbs

A.

1. The average person in the United States eats too much junk food. But these days nutritionists are trying to change this situation. They want people to eat less junk food and more fruits and vegetables.

2. This week Dan is working extra hours because one of his co-workers is on vacation.

3. Lilly has a job as a baby-sitter for two little girls. Usually the girls behave very well. But this week the girls are acting like devils. They are driving Lilly crazy. Lilly doesn't know the reason for the sudden change in their behavior.

B.

1. But today that store isn't open, so right now she's shopping at GrandRite.

2. B: Right now we own one dog and one cat.

3. She doesn't like her job very much, but she earns a lot of money.

4. A: What are you doing?

5. He's wearing a T-shirt in the middle of winter!

6. Correct

7. B: It seems a little small on you.

8. Do you know his telephone number?

9. Correct

10. These cookies contain milk, butter, eggs, and sugar.

CHAPTER 2 Diagnostic Quiz

Adverbs of Frequency

A.

FORM

1. Tom always eats eggs for breakfast.

2. Correct

3. Correct

4. Are you ever late?

5. Stephanie never takes public transportation.

6. I never eat cold cereal.

7. Correct

MEANING AND USE

8. Paul never goes to the opera./Paul doesn't ever go to the opera.

9. Kathleen and Craig rarely eat in restaurants.

10. Correct

11. Correct

12. B: No, I never do./Yes, I always do.

B.

1. d

2. f

3. a

4. b

5. g

6. c

7. e

CHAPTER 2 Diagnostic Quiz

There Is and *There Are*

FORM

1. Correct

2. Receptionist: Ms. Drake, there's a call for you on line 1.

3. There aren't any swimming pools in my neighborhood./There are no swimming pools in my neighborhood.

4. There are a lot of interesting programs on television tonight.

5. B: There aren't any apples in the refrigerator.

6. Correct

7. B: Yes, there's one.

8. A: Is there anything you can do to help me?

MEANING AND USE

9. Correct

10. There's a pile of dirty dishes in the sink and bread crumbs all over the floor!

11. Correct

12. B: There's one on Third Street.

CHAPTER 2 Diagnostic Quiz

Imperatives

FORM

1. Correct

2. Don't walk on the kitchen floor, please.

3. Pay attention to what I tell you.

4. Tell me your address and telephone number, please./Please tell me your address and telephone number.

Note: In conversation, other placements of *please* may be possible with special intonation and pauses. (For example: *Tell me please your address and telephone number*.)

5. Correct

MEANING AND USE

6. Correct

7. Mix at medium speed.

8. Please be careful.

CHAPTER 2 Achievement Quiz

Adverbs of Frequency, *There Is* and *There Are*, and Imperatives

1. Correct

2. There are two children in the average American family.

3. Correct

4. Ursula never wears jeans to school./Ursula doesn't ever wear jeans to school.

5. Open the door, please./Please open the door.

6. Correct

7. Valerie is always talking on the telephone.

8. Susan never comes to school on time.

9. There's nothing to do.

10. Correct

11. A: How many senators are there in Congress?

12. He's always making up some excuse about his busy schedule.

13. That means she is never absent.

14. There are always problems at work./ There's always a problem at work.

15. There are two coats on the sofa.

16. A: Do you usually eat breakfast?

17. Correct

18. Correct

19. There aren't any movie theaters in my neighborhood.

20. A: Is there a problem with unemployment in your country?

CHAPTER 3 Diagnostic Quiz

The Simple Past

FORM

1. Did you make that chocolate cake?

2. Why did Mike and Joe get home late last night?

3. Andrea and Carla were at the party, but I didn't see them.

4. I bought a new stereo in November.

5. Was Andy sick yesterday?

6. Did Veronica go to the dance with Pete?

7. Tony hurt his foot two weeks ago.

8. Were you in the library earlier today?

9. Horace participated in the bowling tournament last month, but he didn't win.

10. B: They built her a treehouse.

11. Several days ago, Helen fell off her bicycle and broke her leg.

MEANING AND USE

12. B: Yes, she did.

13. B: Did you bring your passport?

14. Correct

15. I went to the beach every day and I ate a lot of seafood.

16. B: I missed the bus, so I walked to work.

CHAPTER 3 Diagnostic Quiz

Used to

FORM

1. I didn't use to like vegetables, but now I eat more vegetables than meat.

2. Rick used to be very short.

3. Mr. and Mrs. Brickman used to love each other, but now they are planning to get a divorce.

4. Irene used to have a job she hated.

5. Today Esther lives in California, but she used to live in Arizona.

6. Correct

MEANING AND USE

7. Yesterday I saw a very good movie.

8. Correct

9. Correct

10. Two days ago I had a very difficult exam in my accounting class.

CHAPTER 3 Diagnostic Quiz

The Past Continuous

FORM

1. A: What were you doing at five o'clock yesterday afternoon?

2. A: Where were your parents living twenty years ago?

3. Correct

4. B: Doug was.

5. A: Were you talking on the telephone about an hour ago?

6. A: What was Judy wearing yesterday?

7. B: Two were looking out the window, three were drawing pictures, and one was sleeping.

MEANING AND USE

8. The cat was playing with a ball of string, the parrot was trying to fly out of her cage, and the fish were swimming in their tank.

9. Then suddenly the electricity went out.

10. Correct

CHAPTER 3 Achievement Quiz

The Simple Past, *Used to*, and the Past Continuous

1. Theodore Roosevelt didn't run for president during the 1930s.

2. Correct

3. Correct

4. Some couples were dancing.

5. B: Did I miss something interesting?

6. Abe used to smoke cigars.

7. B: No, they weren't.

8. Correct

9. Correct

10. A: Did you forget to lock the door?

11. Correct

12. A: What did you think of the mayor's speech last night?

13. Correct

14. B: I knew that my Christmas presents came from my parents.

15. Thief: I was eating dinner at Arnie's Bar and Grill.

16. B: I paid the rent and the telephone bill.

17. Student: My grandfather's ghost visited me last night.

18. A: Did your grandmother use to have red hair?

19. Correct

20. Yesterday I heard some interesting news.

CHAPTER 4 Diagnostic Quiz

Be Going to

FORM

1. B: He's going to be in a good mood then.

2. Correct

3. A: What are you going to do this afternoon?

MEANING AND USE

4. Yesterday I talked to my lawyer.

5. Correct

6. B: First he's going to study for his exam.

CHAPTER 4 Diagnostic Quiz

Will

FORM

1. Alicia will know the answer to your question.

2. Lisa won't be in class next week.

3. B: No, I won't.

4. Correct

5. B: He probably won't, but I think he'll come close.

6. Correct

7. I'll bring a blanket and some paper plates to the picnic tomorrow.

8. Correct

9. Correct

10. I promise I won't tell anyone your secret.

CHAPTER 4 Diagnostic Quiz

The Present Continuous as a Future Form

FORM

1. B: Yes. I'm having a party next Monday.

2. She isn't coming to the movies tonight.

3. Correct

MEANING AND USE

4. Correct

5. It's going to snow tomorrow.

6. Correct

7. I think that the Jets are going to win/will win the game this weekend.

8. So he's probably going to get a speeding ticket soon./So he'll probably get a speeding ticket soon.

CHAPTER 4 Diagnostic Quiz

The Simple Present as a Future Form

FORM

1. Correct

2. When does Jane's train arrive tomorrow night?

3. Our bus leaves/is leaving/is going to leave in five minutes.

MEANING AND USE

4. Correct

5. I promise I'll remember to bring you the photographs tomorrow.

6. Who do you think will win/is going to win first prize in the science fair tomorrow?

7. Correct

8. Maybe he'll work for his uncle.

CHAPTER 4 Diagnostic Quiz

Connecting Sentences

FORM

1. Billie Holiday was a singer, and Bessie Smith was too.

2. Correct

Intermediate Grammar: From Form to Meaning and Use
© 1996 Oxford University Press. Permission granted to reproduce for classroom use.

3. Camilla often gets angry at Mrs. Sanders, and so do I.

4. Eve doesn't play tennis very well, and neither does Jenny.

5. I work for a large company, and my husband does too.

6. B: Neither am I./Me neither.

7. B: So does Mary.

MEANING AND USE

8. I won't speak to Josephine again, and neither will Angie.

9. Gertrude never speaks in class, and Rita doesn't either.

10. Correct

11. Correct

12. My stereo isn't working, and neither is my computer.

CHAPTER 4 Achievement Quiz

Be Going to, Will, the Present Continuous, and the Simple Present; Connecting Sentences

1. Correct

2. B: No, we won't.

3. I'll never fall in love again!/I'm never going to fall in love again!

4. The violin is a string instrument, and so is the viola.

5. B: I'm sure that I will.

6. Correct

7. Correct

8. Child: I promise. I won't do it again.

9. Correct

10. I don't have much patience, but my sister does.

11. Unfortunately, Hannah and Colin won't be at the awards ceremony next week.

12. Lance won't play in the basketball game tomorrow, and Eric won't either.

13. A: Which horse are you going to bet on?

14. Correct

15. Correct

16. Employee: Then who's going to be in charge of the store?

17. Correct

18. Director: No, you won't, and neither will anyone else.

19. B: I think she'll stay for a week./I think she is going to stay for a week.

20. Correct

CHAPTER 5 Diagnostic Quiz

Past Time Clauses

FORM

A.

1. After Kate got help from a tutor, her grades improved./Kate's grades improved after she got help from a tutor.

2. Gretchen was shopping while Dan was cleaning the apartment./Dan was cleaning the apartment while Gretchen was shopping.

3. Before his car ran off the road, Mr. Thomas had a perfect driving record./Mr. Thomas had a perfect driving record before his car ran off the road.

4. The prisoner was planning his escape when a guard walked into his cell./When a guard walked into his cell, the prisoner was planning his escape.

5. Mr. James discovered a leak in the radiator after he bought a used car./After he bought a used car, Mr. James discovered a leak in the radiator.

MEANING AND USE

B.

1. Correct

2. Al picked up his hat after he dropped it.

3. Correct

4. Before we bought a cat, we had a problem with mice.

5. Toby was shopping when she lost her wallet.

C.

1. When I opened a can of tuna fish, the cat ran into the kitchen.

2. Before Jerry started school, his mother taught him how to read.

3. The hot water heater stopped working while Peg was washing her hair.

4. Rick spent $200 on new locks after thieves broke into his apartment.

5. I spoke Spanish very poorly before I enrolled in a language school in Madrid.

CHAPTER 5 Diagnostic Quiz

Future Time Clauses

FORM

A.

1. After Brad finishes his book, he'll lend it to me./ Brad will lend his book to me after he finishes it.

2. Before we decide what kind of wedding to have, we'll talk about it with our parents./Before we talk about it with our parents, we'll decide what kind of wedding to have.

3. She'll be surprised when she discovers the truth./ When she discovers the truth, she'll be surprised.

4. We'll show you around the city before you leave./ Before you leave, we'll show you around the city.

5. When they take their next vacation, they'll go to Europe./They'll take their next vacation when they go to Europe.

MEANING AND USE

B.

1. I'll call you when I know the answer.

2. Jill will sell/is going to sell her house after her son finishes high school.

3. Correct

4. Correct

5. Before my hair turns gray, I'll climb Mount Everest.

CHAPTER 5 Diagnostic Quiz

Real *If* Sentences

FORM, MEANING AND USE

1. Correct

2. Callie won't enjoy the trip if we stay in cheap hotels.

3. If you come in late one more time, the boss is going to fire you.

4. Your throat will feel better/is going to feel better if you have some chicken soup now.

5. Correct

6. I'll never speak to you again if you don't tell me the truth.

7. If the bus doesn't arrive soon, we're going to walk.

8. Susan will get the job if she doesn't get nervous during the interview.

9. Will you cancel the picnic if it rains tomorrow?

10. Correct

11. If you don't leave now, you'll miss/you are going to miss the show.

12. You'll get/You're going to get a ticket if you drive that way.

CHAPTER 5 Achievement Quiz

Past Time Clauses, Future Time Clauses, and Real *If* Sentences

A.

1. Last night, Beth was going up the stairs when the phone rang. /Last night, Beth went up the stairs when the phone rang.

2. When my new boss came up to me at the party yesterday, I introduced her to my husband.

3. If Eileen wins the contest, she'll share her prize with me.

4. Keisha will decide/is going to decide which job to take after she talks to her career counselor.

5. Melissa met her husband before she finished the tenth grade.

6. After Craig's father died, his mother moved to Florida.

7. Astrid is going to be happy when she hears the news.

8. Ruby will plant/is going to plant the roses in her garden tomorrow if we help her.

9. When the children came home, Jamal told them about their mother's accident.

10. If Rachel goes to the Caribbean in July, the airfare won't be very expensive.

B.

1. Correct

2. If Mary marries Abe, Abe's mother will have/is going to have a heart attack.

3. Annette gave me the message before she left.

4. Kim won't go to bed before the sun sets.

5. Correct

6. While Corey was playing the piano, Elizabeth was reading/read a book.

7. My neighbors will complain if I have a noisy party.

8. Correct

CHAPTER 6 Diagnostic Quiz

The Present Perfect

FORM

1. Have you gone to any parties this month?

2. Sally has broken three records for women volleyball players this year.

3. Greg has seen/Greg saw that movie five times.

4. Gloria has liked milk since she was a child.

5. Have you ever taken a long train ride?

6. B: Yes, she has.

MEANING AND USE

7. Harry has worked in the same office for six years.

8. Yesterday I wrote several letters.

9. I have lived there for six years.

10. I knew Maria for ten years.

11. Correct

12. Emma was sick for several months when she was four years old.

13. I have owned my car since 1991.

14. Correct

15. They lived here from 1990 to 1995.

16. Thomas Edison invented the electric light bulb.

CHAPTER 6 Diagnostic Quiz

The Present Perfect Continuous

FORM, MEANING AND USE

1. I have been going out with/I have gone out with John for six months, but we're not ready to get engaged.

2. Correct

3. Mimi has been living in Boston for six years.

4. Paul has been playing baseball since he was four years old.

5. Ricky hasn't been talking to/Ricky hasn't talked to his parents since his mother criticized his girlfriend.

6. You have been standing here for twenty minutes.

7. Have you owned your car for a long time?

8. I've already listened to the news four times today.

9. Correct

10. I've been waiting for your telephone call for an hour.

11. Priscilla has known Jeff for twelve years.

12. B: I've just found/I just found my wallet in my car.

Chapter 6 Achievement Quiz

The Present Perfect and the Present Perfect Continuous

1. Alex has been reading that book since noon.

2. Have you ever seen him so interested in a book?

3. He met his new neighbors yesterday.

4. Tim's face is red because he has been working in a hot kitchen for the past two hours.

5. Last year George went on his first trip to California.

6. He has gone to California three times since then.

7. Has Sally told you about her new boyfriend?

8. Since her mother's death, Margaret has never had enough money to take her family on a vacation.

9. Eliza has been talking on the telephone for three hours.

10. What have you been doing since I spoke to you last week?

11. Patty hasn't been feeling well recently.

12. Ted's brothers haven't spoken to him about the party yet.

13. I have watched/I watched that program three times this week.

14. Correct

15. Yesterday Lisa changed her clothes four times.

16. Have you been sick lately?

17. Why hasn't Allen been getting enough sleep lately?

18. So far, I haven't chosen a dress for the party.

19. Maria didn't see her grandfather from 1992 to 1995.

20. Correct

CHAPTER 7 Diagnostic Quiz

Social Modals

A. FORM

1. Penny ought to be home by now.

2. Children must attend school until they are sixteen years old.

3. Should I tell Kate the truth?

4. Correct

5. Latoya might want to meet some of your friends.

6. The report has to be ready on Friday.

7. Aretha has got to be at the airport at six o'clock.

8. You shouldn't give your credit card number to strangers.

9. You had better not be late./You'd better not be late.

10. Why does he have to be home so early?

B. MEANING AND USE

1. must

2. ought to

3. should

4. don't have to

5. Can

6. Could

7. Must

8. must not

9. should

10. Would

11. could

12. have got to

CHAPTER 7 Achievement Quiz

Social Modals

A.

1. You must get a passport if you want to travel outside your country.

2. Why should I go to the store?

3. Brenda may decide to get a new job.

4. Claire has got to finish her report.

5. Correct

6. People shouldn't drive after they drink alcohol.

7. Lillian had better not bother George today.

8. Correct

9. Leonard ought to buy that house.

10. Why does Pauline have to do all the work?

Intermediate Grammar: From Form to Meaning and Use
© 1996 Oxford University Press. Permission granted to reproduce for classroom use.

B.

1. can't
2. cannot
3. Must
4. may not
5. had better
6. doesn't have to
7. ought to
8. Will
9. might
10. may not

CHAPTER 8 Diagnostic Quiz

Modals of Ability and Belief

MEANING AND USE

Note: The form is the same as the form for the modals presented in Chapter 7.

1. will be able to
2. was able to
3. must
4. might
5. must
6. must
7. couldn't
8. could
9. should
10. can
11. must
12. can't
13. will
14. ought to

CHAPTER 8 Diagnostic Quiz

Past Modals

A. FORM

1. It must have rained earlier.
2. I should have taken some food with me.
3. Correct
4. Liz could have worked as an actress when she was a young woman.
5. She might have gone to the beach, or she could have been at her sister's house.
6. Jason could have been the person who answered the phone when you called.
7. The package should have arrived yesterday, but the delivery truck had a flat tire.

B. MEANING AND USE

1. should have
2. couldn't have
3. shouldn't have
4. may have
5. might have
6. must not have
7. may have
8. should have

CHAPTER 8 Achievement Quiz

Modals of Ability and Belief; Past Modals

A.

1. Fiona must have eaten a lot while she was on vacation.
2. Sydney shouldn't have lied to the police.
3. Right after I had my operation, I couldn't walk unless someone held my arm.
4. I should have written Sarah a letter, but I was too busy.
5. Charlie may be on the golf course.

6. Correct

7. I'm not very good now, but I'm sure that by next month I'll be able to skate without falling down.

8. Peter can drive, but he doesn't own a car.

9. Tomorrow I'll bc ablc to hclp you set up the computer.

10. Rodney will be able to pay back his loans next month.

B.

1. should have

2. could

3. can

4. must

5. should

6. couldn't have

7. couldn't have

8. may not

9. was able to

10. could

CHAPTER 9 Diagnostic Quiz

Relative Clauses

FORM, MEANING AND USE

1. Last night I met an interesting woman who/that has lived in China, Russia, and Brazil.

2. Correct

3. I need to see a lawyer who knows about immigration regulations.

4. A rose is a flower that blooms all summer.

5. The path we took was very pretty.

6. Correct

7. Let's make jewelry with the beads Aunt Julia gave us.

8. I looked at the books that/which she was reading./ I looked at the books she was reading.

9. The young man I work with comes from Mexico.

10. The lawyer to whom I am writing has a very good reputation.

11. Correct

12. The students whose grades were under 70 percent were allowed to take the test again.

13. Correct

14. There's the girl whose sister is on the swim team.

15. Mr. Plowright, who used to work for a large company, now runs his own consulting business.

16. B: Mario, who is eighteen, is a senior in high school.

17. Margie's husband, who is seven feet tall, played basketball when he was in college.

18. Prattson University, which has an excellent chemistry department, is going to spend several million dollars to improve its chemistry laboratory.

CHAPTER 9 Achievement Quiz

Relative Clauses

1. Correct

2. Belinda owns a car that/which uses diesel fuel.

3. A veterinarian is a doctor who treats animals.

4. Last night I saw a movie that/which made me cry.

5. Paula has a roommate whose mother is an actress.

6. Carnet Market is the store that has the best selection of fruits and vegetables.

7. Correct

8. Amy, who is only seven years old, is a very talented musician.

9. Correct

10. Mary is the only person in the office whom the boss likes.

11. The band in which my daughter plays just got a record contract./The band my daughter plays in just got a record contract.

12. Correct

13. Your father tells the best jokes that I have ever heard.

14. I'd like to introduce you to Mr. and Mrs. Applethorp, who just moved into the house next door to mine.

15. Correct

16. Kelly, who is a fantastic cook, is opening her own restaurant.

17. This watch, which I bought two days ago, stopped working this morning.

18. Albert and Karen are the people who helped me when my car broke down.

19. These are the dishes that/which my grandmother gave me last year./These are the dishes my grandmother gave me last year.

20. Correct

CHAPTER 10 Diagnostic Quiz

Count and Noncount Nouns

FORM, MEANING AND USE

1. Our class has twelve men and fifteen women.

2. The people in my country usually eat dinner after 8:00 P.M.

3. If you need information about cultural activities, you should talk to Imogene.

4. Sarabeth is studying to be a physical therapist.

5. I don't care about politics, but my sister is very interested in it.

6. Camilla needs advice.

7. I like cake, fruit, and ice cream, but I don't like cookies.

8. It's a crime if you don't report all of your income on your tax return.

9. Alex has an interesting job.

10. When I take my daughter on a trip, I have to bring bottles, milk, and a stroller.

11. The police don't patrol this neighborhood too often.

12. Mathematics is easy for some people.

13. If you have homework, I'll help you./If you have some homework, I'll help you.

14. Correct

15. He put his luggage down for a moment.

CHAPTER 10 Achievement Quiz

Count and Noncount Nouns

1. There were three men and two women at the dinner party.

2. Jenny's feet are very large.

3. I'm going outside to get fresh air./I'm going outside to get some fresh air

4. The leaves on maple trees turn red in October.

5. She likes it a lot, but I think she wasted a great deal of money.

6. She told it to all the other people in the office.

7. When you go to the drugstore, please get shampoo, suntan lotion, and a toothbrush.

8. Carla is going to be a lawyer when she gets older.

9. I'm going to donate blood at the hospital./I'm going to donate some blood at the hospital.

10. There was a serious crime in my neighborhood last night.

11. Correct

12. I think he should go to San Diego because it has good weather.

13. Henrietta owns beautiful jewelery.

14. If you want information about computers or stereo systems, you should talk to her.

15. Correct

16. Yvette left all her stuff at her mother's house.

17. He especially likes her long, red hair.

18. Correct

19. Mimi wants a new bicycle for her birthday.

20. I see smoke!

CHAPTER 11 Diagnostic Quiz

Quantity Expressions

FORM, MEANING AND USE

1. How much money do you have in the bank?

2. On Valentine's Day, Bert bought a box of chocolates for his wife.

3. There's a lot of orange juice in the refrigerator, so please help yourself.

4. There are too many people at the gym in the morning, so I always go in the afternoon.

5. There are a few slices left.

6. Benny has little hope/some hope that the situation will improve.

7. Correct

8. Solomon gave me several ideas for the show.

9. Correct

10. Please buy a tube of toothpaste at the supermarket.

11. Let me give you a piece of advice.

12. Correct

13. Apples cost eighty-nine cents a pound today.

14. How much does a bunch of bananas cost?/How much does a head of lettuce cost?

CHAPTER 11 Diagnostic Quiz

Articles

FORM, MEANING AND USE

1. Botany is a branch of biology.

2. B: Margarine is a substitute for butter.

3. B: When I turn the steering wheel, it squeaks very loudly.

4. B: I only have a dime.

5. A trapezoid is a geometric shape.

6. B: She doesn't like country music.

7. B: He always drinks water.

8. The cockroach is an insect that almost no one likes.

9. Tammy is scared of dogs.

10. Correct

11. Sam needs a new coat.

12. The capital of England is London.

13. He's been playing the piano since he was a very young child.

14. Scientists think the sun will run out of energy some day.

CHAPTER 11 Achievement Quiz

Quantity Expressions and Articles

1. Did Mrs. Burgos give you a lot of information/much information/any information about Mexico?

2. B: Apples are healthy and are very good for snacks.

3. Correct

4. B: Well, she doesn't like basketball, but she loves baseball.

5. There's very little traffic today because it's a holiday.

6. Marilyn ate two pieces of cake for dessert.

7. Correct

8. Correct

9. What happened to the milk I put in the refrigerator yesterday?

10. When you open this jar, please don't dent the lid.

11. We have very little olive oil left.

12. You can't buy a lot of things/lots of things for a nickel.

13. She has few friends there, so she feels very lonely.

14. Marcus didn't like pizza until he visited Renata's family.

15. How many hours a week is your Italian class?

16. Ivy brought two bags of ice cubes to the party.

17. Correct

18. The basketball team has very good players this year.

19. Eliza won a prize in an art contest for the portrait of her mother that she painted last year.

20. Correct

CHAPTER 12 Diagnostic Quiz

Comparative and Superlative Adjectives and Adverbs

FORM, MEANING AND USE

1. Joan's house has a smaller kitchen than my house does.

2. Kay's Market has the cheapest prices in the city.

3. Correct

4. I think that Bob's idea is better than Aaron's.

5. Barbara is one of the best singers in the chorus.

6. Seth behaves badly, but his little brother's behavior is even worse.

7. The Sears Tower in Chicago is the highest office building in the world.

8. B: It was the worst movie I've seen this year.

9. Of all the houses that we looked at, I liked the one on Elm Street the least.

10. The fruit store is more expensive than the supermarket.

11. He's stronger than I am.

12. Correct

13. She's probably the richest woman in the world.

14. Last night was the coldest night of the entire winter.

CHAPTER 12 Diagnostic Quiz

Comparative and Superlative Nouns, As…As, The Same…As, and So…That/Such(a)…That

FORM, MEANING AND USE

1. I'm not able to run as fast as I could when I was in high school.

2. Correct

3. Of all the English classes in the school, my class has the fewest students.

4. Japan has fewer natural resources than Russia.

5. Correct.

6. It's so warm outside today that you don't need to wear a jacket.

7. Melissa slammed the door so hard that I could feel the vibrations.

8. Correct

9. Strawberries have fewer calories than raisins.

10. Of all the men in his family, Arthur earns the least money.

11. Maureen used to wear more makeup than she does now.

12. Are you the same weight as your sister?

13. Greta made such a good impression at the interview that she was offered the job one day later.

14. Your face is as red as a fire engine.

15. Correct

16. This shirt is the same price as that one, but the quality is not as good.

CHAPTER 12 Achievement Quiz

Expressing Differences and Similarities

1. California is bigger than New Hampshire.

2. Audiocassettes cost less than compact discs.

3. John is the fastest runner on the team.

4. Sue has traveled less extensively than the other people in her family.

5. Correct

6. California is the most populous state in the United States.

7. Abigail works as many hours as I do.

8. Correct

9. Correct

10. The music was so loud that it gave me a headache.

11. Carol is the tallest player on the women's basketball team.

12. Delaware has fewer people than New Jersey.

13. Gracie ate so much that she couldn't move.

14. Allie is not as intelligent as Martiza.

15. The doctor says your condition is going to get worse unless you have an operation.

16. Kathleen is not prettier than Rachel./Kathleen is not as pretty as Rachel.

17. Correct

18. Martha has more children than I do.

19. Candace is the same age as Jolene./Candace is as old as Jolene.

20. Everett is the least serious student in the class.

Wish Sentences and Imaginary *If* Sentences

FORM, MEANING AND USE: *WISH* SENTENCES

1. Ella wishes that she lived in a quiet place, but she doesn't.

2. I wish I could go to the party, but I can't because I have to take care of my little brother.

3. But I hope that I will/I'll be able to get a new one soon. OR But I hope that I am/I'm able to get a new one soon.

4. I wish she would ask for my permission.

5. B: No, but I wish it were/was. (Note: The second form is acceptable in informal, conversational style.)

6. I wish her boss would give her a raise soon.

7. He wishes he had more time.

8. I wish I were/was stronger. (Note: The second form is acceptable in informal, conversational style.)

FORM, MEANING AND USE: IMAGINARY *IF* SENTENCES

9. If they were older, you could explain it to them.

10. I wouldn't decide what to do so quickly if I were you.

11. Correct

12. What would you do if you won a million dollars in a lottery?

13. If I were president, I would eliminate all taxes.

14. If she weren't able to help me, I would/I'd never be able to finish.

15. Correct

Wish Sentences and Imaginary *If* Sentences

A.

1. won

2. would move

3. saw

4. would read

5. could

6. can

7. were

8. didn't have

9. smoked

10. wouldn't worry/didn't worry

B.

1. If I were you, I wouldn't tell the truth about what really happened.

2. B: I wish I were able to/was able to, but I don't have any money. (Note: The second form is acceptable in informal, conversational style.)

3. I wish she would move.

4. Does Tara wish her brothers weren't so protective?

5. What would you do if you lost your wallet?

6. Peter wouldn't be so depressed if his parents were healthy.

7. Correct

8. Correct

9. Paulette would be shocked if she knew Julie's secret.

10. If machines never broke, mechanics wouldn't have any work.

Gerunds and Infinitives

FORM, MEANING AND USE

1. Eating chocolate makes Annabeth happy.

2. Trying to understand complicated grammar points gives some students a headache.

3. Before moving to Los Angeles, Lawrence lived in Nevada.

4. Penny went to the library to return/in order to return a book.

5. Would you mind calling me back in a few minutes?

6. When I was very young, I used to believe that animals could speak.

7. Richard and Jane look forward to visiting their daughter next week.

8. Correct

9. Carl used to weigh 200 pounds until he stopped eating junk food all the time.

10. Don't forget to call Aunt Jenny tonight.

11. When Meredith finished reading the newspaper, she gave it to her husband.

12. Kate spent a lot of time working on her project.

13. You can contact me by leaving a message with my secretary.

14. Amber expects to find a new job within the next three months.

15. I need to tell you something.

16. Instead of leaving work at five, she stayed late.

17. Read the manual in order to operate the machine properly.

18. He regrets not attending the show.

19. Correct

20. B: I don't want to.

Gerunds and Infinitives

1. By using electronic mail, people can communicate quickly and cheaply with friends in different parts of the world.

2. He promised not to drive so fast anymore.

3. Correct

4. So she's trying to avoid her landlord.

5. They talked about not going anywhere all weekend.

6. Instead of complaining about your boss, you should get another job.

7. So we stopped to take some pictures, and then we continued our drive.

8. There's no point in cleaning this house.

9. Correct

10. Wearing a suit and tie makes Lou uncomfortable.

11. Fred enjoys playing basketball.

12. Correct

13. Speaking several languages can help you get a good job.

14. Correct

15. It's important to sleep.

16. Leslie is not accustomed to eating a large breakfast.

17. Did you go shopping last night?

18. Aaron dislikes waiting for other people.

19. Callie forgot to tell me about what happened yesterday.

20. Driving a car requires a lot of concentration.

CHAPTER 15 Diagnostic Quiz

The Past Perfect and the Past Perfect Continuous

FORM, MEANING AND USE

1. c	6. c	11. c
2. b	7. c	12. a
3. a	8. b	13. c
4. a	9. a	14. a
5. c	10. b	15. b

CHAPTER 15 Diagnostic Quiz

Past *Wish* Sentences and Past Imaginary *If* Sentences

FORM, MEANING AND USE

1. c	6. b	11. c
2. b	7. a	12. b
3. a	8. a	13. b
4. c	9. a	14. c
5. b	10. b	15. a

CHAPTER 15 Achievement Quiz

The Past Perfect and the Past Perfect Continuous, Past *Wish* Sentences, and Past Imaginary *If* Sentences

A.

1. c	5. c
2. a	6. a
3. c	7. a
4. c	8. c

B.

1. I wish it were/was sunny right now. (The second form is also acceptable in informal, conversational style.)
2. The boys wish they could have gone on the trip last year.
3. Nick wishes he had a car.
4. B: If I were/was you, I'd call the manufacturer's Help Line right now. (The second form is also acceptable in informal, conversational style.)
5. Correct
6. If it hadn't been raining yesterday, we would have gone on a picnic.
7. Teresa would have won the contest if Jamie hadn't been playing also.
8. If she had known about the delay, Clara wouldn't have driven to the airport.

CHAPTER 16 Diagnostic Quiz

Passive Sentences

FORM, MEANING AND USE

1. The omelette is being cooked right now.
2. Correct
3. Pets are not allowed in my apartment building.
4. All students will be expected/are expected to attend class regularly.
5. This shirt has been washed in hot water twice since last week.
6. While I was visiting June, her house was being painted/was painted.
7. Bills must be paid by cash or money order.
8. Eve should be permitted/should have been permitted to enter the discotheque.
9. Five people were injured in a fire at a warehouse yesterday.
10. The flight arrived/was arriving twenty minutes ago.
11. The doctor should have been called immediately, but the phone was broken.
12. All the children were weighed by the school nurse.
13. Correct

14. Every day my mail is delivered at noon.

15. My house has been robbed by the same person two times.

CHAPTER 16 Achievement Quiz

Passive Sentences

1. At the present time, French is spoken in many African countries.

2. The rent must be paid on the first day of the month.

3. This book was written ten years ago.

4. If you go to the new Japanese restaurant, you will be asked to take off your shoes.

5. Harry wasn't invited to the party.

6. Correct

7. Your calculations should be checked by another person so that you are certain there are no mistakes.

8. That fabric might have been manufactured in India.

9. Sugarcane is cultivated in tropical countries.

10. Amy will be surprised by the news.

11. Correct

12. But now, bonuses are not given to anyone.

13. Last week, Alison was hired to take care of three little girls.

14. The dog was taken to the veterinarian this morning.

15. It cost/was twenty dollars.

16. Max has been promoted recently.

17. Nancy should be chosen for the basketball team.

18. All the passengers could have been killed in an accident!

19. Correct

20. The baby weighed ten pounds./The baby was weighed.

CHAPTER 17 Diagnostic Quiz

Noun Clauses

FORM, MEANING AND USE

1. Frederica didn't understand what the teacher was saying.

2. Correct

3. Jeremy believed that his friends were going to help him.

4. Does Sandy know if/whether or not the children will be home for dinner?
Does Sandy know whether the children will be home for dinner or not?

5. Faye couldn't remember why her sister wasn't coming to the meeting.

6. Kari knows how a computer works.

7. B: Yes, I think so.

8. Could you please tell me where Amsterdam Avenue is?

9. Correct

10. I thought she would call me last week, but she didn't.

11. Do you understand what this means?

12. I need John's phone number, but I don't know where the phone book is.

13. Can you please tell me if/whether/whether or not there are any seats left?
Can you please tell me whether there are any seats left or not?

14. I wonder what she said.

15. Correct

CHAPTER 17 Diagnostic Quiz

Reported Speech

FORM, MEANING AND USE

1. Mark explained that he had lived in Ecuador a long time ago.

2. Rachel asked her husband if Leona was going to be home that afternoon.

3. Gayle asked Harry why he was smiling.

4. Richard asked Danny when the class would be over.

5. The teacher told the class that Manitoba is/was in Canada.

6. George told Becky to go to the store and buy some milk.

7. Mrs. Gibson told her son not to forget his umbrella.

8. Clark suggested that Andrea go/should go to the beach.

9. Tammy said that she hadn't talked to Betty since the day before.

10. Abigail said that she couldn't speak French when she was in high school.

11. The teacher told Lucy that she had to hand in her homework the next day.

12. John said that he has just started/had just started a new book.

13. Scott answered that he'll/he will be home in a couple of hours.
    Scott answered that he'd/he would be home in a couple of hours.

14. Carolyn complained that this weather makes/made her feel depressed.

CHAPTER 17 Achievement Quiz

Noun Clauses and Reported Speech

A.

1. Audrey said that she had changed her plans./Audrey said to me that she had changed her plans./Audrey told me that she had changed her plans.

2. Harold wants to know why Patricia decided to sell her house.

3. B: No, I don't think so./No, I think not.

4. Ruth told me where you had put the book.

5. Mimi asked me if I would like to join the club.

6. B: He recommended that we buy/should buy a used car.

7. Barbara thought the movie was very interesting.

8. Correct

9. I need to know if/whether or not you will be home for dinner.
   I need to know whether you will be home for dinner or not.

10. Last night Laura asked me if she could take my notes home.

11. We believed that the store would be open on Monday, but it wasn't.

12. I suggested that Nancy hire/should hire a new secretary.

B.

1. Kate told Allen to take her with him.

2. Vicky asked her sister why she wasn't ready.

3. Susan asked Paul if he had liked/liked Jerry's new girlfriend.

4. Alice remarked that she hadn't seen Tim that morning.

5. Amy told Bob that she probably could help him with his math homework.

6. Craig told James not to answer the telephone.

7. Jeff explained to Arthur that Kay wouldn't be/won't be at work tomorrow.

8. Debbie said that she was taking/is taking a very difficult physics class this semester.

STUDENT BOOK
ANSWER KEY

Chapter 1

Exercise 1 (page 3)

1. A: *gives*
   B: *doesn't give; do you get*

2. A: lives; think
   B: do they visit you
   A: refuse, snows; come

3. A: does Ellen watch
   B: do you mean
   A: watches, do, makes

4. A: does your brother do
   B: sells; works

5. A: does the bus come
   B: arrives
   A: Does this happen
   B: comes, has; doesn't drive

6. A: don't grow
   B: don't you try

Exercise 2 (page 4)

1.

Who defends people in trouble? — A lawyer does.
Who studies weather patterns? — A meteorologist
   does.
Who serves people in a restaurant? — A waiter does.
Who prepares drinks in a bar? — A bartender does.
Who teaches in a university? — A professor does.
Who runs a city government? — A mayor does.
Who treats heart patients? — A cardiologist does.

Who reports the news? — A newscaster does.
Who cleans buildings? — A janitor does.
Who performs operations? — A surgeon does.
Who runs the state government? — A governor does.
Who fixes cars? — A mechanic does.
Who investigates crimes? — A detective does.

2.
Answers will vary. For example:

What does a bus driver do? She drives a bus.
What does a carpenter do? He builds houses.
What does a pharmacist do? She prepares
   medical drugs.

Exercise 3 (page 6)

1. *True.*

2. *False. Water doesn't freeze at 0° Fahrenheit.
   It freezes at 0° centigrade.*

3. False. The earth doesn't revolve around the moon.
   It revolves around the sun.

4. True.

5. False. Palm trees don't grow in cold climates.
   They grow in warm climates.

6. False. Magnets don't attract pieces of glass.
   They attract pieces of metal.

7. False. Penguins don't live in the desert. They live
   in the Antarctic.

8. False. The sun doesn't rise in the north. It rises
   in the east.

9. True.

10. False. Birds don't spin webs. Spiders spin webs.

11. False. Spiders don't make wax and honey.
    Bees make wax and honey.

12. True.

Exercise 4 (page 7)

Answers will vary. For example:

1. *Many people*

2. Most Americans

3. Some children

4. Many children

5. Some adults

6. Not many Americans

7. Many people

8. Some adults

9. Many Americans

10. Not many people

11. Few Americans

12. Most teenagers

Exercise 5 (page 7)

Answers will vary. For example:

1. *retire before they are sixty.*
2. attend kindergarten.
3. get student loans.
4. have enough free time.
5. work on Sundays.
6. eat hamburgers and hot dogs.
7. teachers work from September to June.
8. people take night courses.

Exercise 6 (page 8)

1.
instruct — teach
permit — allow
phone — call
start — begin
compliment — praise
choose — select
fix — repair
speak — talk

3.
rough — smooth
near — far
rude — polite
special — ordinary
safe — dangerous
simple — complex
wrong — right

Exercise 7 (page 11)

1. Parent: *You're getting mud on the floor.*
2. Sue: The bag is tearing, and I'm dropping groceries on the floor.
3. Joe: What are you doing?
   Roommate: I'm looking for a pencil.
   Joe: Why are you making such a mess?
4. Linda: Why are you walking so fast?
   Julie: I'm trying to hurry.
5. Lee: Why are you kicking the machine?
   Sam: I'm trying to get my money back.

Exercise 8 (page 11)

1. B: *Yes, they are./No, they're not./No, they aren't.*
2. B: Yes, I am./No, I'm not.
3. B: Yes, I am./No, I'm not.
4. B: Yes, I am./No, I'm not.
5. B: Yes, they are./No, they're not/No, they aren't.
6. B: Yes, it is./No, it isn't.
7. B: Yes, it is./No, it isn't.
8. B: Yes, they are./No, they aren't./No, they're not.
9. B: Yes, I am./No, I'm not.
10. B: Yes, I am./No, I'm not.

Exercise 9 (page 13)

Answers to questions will vary. For example:

1. A: *What are you doing?*
   B: *I'm cleaning out my closet.*
   A: *Why are you doing that?*
   B: *It was a mess!*
2. A: What are you making?
   B: Some chicken noodle soup.
3. A: Where are you going?
   B: To the bus stop.
   A: Why are you rushing?
   B: I'm late!
4. A: Who's knocking?
   B: It's my friend Tom.
   A: Why are you laughing?
   B: He's wearing a funny hat.
   A: What's going on?
   B: It's his birthday.
5. A: What number are you calling, please?
   B: 668-8668
6. A: Who's calling, please?
   B: It's Joe.

Exercise 10 (page 14)

Answers will vary. For example:

1. *I'm learning to swim this year and I'm also jogging a lot.*
2. I'm taking four courses this semester.
3. I'm studying a lot these days.

Exercise 11 (page 14)

1. (a) *No.*
   (b) It's not clear.
   (c) Probably not.

2. (a) No.
   (b) Probably.
   (c) Probably not.

3. (a) No.
   (b) Probably not.
   (c) It's not clear.

4. (a) It's not clear.
   (b) Yes.
   (c) No.

Exercise 12 (page 15)

Tom lives on Dryden Road. — He has lived there for a long time.
Peter is living on Dryden Road. — He just moved there a few weeks ago.
Alex wears a tie to school. — He's a very formal dresser.
Matt is wearing a tie to school. — He usually wears jeans and a T-shirt, however.
James works at the bank. — He has worked there since 1980.
Andrew is working at the bank. — He started the job a few days ago.

Exercise 13 (page 16)

1.

He is 5 feet 11 inches tall.
He weighs 165 pounds.
His hair is short.
He has straight, brown hair.
His eyes are brown.
He has a mustache, a beard, and freckles.

2.

Answers will vary. For example:

She is *5 feet 5 inches tall. She weighs about 120 pounds. She has short, brown hair. Her hair is curly. Her eyes are brown.*

Exercise 14 (page 17)

Answers will vary. For example:

A: *You have a nice apartment.*
B: *Thank you.*
A: *This chicken tastes delicious!*

B: *Thank you. I'm glad you like it.*
A: I love the pictures you have.
B: Oh, thank you.

Exercise 15 (page 17)

Answers will vary. For example:

1. You: *I don't like it. It's too crowded.*

2. You: I don't like it. It smells strong/bad/awful.

3. You: They cost too much. I don't like them.
   You: They seem too big.

4. You: I don't like it. It looks cheap.

5. You: It's too loud. It sounds awful.
   You: He's strange.

6. You: It's too salty.
   You: It's too sweet.

7. You: It weighs too much. It feels heavy.

8. You: It's too big.

Exercise 16 (page 19)

1. A: *is calling*
   B: *know, 'm doing*

2. A: are you taking/do you take
   A: Is it
   B: depends; guess, 's, 's getting; 'm having

3. A: hope, 'm not being, need
   B: seems
   A: is smoking

4. A: complains/is complaining
   B: sounds, needs
   A: think, 's looking for; hope; 'm getting/get

5. A: 'm calling; is
   B: has

6. A: are you doing
   B: 'm looking for, 'm preparing
   A: Do you want

Exercise 17 (page 20)

They could refer to children, birds, dogs, and guests, because children, birds, dogs, and guests can control their behavior. Flowers and raindrops cannot decide to be quiet.

Exercise 18 (page 21)

Answers will vary. For example:

1. *He is usually very rude./He often insults people./ His behavior is unusual.*

2. She always answers everyone's questions.

3. It usually isn't generous. This is unusual.

4. They usually complain a lot./They usually argue a lot.

5. He doesn't treat everyone the same./He always criticizes us.

Summary Exercise (page 21)

1. *It's snowing!*

2. The baby is very big now.

3. What does this mean?

4. I don't know his number.

5. What does your father do?

6. We eat there all the time.

7. Do you know that water freezes at 0° centigrade?

8. Susan doesn't go there anymore.

9. We take the bus every morning.

10. Ron goes to work every Sunday.

Chapter 2

Exercise 1 (page 27)

1. *always*

2. Sometimes/Occasionally

3. never

4. usually

5. always

6. hardly ever/seldom/rarely, always

Exercise 2 (page 28)

1. *She always listens to the morning news on the radio.*

2. He always remembers to send his aunt a birthday card.

3. We often go to the movies.

4. She hardly ever watches television.

5. He hardly ever cooks dinner.

6. He frequently visits his girlfriend in another city.

7. We often/frequently call each other.

8. I sometimes/occasionally see her.

Exercise 3 (page 30)

1. *They often eat dinner at six o'clock.*

2. On Saturday morning, I usually sleep late. Sometimes I sleep until eight or nine o'clock. On weekdays, my alarm always rings at 6:00 A.M. I rarely go to bed before midnight. Therefore, I am often very tired by lunchtime.

3. Jack is normally very slow in the morning. He always needs a lot of time. He usually takes a shower after his alarm rings. Occasionally, he spends half an hour in the shower. He typically spends a lot of time getting dressed and eating breakfast. As a result, he is often late for work.

4. The baby usually sleeps through the night. Occasionally, she wakes up in the middle of the night. Frequently, this happens when she has a long nap during the day. We always try to wake her from her nap after two hours. But sometimes we can't wake her up.

Exercise 4 (page 31)

Answers will vary. For example:

A: *Do you ever wake up early to study for an exam?*
B: *Yes, I sometimes do./No, I never do.*

A: Do you ever study at night?
B: No, I never do./Yes, I always do.

Exercise 5 (page 31)

Answers will vary. For example:

Anna never studies at night. Sometimes she wakes up early to study for an exam.

Exercise 6 (page 32)

Answers will vary. For example:

My father is always smoking a cigar.
The mayor is constantly exaggerating.
The governor is always losing his temper.
She is forever complaining about her work.
Her husband is constantly threatening to leave.

Exercise 7 (page 32)

Answers will vary. For example:

1. Situation: You are complaining that every time you go to Joe's office, he is busy. Other ways of saying it are:
   Joe is forever talking on the phone.
   Joe is constantly talking on the phone.
   Joe is continually talking on the phone.
   Joe talks on the phone too much and I don't like it.

2. This sounds more like the speaker is just expressing a fact. It is not as negative as *Joe is always talking on the phone.* However, with stress on *always*, this sentence could also convey a negative attitude.

Exercise 8 (page 33)

Time
How many days are there in a year? (There are) 365.
How many hours are there in a day? (There are) 24.
How many weeks are there in a year? (There are) 52.
How many years are there in a century? (There are) 100.
How many decades are there in a century?
   (There are) 10.

Weight
How many ounces are there in a pound? (There are) 16.
How many pounds are there in a ton? (There are) 2,000.
How many grams are there in a kilogram?
   (There are) 1,000.
How many pounds are there in a kilogram?
   (There are) about 2.2.
How many milligrams are there in a gram?
   (There are) 1,000.

Distance
How many inches are there in a foot? (There are) 12.
How many feet are there in a yard? (There are) 3.
How many meters are there in a kilometer?
   (There are) 1,000.
How many kilometers are there in a mile?
   (There are) about 1.6.
How many centimeters are there in an inch?
   (There are) about 2.5.

Money
How many pennies are there in a dollar?
   (There are) 100.
How many nickels are there in a quarter? (There are) 5.
How many quarters are there in a dollar? (There are) 4.
How many nickels are there in a dime? (There are) 2.
How many dimes are there in a dollar? (There are) 10.

Exercise 9 (page 34)

Answers will vary. For example:

A: *Are there six nickels in a quarter?*
B: *No, there aren't. There's only five./There're only five.*

A: Are there a thousand meters in a kilogram?
B: No, there aren't. There are a thousand meters in a kilometer.

Exercise 10 (page 34)

1. *Ms. Malik, there's a message for you.*
2. Ms. Stern, there's a package for you.
3. Mr. Blake, there's a special delivery letter for you.
4. Mr. Blake, there's an emergency meeting at two o'clock.
5. Ms. Stern, there's a phone call for you.

Exercise 11 (page 35)

1. Rental agent: *Yes, there are three large closets.*
2. Rental agent: I don't know.
3. Rental agent: There's a refrigerator, a stove, a dishwasher and a microwave oven.
4. Rental agent: Yes, there's a tub with a shower.
5. Rental agent: There's gas heat.
6. Rental agent: There are four apartments in the building.
7. Rental agent: Yes, there's a bus stop on the corner.

8. Rental agent: Yes, there's a supermarket one block away.

9. Rental agent: I don't know.

10. (⌣⌢⌣⌣) Apartment hunter: Is there parking available?
    Rental agent: Yes, there's a parking lot behind the building.
    Apartment hunter: Is the apartment carpeted?
    Rental agent: There's carpeting in the living room and in the bedrooms.

Exercise 12 (page 36)

1. *Please call me later.*
2. *Go three blocks and turn left.*
3. Please don't worry about me.
4. Please don't speak so fast.
5. Go downstairs and then straight ahead.
6. Don't drive over the speed limit.
7. Please take my seat.
8. Please don't work so hard.
9. Please wait for me after class.
10. Don't drink and drive.

Exercise 13 (page 38)

Answers will vary. For example:

1. *Check the battery.*
2. *Don't stick a fork in the toaster! Unplug it first.*
3. Fill it up.
4. Drink plenty of fluids.
5. Read for a while.
6. Get a job.
7. Throw it out.
8. Look it up in the telephone directory.

Exercise 14 (page 38)

Answers will vary. For example:

Walk the dog every day at 7:00 A.M. and 7:00 P.M.

Bring in the newspaper every morning.

Water the plants twice a week.

Feed the fish every morning and evening.

Send me any important mail.

Separate recyclable materials from trash.

Put recyclable material in the green bins.

Put the trash cans and recycling bins out on Tuesdays and Thursdays.

Exercise 15 (page 39)

Answers will vary. For example:

Dear ___Rita___   December 5

I have been worrying about your trip next week. You know that the city is very expensive, so ___figure out how much money you will need___ and ___then get some traveler's checks.___

Also, it can be very dangerous. The crime rate is very high. Please ___be careful and keep your money out of sight.___

And another thing—the weather is bad this time of year. There are frequent snowstorms and cold winds. ___Take a warm coat, a scarf, and some gloves.___

I know the city can be a lot of fun, too. ___Don't forget to visit the zoo and the natural history museum.___

Now remember, I'm going to worry about you so ___please call me as soon as you get back.___

Love,
_____

P.S. I almost forgot! ___Have fun!___

Summary Exercise (page 41)

1. *Suzanne, there's someone at the door.*
2. It always arrives late.
3. Here. Take this one, OK?
4. We never take a trip in August.
5. There's a hole in your shoe.
6. I seldom eat pizza.
7. I think there are nine people in line.
8. She's forever waking me up in the morning.
9. Please don't smoke.
10. Mark, there's a message for you.

CHAPTER 3

Exercise 1 (page 46)

1.

Column 1		Column 2		Column 3	
worked	1	tried	1	invited	3
looked	1	arrived	2	started	2
asked	1	sprained	1	rented	2
picked	1	closed	1	reported	3
dropped	1	allowed	2	waited	2
wished	1	traveled	2	needed	2
laughed	1	judged	1	added	2
sliced	1	robbed	1	decided	3
watched	1	stayed	1	attended	3

2.

In Column 1, *-ed* is pronounced as /t/.

In Column 2, *-ed* is pronounced as /d/.

In Column 3, *-ted* or *-ded* are pronounced as an extra syllable, so the number of syllables increased by one.

Exercise 2 (page 46)

Simple Past Verb		Column 1 /t/	Column 2 /d/	Column 3 /id/
walked	1	☑	☐	☐
phoned	1	☐	☑	☐
bumped	1	☑	☐	☐
twisted	2	☐	☐	☑
pushed	1	☑	☐	☐
happened	2	☐	☑	☐
traded	2	☐	☐	☑
answered	2	☐	☑	☐
studied	2	☐	☑	☐
waved	1	☐	☑	☐
punched	1	☑	☐	☐
admitted	3	☐	☐	☑
wanted	2	☐	☐	☑
missed	1	☑	☐	☐
pretended	3	☐	☐	☑

Exercise 3 (page 47)

1. A: *rented*
   B: *decided, traveled*

2. A: dropped
   B: tried, bumped

3. A: studied
   B: answered; called, wanted

4. A: happened
   B: missed, walked

5. A: watched; laughed, frightened
   B: Did you rent

6. A: stayed, injured, sprained, bumped
   B: phoned, asked

Exercise 4 (page 48)

1. A: *came*
   B: *Yes, she did; had*

2. A: *didn't pay*
   B: *No, I didn't; made*

3. A: left
   B: Yes, they did; got, ran

4. A: forgot
   B: Yes, I did; brought; found

5. A: didn't give
   B: No, she didn't; gave

6. A: made
   B: Yes, I did; saw, thought

7. A: didn't take out
   B: No, you didn't; took it out, woke up

8. A: heard, broke
   B: Yes, she did; spoke; fell; hurt

Exercise 5 (page 49)

Who wrote Macbeth? — *Shakespeare did.*/
What did Shakespeare write? — He wrote Macbeth.
Who painted *Guernica?* — Pablo Picasso did.
What did Beethoven compose? — He composed
the Ninth Symphony.
Who wrote *Don Quixote?* — Cervantes did.
What did Yasunari Kawabata write? — He wrote
Snow Country.
Who wrote *Crime and Punishment?* —
Dostoyevsky did.
What did Gabriel García Márquez write? — He wrote
One Hundred Years of Solitude.
Who sculpted the Statue of Liberty? —
Frédéric Bartholdi did.
What did Frida Kahlo paint? — She painted
Self-Portrait, 1926.
Who wrote *The Divine Comedy?* — Dante did.

Intermediate Grammar: From Form to Meaning and Use

Exercise 6 (page 51)

1. A: *were*
   B: *was*

2. A: were, were
   B: were

3. A: were
   B: was

4. A: were
   B: were

5. A: was
   B: was

6. A: were
   B: were

7. A: was
   B: was

8. A: was
   B: was

Exercise 7 (page 52)

1. *Who was Genghis Khan?*
   What happened in the 1200s?
   What did Genghis Khan do in the 1200s?
   When did Genghis Khan conquer Persia and
   much of China?

2. Who led the movement against British rule in India
   in the 1940s?
   When did Mahatma Gandhi lead the movement
   against British rule in India?

3. Who celebrated the first Thanksgiving?
   What did the Pilgrims celebrate in 1621?

4. Who was Julius Caesar?
   What did Julius Caesar do?

5. Who became emperor of the western Roman
   Empire in the year 800?
   When did Charlemagne become emperor
   of the western Roman Empire?

6. Who calculated the value of *pi*?
   What did Archimedes do?

7. Who defeated Napoleon at Waterloo?
   When did the British and Prussians defeat
   Napoleon at Waterloo?

8. Who was a hero of the South American wars
   of independence in the nineteenth century?
   What did Simón Bolívar do?

Exercise 8 (page 54)

Answers will vary. For example:

1. A: *Did you get your bathing suit?*
   B: *Yes, I did./No, I didn't.*

2. A: Did you pack your toothbrush?
   A: Did you bring your raincoat?
   A: Did you take your ticket?
   A: Did you remember your glasses?
   A: (～～) Did you bring your wallet?

   A: Did you water the plants?
   A: Did you take out the garbage?
   A: Did you stop the mail delivery?
   A: Did you lock the doors?
   A: (～～) Did you lock the windows?

3. A: Did you brush your teeth?
   A: Did you wash your face?
   A: Did you sharpen your pencils?
   A: Did you do your homework?
   A: (～～) Did you finish your book?

   A: Did you remember your lunch money?
   A: Did you take your gym shoes?
   A: Did you bring your backpack?
   A: Did you get your jacket?
   A: (～～) Did you get your glasses?

Exercise 9 (page 55)

1. *I'm sorry I'm late. I missed the bus.*

2. My watch stopped.

3. I got lost.

4. I overslept.

5. The electricity went off in my apartment.

6. My goldfish jumped out of the tank.

7. My cat died.

8. I fell into a manhole.

9. A mugger took all my money.

10. My cousin called long distance from Antarctica.

11. Aliens from outer space kidnapped me.

12. (～～) A spaceship landed in my apartment.

Exercise 10 (page 56)

1. *Why didn't the little boy want to use toothpaste?*
2. Why did the banana go out with the prune?
3. Why did the house seem empty?
4. Who got up last night when the baby cried?
5. What did the digital watch say to its mother?
6. What did the Beatles say during a rockslide?
7. What caused a lot of trouble when it stopped smoking?
8. Why did the turkey join the band?
9. What kind of chair did the geologist like?
10. Why did the jogger go to the veterinarian?

Exercise 11 (page 57)

Answers will vary. For example:

1. *He probably had an accident or a fight.*
   He probably broke his arm.
   He probably needed an X ray.
2. He probably built it himself.
3. He probably missed the bus.
4. His dog probably ran away.
5. He probably found his dog.
6. Her car probably ran out of gas.
7. She probably won the lottery.
8. He probably stole the purse.
9. The Browns probably went on vacation.
10. She probably woke up late.
11. She probably fell down and scraped her knee.

Exercise 12 (page 59)

Answers will vary.

Exercise 13 (page 59)

1. B: No, *it wasn't. It was hard.*
2. B: *Yes, you were. In fact, you were very helpful.*
3. B: No, it wasn't. It was very nice.
4. B: Yes, they were. They were fine.
5. B: No, it wasn't. It was just right.
6. B: Yes, you were. I called you at 7:00 P.M.
7. B: Yes, it was. It was terrific.
8. B: Yes, it was. It had good explanations.
9. B: Yes, he was. He sat in the back.
10. B: Yes, there were. There were three.
11. B: No, you weren't. You were right.
12. B: No, I wasn't. I just disagreed with her.

Exercise 14 (page 60)

1. *False. John F. Kennedy didn't die in the seventeenth century. He died in the twentieth century.*
2. False. Hawaii became part of the United States in the twentieth century.
3. True.
4. False. Alexander Graham Bell didn't invent the piano. He invented the telephone.
5. True.
6. False. Astronauts didn't land on Mars in 1969. They landed on the moon.
7. False. Mozart didn't write novels. He wrote music.
8. False. Rembrandt didn't paint the *Mona Lisa*. Leonardo da Vinci did.
9. False. Mao Zedong didn't establish the Communist People's Republic of China in 1965. He established it in 1949.
10. True.
11. False. Romeo and Juliet didn't get married at the end of the story. They died.
12. True.

Exercise 15 (page 61)

Answers will vary.

Exercise 16 (page 63)

1. A: *did you use to*
   B: *didn't use to*

2. A: used to
   B: Didn't she use to

3. A: used to
   B: used to

4. A: Did you use to; used to
   B: used to

5. A: did the library use to
   B: used to

Exercise 17 (page 65)

1. *I used to visit my grandmother every Sunday.*

2. Every year my grandmother used to cook a big dinner for the holidays.

3. My father used to have a Ford station wagon.

4. In the fifties, a candy bar used to cost ten cents and a quart of milk used to cost a quarter.

5. My brother and I used to play a lot of *Monopoly*.

6. I used to have a cat named Sylvester.

7. My brother and I used to quarrel a lot.

8. We used to spend summers in a cabin near Lake George.

Exercise 18 (page 65)

Answers will vary. For example:

1. I used to run a mile in four and a half minutes.

2. I used to hate vegetables.

3. I used to work late at night.

Exercise 19 (page 66)

1. *Offices used to have only typewriters. Now they have computers.*

2. Many Americans used to live on farms. Now they live in or near large cities.

3. A trip from Chicago to New York used to take two days. Now it takes one and a half hours by plane.

4. We used to have a small variety of fresh fruit and vegetables. Now we have a wide variety.

5. Businesses often used to close in the summer because of the heat. Now we have air-conditioning.

6. House keys used to be almost four inches long. Now they're only two inches long.

7. Mothers used to stay home with their children. Now many mothers work outside the home.

8. Most Americans used to go to work right after high school. Now many Americans go to college.

9. Americans used to have large families. Now they have small ones.

10. Girls used to have to wear skirts or dresses to school. Now they wear jeans and sweatshirts.

Exercise 20 (page 66)

Answers will vary.

Exercise 21 (page 68)

1. A: *What were you doing last night at ten o'clock?*
   B: *I was studying.*
   A: *What were you doing last night at midnight?*
   B: *I was sleeping.*

2. A: What were you doing last night at 7:30 P.M.?
   A: What were you doing this morning at 6:00 A.M.?
   A: What were you doing this morning at 8:00 A.M.?
   A: What were you doing an hour ago?

3. A: Where were you living last year?
   A: Where were you living five years ago?
   A: Where were you living ten years ago?

4. A: What were you thinking about when you went to sleep last night?
   A: What were you thinking about when you woke up this morning?
   A: What were you thinking about when you were coming to class?
   A: What were you thinking about when the class started?
   A: What were you thinking about a minute ago?

Exercise 22 (page 69)

Answers will vary. For example:

1. *I was sleeping.*
   My roommate was taking a shower.
   The cat was meowing in the kitchen.

2. I was sitting in the front of the room.
   I was biting my nails.
   Some students were looking for seats.

3. Music was playing softly.
   I was sitting on the couch.
   The children were sleeping.

4. The students were making a lot of noise.
   Some people were smoking.
   I was sitting near the window.

5. People were standing in line.
   Two tellers were counting money.
   The manager was talking on the phone.

Exercise 23 (page 70)

Answers will vary.

Summary Exercise (page 73)

1. *Did you find the umbrella?*

2. What did she do last night?

3. When did you call this morning?

4. He didn't go out.

5. She used to work at the library.

6. The wind was howling.

7. Did you use to live in an apartment?

8. Did they have any refreshments?

9. Did he go to class yesterday?

10. You weren't here on December 10.

Chapter 4

Exercise 1 (page 77)

1. A: *are you going to do*
   B: *'m going to look for*

2. A: Are you going to apply
   B: 'm not going to send

3. A: is going to break
   B: is going to fall

4. A: 's going to help
   B: 're going to bring

5. A: are you going to wear
   B: 'm going to buy

6. A: 's going to rain
   B: 'm not going to walk, 'm going to ask

Exercise 2 (page 79)

Answers to questions will vary. For example:

1. A: *When are you going to take a vacation?*
   B: *This summer.*

2. A: When are you going to get a medical checkup?
   B: Next month.

3. A: When are you going to take the day off?
   B: Next Friday.

4. A: When are you going to clean your apartment?
   B: Tomorrow morning.

5. A: When are you going to take a trip?
   B: Next summer.

6. A: When are you going to go out to dinner?
   B: This Sunday.

7. A: When are you going to do the laundry?
   B: Tomorrow evening.

8. A: When are you going to shop for groceries?
   B: The day after tomorrow.

9. A: When are you going to read a novel?
   B: This month.

10. (⌒⌒) A: When are you going to see
    the new movie?
    B: Next Saturday.

Exercise 3 (page 80)

Answers will vary. For example:

1. *This afternoon I'm going to play tennis.*

2. I'm going to clean my apartment this weekend.

3. I'm going to work out tomorrow afternoon.

4. I'm going to visit my grandparents in three months.

5. The day after tomorrow I'm going to get a haircut.

6. Next semester I'm going to take only five courses.

Exercise 4 (page 81)

Answers will vary.

Exercise 5 (page 81)

Answers may vary. For example:

1. *He's going to spill the milk.*

2. He's going to cut down the tree.

3. There's going to be a storm./It's going to rain.

4. She's going to fall.

5. He's going to take a trip.

6. They're going (to go) ice-skating.

7. The plane is going to land.

8. Number 7 is going to win.

9. She's going to take photographs.

Exercise 6 (page 83)

1. B: *'ll get*

2. A: will you help
   B: 'll help

3. A: will be
   B: 'll come

4. A: will win
   B: 'll have to

5. A: will be
   B: 'll be

6. A: 'll lock
   B: 'll take

Exercise 7 (page 84)

Answers to questions will vary. For example:

1. A: *When will the exam be?*
   B: *The day after tomorrow.*

2. A: *Will there be true/false questions?*
   B: *Yes, there will.*

3. A: Will there be fill-in-the-blank questions?
   B: Yes, there will.

4. A: How long will the exam be?
   B: Two hours.

5. A: Will there be multiple-choice questions?
   B: No, there won't.

6. A: Will it be difficult or easy?
   B: Difficult.

7. A: Will there be a review session?
   B: Yes, the day before.

8. A: Will there be essay questions?
   B: I'm not sure. Maybe we should ask the teacher.

9. A: When will we get our grades back?
   B: At the end of the week.

10. (⁓) A: What time will the exam be?
    B: From 10:00 to 12:00 A.M.

Exercise 8 (page 86)

Teenager's answers to numbers 6–8 will vary.

1. Parent: We hope you'll be home on time.
   Teenager: I promise I won't break the rules.

2. Parent: I hope you won't make a mess.
   Teenager: Don't worry. I'll clean up the house.

3. Parent: We hope you won't have a wild party.
   Teenager: I promise I won't. I won't invite more than two friends over.

4. Parent: I hope you won't stay out late.
   Teenager: I promise I'll follow the rules.

5. Parent: I hope you'll lock the doors.
   Teenager: I will, and I promise I won't open the door to strangers.

6. Parent: We hope you'll drive carefully.
   Teenager: (⁓) I promise I won't go over the speed limit.

7. Parent: I hope you'll do your homework.
   Teenager: (⁓) I promise I'll do everything as usual.

8. Parent: We hope you'll turn off the stove.
   Teenager: (⁓) I promise I'll check it before I leave the house.

Exercise 9 (page 87)

Answers will vary.

Exercise 10 (page 88)

Answers will vary.

Exercise 11 (page 89)

Answers will vary.

Exercise 12 (page 89)

Answers will vary.

Exercise 13 (page 90)

1. *I won't make any exceptions. All papers are due on Thursday.*

2. I won't clean up your room. You('ll) have to do it yourself.

3. I won't let you pay. It's my treat for your birthday.

4. I won't pay this bill because you didn't fix my car. It still makes the same noise.

5. I won't discuss it with anyone because it's a secret.

6. I won't let you ride your bicycle on this street. There's too much traffic.

7. I won't pay this late fee. I paid my bill on time.

8. I won't climb up twenty-four flights of stairs in this heat. It's crazy.

Exercise 14 (page 91)

Situations will vary. For example:

1. Situation: radio weather forecast
   Restatement: It's going to be cool tomorrow with a chance of rain.

2. Situation: TV news broadcast
   Restatement: The president is going to meet the Polish ambassador early tomorrow morning.

3. Situation: Airport loudspeaker announcement
   Restatement: Flight 276 is going to be delayed until 6:35.

4. Situation: Sign on the door of a store
   Restatement: Smith's is going to close at nine o'clock tonight.

5. Situation: College course schedule
   Restatement: Classes are going to resume on January 22.

6. Situation: A college biology textbook
   Restatement: This chapter is going to summarize recent research on this problem.

7. Situation: An English teacher in class
   Restatement: Tonight we're going to begin with a short poem.

8. Situation: A sign in a bus
   Restatement: On April 1 the fare is going to increase to $1.25.

Exercise 15 (page 92)

1. Sue: *'s going to visit*
   Ann: *Are you going to make*

2. Host: 'll get

3. Husband: 'm going to bake

4. Kyoko: 're going to rent

5. Answering machine: 'll get back to
   Caller: 're going to play

6. Salesperson: 'll be

7. Alexander: Will you marry
   Josephine: 'm going to marry

8. Paul: are you going to do
   Matt: 'll stay

Exercise 16 (page 93)

1. (a) Something spilled.
   (b) Right after the spill happened.
   (c) No.
   (d) With *maybe* the sentence has a different use. In *Maybe I'll get a sponge*, the speaker is not volunteering to get a sponge. The speaker is mentioning a possibility about the future.

2. Sentence (b) can appropriately be followed by the decision *I'll have a bowl of soup*. The other sentences, (a) and (c), would require responses with *going to* because they ask about intentions and plans.

3. A: Joe, the phone is ringing and my hands are full of paint.
   B: *OK, I'll get it.*
   A: Who wants to get me the hammer over there?
   B: I'll get it.
   A: Who volunteered to pick up the pizza for the party tonight?
   B: I did. I'm going to get it.
   A: Are you going out? We need a quart of milk.
   B: Sure, I'll get it on my way home.

Exercise 17 (page 94)

1. *'re having*

2. *is going to win*

3. *'m flying*

4. *'s going to snow*

5. *'is leaving*

Intermediate Grammar: From Form to Meaning and Use

6. Are you staying

7. 'm signing/'m returning

8. is going to win/is going to lose

9. 're going to cut

10. are returning

Exercise 18 (page 95)

These events can be planned, so they can substitute for *one*: a party, a meeting, an exam, a sale, a barbecue, an election.

These events cannot substitute for *one* because they are natural occurrences or accidents: an accident, an earthquake, a fire, a tornado.

Exercise 19 (page 96)

Classes start on September 1.
Fall vacation begins on October 12 and (it) ends on October 15.
Thanksgiving recess starts on November 22 and (it) ends on November 25.
Classes end on December 6.
Final exams begin on December 13 and (they) end on December 20.

Exercise 20 (page 96)

1.
European Trip
Travel Agent:
You leave New York at 7:00 P.M. on July 5.
You arrive in Paris on July 6 and you spend five days there.
On July 11, you fly to London at 11:00 A.M. on Air Britain.
You spend four days in London.
On July 15 you travel to Scotland by car.
You stay in Scotland through July 22.
You return to London on July 23 and you stay overnight in London.
You leave for New York on July 24.

Washington, D.C./Georgia/Florida Trip
Travel Agent:
You fly from Newark Airport to Washington, D.C., on August 19.
You spend three days in Washington, D.C.
On August 22, you fly to Atlanta and you stay there for four days.

You fly to Orlando on August 26 and you spend four days there.
On August 30, you drive to West Palm Beach and you spend one more day there.
You drive to Miami Beach on September 1 and you stay there for six days.
You leave for New York on September 7.

2.
Answers will vary.

Exercise 21 (page 98)

These events occur according to the calendar or according to a schedule, so they can substitute for *it*: winter vacation, school, a sale, my new job, spring.

A snowstorm, an explosion, and a hurricane are not possible because they are not scheduled events. A snowstorm and a hurricane are naturally occurring events, and an explosion is usually an accident.

Exercise 22 (page 98)

1. Yes.

2. A trip itinerary.

3. No. It's a planned trip, so only an unforeseen event such as an accident or illness would change it.

Exercise 23 (page 98)

Answers will vary. For example:

1. *backpack, Jill doesn't.*

2. *a sweater, Rosa is.*

3. *meat, Abdul does.*

4. car, Anna doesn't.

5. Spanish, Pablo does.

6. in Ecuador, Maria wasn't.

7. a garage, Paul's doesn't.

8. have a car, now I do.

9. a bicycle, Peter does.

10. fast food, Joe often does.

11. my uncle, Martin isn't.

12. home, Diana isn't.

Exercise 24 (page 100)

Geography

1. *Tokyo is in Japan, but Jakarta isn't.*
2. Bangkok is in Thailand, but Istanbul isn't.
3. Egypt has a canal, and Panama does too.
4. Guam is an island, and Puerto Rico is too.

History

5. The Vikings were from Scandinavia, but Cleopatra wasn't.
6. Albert Einstein wasn't an American president, and Thomas Edison wasn't either.
7. World War I occurred in the twentieth century, and World War II did too.

Music

8. The trumpet is not a string instrument, and the flute isn't either.
9. The sitar is a musical instrument from India, but the piano isn't.
10. Beethoven wrote sonatas, and Mozart did too.

Food

11. Beets are root vegetables, and carrots are too.
12. Yogurt isn't made of bean curd, but tofu is.
13. Strawberries are red, but cantaloupes aren't.

Animals

14. Horses are vertebrates, and humans are too.
15. Mice don't lay eggs, and raccoons don't either.
16. Chickens don't live in the water, but fish do.

Famous People

17. Charles de Gaulle was a French president, but Louis Pasteur wasn't.
18. Galileo was an astronomer, and Copernicus was too.
19. Mikhail Baryshnikov is a dancer, but Woody Allen isn't.

Movies

20. Humphrey Bogart was in *Casablanca*, but Kevin Costner wasn't.
21. Pelé is not an actor, but Sylvester Stallone is.
22. *Star Trek* isn't a cartoon, and *Star Wars* isn't either.

Exercise 25 (page 101)

Answers will vary. For example:

1. *and so is sledding.*
2. *and neither does my roommate.*
3. and so does gasoline.
4. and so is clothing.
5. and neither does *story.*
6. and neither did Tom.
7. *I resemble my mother*
8. Europe is not in the Southern Hemisphere
9. Maria went swimming this morning
10. I don't have a guitar
11. Women should vote in the election
12. Volleyball is a sport
13. I don't like peanut butter, and neither does Mae.
14. I like lemon sherbet, and so does my son.

Exercise 26 (page 103)

1. B: *I do too./Me too.*
2. B: *I don't either./Me neither.*
3. B: I do too./Me too.
4. B: I did too./Me too.
5. B: I don't either./Me neither.
6. B: I don't either./Me neither.
7. B: I did too./Me too.
8. B: I'm not either./Me neither.

Exercise 27 (page 104)

1. B: *So am I./Me too.*
2. B: *Neither do I./Me neither.*
3. B: So do I./Me too.
4. B: Neither do I./Me neither.
5. B: Neither do I./Me neither.
6. B: Neither was I./Me neither.
7. B: So am I./Me too.
8. B: So did I./Me too.

Exercise 28 (page 104)

Answers will vary.

Summary Exercise (page 108)

1. *I promise I'll help you later.*
2. I think it's going to rain tomorrow.
3. B: I'm going to bake a cake.
4. You'll be in Santa Fe on Tuesday, won't you?
5. He finished early, and so did I.
6. I need a vacation, and he does too.
7. Child: No, I won't.
8. B: Neither did I.
9. B: Maybe I'll work at the pharmacy again.
10. I think Taylor is going to win the election next week.
11. When are you going to take a vacation?
12. The receptionist was talking on the phone, but the secretary wasn't.

Chapter 5

Exercise 1 (page 110)

1. *When I went home, I finished my work./When I finished my work, I went home./I went home when I finished my work./ I finished my work when I went home.*
2. He was reading while he was listening to music./ While he was listening to music, he was reading./ While he was reading, he was listening to music./ He was listening to music while he was reading.
3. After he was sick for a long time, he died./He died after he was sick for a long time. (Note: Using *after* with *he died* results in the following inappropriate sentences: *After he died, he was sick for a long time. *He was sick for a long time after he died. These sentences are incorrect.)
4. Before she fell asleep, the doorbell rang./The doorbell rang before she fell asleep./Before the doorbell rang, she fell asleep./She fell asleep before the doorbell rang.

5. When the fire started, we were sleeping./We were sleeping when the fire started./The fire started when we were sleeping./When we were sleeping, the fire started.

Exercise 2 (page 113)

1. When <u>I went home</u>, I opened the mail.
2. After <u>I played tennis</u>, I took a shower.
3. <u>I finished my work</u> before I went home.
4. The phone rang while <u>I was fixing the bathroom sink.</u>
5. <u>She came home</u> before it started to rain.
6. While <u>I was waiting for John</u>, I saw Erica.
7. Before I ate breakfast, <u>I took a walk.</u>
8. After <u>Jim got up</u>, he called me.
9. When <u>I shouted</u>, she turned around.
10. The water ran out when <u>I opened the drain.</u>
11. After <u>I called the operator</u>, she connected me with Bogotá.
12. A few minutes after <u>the elections ended,</u> the TV reporters declared a winner.

Exercise 3 (page 113)

1. *was raining, arrived*
2. closed, was reading
3. struck, were watching
4. began, was living
5. were talking, remembered
6. was studying, decided
7. stopped, was driving
8. broke, was copying
9. was eating, heard
10. slipped, was climbing

Exercise 4 (page 114)

1. *cause*
   effect
   When the temperature dropped below freezing, the roads became icy.

2. cause
   effect
   When they painted their house bright pink, the neighbors refused to talk to them.

3. effect
   cause
   When the lightning struck, the lights went out.

4. effect
   cause
   When the computer system went down, all work stopped.

5. effect
   cause
   When they ran out of gas, they had to call for help.

6. effect
   cause
   When his best suit didn't fit anymore, he went on a strict diet.

7. cause
   effect
   When he sneezed, everyone jumped.

8. effect
   cause
   When a mosquito bit her, her arm started to itch.

9. cause
   effect
   When the doorbell rang, he answered the door.

10. cause
    effect
    When she found the lost jewelry, she got a reward.

Exercise 5 (page 116)

You wouldn't believe what a terrible day I had! (I try to sleep/the cat jump on my chest) *While I was trying to sleep, the cat jumped on my chest.* So I got up to let him go out, but (I go down the stairs/I trip on a shoe) *while I was going down the stairs, I tripped on a shoe.* By this time, I was fully awake even though it was just 5:15 in the morning. So I decided to make breakfast. Would you believe that (I make coffee/I spill nearly a whole can of coffee on the floor) *while I was making coffee, I spilled nearly a whole can of coffee*

on the floor? I tried to calm down, eat my breakfast, and get washed. But (I take a shower/the phone ring) *while I was taking a shower, the phone rang.* (I rush out of the shower/I slip on the wet floor) *While I was rushing out of the shower, I slipped on the wet floor.* Who was it, but an old friend who drives me crazy! He asked to come and stay with me for two weeks. (I try to explain how busy I am/he hang up on me) *While I was trying to explain how busy I am, he hung up on me.*

Well, I got to school all right. The most important thing that I had to do today was to type a paper for my economics class. Well, guess what? (I type the paper/the computer system go down) *While I was typing the paper, the computer system went down.* I had to go to class without my paper. On my way there, (elevator go up/it suddenly stop and the alarm go off) *while the elevator was going up, it suddenly stopped and the alarm went off.* I was thirty-five minutes late, so I missed most of my class. Fortunately, my professor has a sense of humor. (I explain what happened/he begin laughing) *While I was explaining what happened, he began laughing.*

Now I'm safe at home and I'm not leaving here until tomorrow morning. Thanks for listening to all of this nonsense! How was your day?

Exercise 6 (page 117)

Answers will vary.

Exercise 7 (page 117)

Answers will vary. For example:

1. *Before the guests arrived, they were fighting./*
   Before the guests arrived, they were yelling at each other.
   After the guests arrived, they were holding hands./
   After the guests arrived, they calmed down.

2. Before he fell in love, he looked sloppy./Before he fell in love, he was poorly dressed.
   After he fell in love, he was neat and well-groomed./After he fell in love, he dressed well.

3. Before the realtors developed the land, there were many trees./Before the realtors developed the land, there was a lot of wildlife in the area.
   After the realtors developed the land, there were many houses and apartments./After the realtors developed the land, there weren't many trees.

Exercise 8 (page 119)

1. *When I go home, I'll finish my work./When I finish my work, I'll go home./I'll finish my work when I go home./I'll go home when I finish my work.*

2. Before I go shopping, I'm going to/I'll call you./ I'm going to/I'll call you before I go shopping./ I'm going to/I'll go shopping before I call you./ Before I call you, I'm going to/I'll go shopping.

3. After the mail arrives, I'm going to/I'll eat breakfast./ I'm going to/I'll eat breakfast after the mail arrives./ The mail is going to/will arrive after I eat breakfast./ After I eat breakfast, the mail is going to/will arrive.

4. When he reads the newspaper, he's going to/he'll fall asleep./He's going to/he'll fall asleep when he reads the newspaper.
*When he falls asleep, he's going to/will read the newspaper. (INCORRECT)
*He's going to/will read the newspaper when he falls asleep. (INCORRECT)

5. Before he sets the table, he's going to/he'll cook dinner./ He's going to/he'll cook dinner before he sets the table./Before he cooks dinner, he's going to/he'll set the table./He's going to/he'll set the table before he cooks dinner.

Exercise 9 (page 120)

Answers will vary. For example:

1. *Before I leave home, I'll eat dinner.
When I arrive, I'll buy a ticket and some popcorn.
After the movie begins, I'll eat my popcorn.*

2. Before I leave, I'll put the tickets in my wallet.
When I arrive, I'll go to my seat.
After the concert begins, I'll sit back and enjoy it.

3. Before I leave, I'll eat breakfast.
When I arrive, I'll find a seat near the window.
After the class begins, I'll take notes.

4. Before I leave, I'll sharpen some pencils.
When I arrive, I'll talk to my classmates.
After the exam begins, everyone will be quiet.

5. Before I leave, I'll dress carefully.
When I arrive, I'll speak to the receptionist.
After the interview begins, I'll do my best.

6. Before I leave, I'll try to relax.
When I arrive, they'll greet me at the door.
After the meal begins, they'll probably ask me a lot of questions.

7. Before I leave, I'll practice one more time.
When I arrive, I'll sit in the front row.
When the recital begins, I'll wait for my turn.

8. Before I leave, I'll pack my notes.
When I arrive, I'll get everything ready.
After I begin the lecture, I'll check my watch.

Exercise 10 (page 121)

Answers will vary. For example:

1. Child: *I'll take out the garbage before I go to bed.*

2. Wife: I'll call her before I go to bed.

3. Teenager: I'll mow the lawn after I eat lunch.

4. Boss: I'll sign the letters when I'm ready to leave.

5. Roommate B: I'll call him before I leave for school.

6. Husband: I'll make dinner when I finish reading the newspaper.

7. Friend B: I'll apply for that job after I finish my résumé.

8. Co-worker B: I'll tell him I'm going to resign when he's in a good mood.

Exercise 11 (page 123)

Answers will vary.

Exercise 12 (page 124)

Answers will vary.

Exercise 13 (page 124)

Answers will vary. For example:

1. *you won't have a balanced diet.*

2. you'll get cavities.

3. you'll gain weight.

4. you'll damage your liver.

5. you won't have strong bones.

6. you won't lose weight.

7. you won't stay healthy.

8. you'll ruin your teeth.

Exercise 14 (page 125)

Answers will vary. For example:

1. *you don't pay your taxes*
2. you don't add oil
3. you park illegally
4. you steal something
5. you spend all your money
6. you walk on the wet floor
7. you touch that wire
8. you're not careful

Exercise 15 (page 126)

Answers will vary. For example:

1. *If the music doesn't stop immediately, I'm going to call the police.*
2. If I don't get my sandwich right away, I'm going to leave.
3. If you park here again, I'm going to call the manager.
4. If you hand in your work late, you're going to get a lower grade.
5. If you do that again, you're going to be punished.
6. If the lies don't stop immediately, I'm going to end our friendship.

Exercise 16 (page 126)

1. *If you turn down your thermostat at night, you won't use so much fuel.*
2. If you take my advice, your troubles will be over.
3. If you go to sleep early, you'll feel better in the morning.
4. If you call at night, your telephone bill won't be so high.
5. If you don't eat so much, you won't get indigestion.
6. If you read for a while, you'll fall asleep easily.
7. If you pick the baby up, he'll stop crying.
8. If you don't yell at her, she won't yell back.
9. If you take a break every few hours, you won't get so tired.
10. If you call the doctor, she'll tell you what to do.

Exercise 17 (page 127)

Answers will vary. For example:

1. *If I am elected mayor, I will create jobs./If I am governor, I will create jobs./If I become president, I will create jobs.*
2. If I become president, I'll give money for education/health care.
3. If I am mayor, I'll build new schools/hospitals/day-care centers/airports.
4. If I am elected president, I'll help the poor.
5. If I am president, I'll work for peace.
6. If I become president, I'll clean up the environment.
7. If I am president, I won't raise/I'll lower taxes.
8. If I'm elected president, I'll solve the drug/crime/unemployment/pollution problem.
9. If I am governor, I'll hire more police/firefighters/women/minorities in the government.
10. (‿‿‿) If I'm elected president, I'll keep my promises.

Exercise 18 (page 128)

Answers will vary.

Summary Exercise (page 130)

1. *When he gets a letter, he'll be happy.*
2. Correct
3. If I press the button, the machine will start.
4. I was talking on the phone when I dropped the glass.
5. You'll get a speeding ticket if you drive too fast.
6. Before he fell asleep, he was reading a book.
7. Before she leaves the house, she's going to call you.
8. Correct
9. I dialed again after I heard the dial tone.
10. Correct
11. I'll call you before I leave.
12. Correct
13. He jumped up when I called.
14. B: I'll clean it up after I take a nap.

Chapter 6

Exercise 1 (page 136)

1. A: *haven't eaten, Have you tried*
   B: 've heard; has finally begun

2. A: Have you found
   B: haven't had; 've looked, 've checked, 've applied; has gotten
   A: 've thought, haven't called; 's been; have worked

3. A: has Tom been
   B: 's been, 's known

4. A: haven't written; has happened
   B: haven't called; Have you ever used

5. A: has been; haven't gone; haven't played
   B: haven't spent; haven't taken, haven't ridden

6. A: 've seen; have you done
   B: 've done, 've swept, 've made, 've written; haven't taken

Exercise 2 (page 138)

Answers to questions will vary. For example:

1. A: *Have you ever had a flat tire?*
   B: *Yes, I have. I've had a flat tire once./*
   No, I haven't. I've never had a flat tire.

2. A: Have you ever skied in the Rockies?
   B: Yes, I have. I've skied once at Steamboat in Colorado.

3. A: Have you ever bounced a check?
   B: Yes, I have. I've accidentally bounced a check once.

4. A: Have you ever lost your wallet?
   B: No, I haven't. I've never lost my wallet.

5. A: Have you ever run out of gas?
   B: Yes, I have. I've run out of gas once on the freeway.

6. A: Have you ever told a lie?
   B: Yes, I have. I've told a lie a few times.

7. A: Have you ever written a poem?
   B: Yes, I have. I've written a poem once or twice.

8. A: Have you ever met a movie star?
   B: Yes, I have. I've met a movie star once in Beverly Hills, California.

9. A: Have you ever eaten raw fish?
   B: Yes, I have. I've eaten raw fish many times.

10. A: Have you ever taken a bus trip?
    B: No, I haven't. I've never taken a bus trip.

11. A: Have you ever seen a shooting star?
    B: Yes, I have. I've seen a shooting star once or twice.

12. (～～～) Have you ever ridden an elephant?

Exercise 3 (page 139)

Answers will vary.

Exercise 4 (page 140)

Answers will vary.

Exercise 5 (page 141)

1. *Have you taken the sunscreen?*

2. Have you gotten a haircut?
   Have you shined your shoes?
   Have you picked up your suit at the cleaners?
   Have you chosen a matching shirt and tie?
   (～～～) Have you read up on the company?

3. Have you checked the mileage?
   Have you taken it to a mechanic?
   Have you driven it?
   Have you talked to your bank about a car loan?
   (～～～) Have you spoken to other dealers?

4. Have you enclosed a check or money order?
   Have you written your account number on the front of your check or money order?
   Have you signed your check?
   Have you included the top portion of your bill?
   Have you placed a stamp on the envelope?
   (～～～) Have you kept the bottom portion of your bill for your own records?

Exercise 6 (page 141)

Answers to questions may vary. For example:

1. B: *I've already eaten.*

2. B: I've already read it.

3. B: I've already called my friend.

4. B: I've already seen it.

5. B: I still haven't finished.

6. B: I haven't saved enough money yet.

Exercise 7 (page 143)

1. *has raised gasoline and cigarette taxes*
2. has signed anti-pollution legislation
3. have discovered two new cancer drugs
4. has found rare fossils
5. have fallen rapidly
6. has cost taxpayers one million dollars
7. has won two million dollars
8. has selected

Exercise 8 (page 144)

Answers may vary. For example:

1. *(I think) she has just won a contest.*
2. (I think) he has just picked some flowers.
3. (I think) her sister has just hit her.
4. (I think) he has just graduated.
5. (I think) she has just won the lottery.
6. (I think) he has just gone shopping.

Exercise 9 (Page 145)

Answers will vary.

Exercise 10 (page 146)

Answers to questions will vary. For example:

1. A: *How long have you been in this room?*
   B: *I've been in this room for ten minutes.*
   C: *I've been in this room since ten o'clock.*

2. A: How long have you known how to speak English?
   B: I've known how to speak English for one year.
   C: I've known how to speak English since 1994.

3. A: How long have you had your driver's license?
   B: I've had my driver's license for five years.
   C: I've had my driver's license since 1988.

4. A: How long have you owned this book?
   B: I've owned this book for three months.
   C: I've owned this book since March.

5. A: How long have you been a student?
   B: I've been a student for years.
   C: I've been a student since 1991.

6. A: How long have you lived in your apartment/dorm?
   B: I've lived in my apartment for a year.
   C: I've lived in my dorm since September.

7. A: How long have you known the students in this class?
   B: I've known the students in this class for five weeks.
   C: I've known the students in this class since the beginning of the semester.

8. A: How long have you been able to understand English?
   B: I've been able to understand English for a few years.
   C: I've been able to understand English since I started high school.

9. A: How long have you owned your car/bicycle?
   B: I've owned my car for a year and a half.
   C: I've owned my bicycle since school began.

10. A: How long have you known how to use a computer?
    B: I've known how to use a computer for many years.
    C: I've known how to use a computer since 1990.

11. A: How long have you had your student ID?
    B: I've had my student ID for a year.
    C: I've had my student ID since school began.

12. A: How long have you been in this country?
    B: I've been in this country for a month.
    C: I've been in this country since August 1.

Exercise 11 (page 149)

1. A: *Has the juggler already performed?*
   B: *Yes, he has. He finished two and a half hours ago.*

2. A: *Has the jazz band played yet?*
   B: *No, they haven't. They play this afternoon at four.*

3. A: Has the mayor spoken yet?
   B: Yes, he has. He spoke at 9:00.

4. A: Has the picnic started yet?
   B: Yes, it has. It started a half hour ago.

5. A: Have the fireworks begun?
   B: No, they haven't. They begin at 9:30.

6. A: Has the three-legged race occurred?
   B: Yes, it has. It ended a half hour ago.

7. A: Has the pie-eating contest ended?
   B: Yes, it has. It ended at 3:00.

8. A: Have the Melodians sung yet?
   B: Yes, they have. They sang from 1:00 to 1:30.

9. A: Has the sing-along taken place?
   B: No, it hasn't. It starts at 7:30.

10. A: Have the Harem belly dancers danced yet?
    B: Yes, they have. They finished at 3:30.

Exercise 12 (page 150)

Answers will vary. For example:

1. *I did all my assignments on a word processor last semester.*

2. there were three hurricanes last fall.

3. I lost contact with some of my high school friends after I went to college.

4. last December the government changed the monetary system.

5. I learned last year that friends are very important.

6. last summer we drove to Yellowstone National Park.

Exercise 13 (page 152)

1. B: 've been trying
   B: haven't been feeling
   A: Have you been getting; 've been working; 've been thinking

2. A: haven't been going
   A: 've been going; 've been helping, hasn't been feeling

3. A: has been giving
   B: haven't been making, has been getting

4. A: have you been doing
   B: 've been exercising, haven't been eating

Exercise 14 (page 153)

Answers to questions will vary. For example:

1. A: *How have you been feeling lately?*
   B: *I've been feeling fine. What about you?*
   A: *I've been feeling great.*

2. A: Who have you been writing to lately?
   B: I've been writing to my great aunt.
      What about you?
   A: I've been writing to my cousin in Mexico.

3. A: Have you been sleeping well lately?
   B: Yes, I have. What about you?
   A: No, I haven't. I often wake up in the middle of the night.

4. A: Have you been working hard this semester?
   B: Yes, I have. What about you?
   A: I've been working very hard this semester.

5. A: Have you been learning anything lately?
   B: Yes, I have. What about you?
   A: I've been learning a new computer program.

6. A: What time have you been getting up recently?
   B: I've been getting up around 6:30.
      What about you?
   A: I've been getting up at 6:00.

7. A: What have you been doing in the evening?
   B: I've been reading a new novel. What about you?
   A: I've been studying most evenings.

Exercise 15 (page 155)

Dear Ellen,   March 20th
     How are you and how's your family? Has your father
_____ been feeling _____ (your father/feel) better? I hope so.
I _____ haven't received _____ (not/receive) a letter from you since
last month. I've been thinking/'ve thought _____ (think) about you a lot and
_____ wondering/wondered _____ (wonder) if everything is OK.
     _____ I've been reading _____ (read) the book that you sent me
for my birthday, but I _____ haven't finished _____ (not/finish) it yet.
So far, I _____ 've read _____ (read) about a hundred pages and
I'm really enjoying it. I _____ 've been _____ (be) so busy
lately that I _____ haven't had _____ (not/have) much
time to read, but hope to finish it soon.
     Right now, I'm writing a paper for one of my courses. I've _____
_____ been writing _____ (write) it for two weeks. It's
going to be long. So far, I _____ 've changed _____
(change) the topic four times, but now I'm finally pleased with it.
     What _____ have you been doing/have you done _____ (you/do) during the
past few weeks? _____ Have you been working/Have you worked _____ (you/work)
hard? _____ Have you had _____ (you/have) any exams yet?
I _____ 've had _____ (have) two so far, and I did
pretty well on them. I _____ 've been working/'ve worked _____ (work)
very hard.
     _____ Have you decided _____ (you/decide) what
you're going to do this summer? We really need to make plans soon!
Please write!
                              Love,
                              Pat

Exercise 16 (page 156)

Answers will vary. For example:

1. *I'm sorry. I've been thinking about something else.*

2. I'm sorry. I've been trying to find a birthday gift for my father.

3. I'm sorry. I've been working on it all week, but I'm not finished.

4. I'm sorry. I've been studying for two exams.

5. I'm sorry. I've been trying to finish my work before our vacation.

6. I'm sorry. I've been worrying about the weather. It's supposed to snow.

7. I'm sorry. We've been cleaning the carpets.

8. I'm sorry. I've been using it in the living room.

Exercise 17 (page 157)

1. *she has been crying.*

2. he has been smoking.

3. he has been studying.

4. she has been jogging.

5. someone has been cooking.

6. she has been sleeping.

Exercise 18 (page 158)

Answers will vary. For example:

1. *Have you been trying to lose weight without success? Have you been starving yourself?*

2. Have you been looking for a companion? Have you been feeling lonely?

3. Have you been paying too much for groceries?

4. Have you been feeling out of shape? Have you been trying to get more exercise?

5. Have you been looking for an apartment?

6. Have you been working too hard? Have you been dreaming about a vacation?

Exercise 19 (page 159)

Answers will vary.

Exercise 20 (page 159)

1. (a) T   6. (a) T
   (b) ?   (b) T

2. (a) F   7. (a) F
   (b) T   (b) ?

3. (a) T   8. (a) F
   (b) ?   (b) T

4. (a) F   9. (a) F
   (b) ?   (b) F

5. (a) T   10. (a) T
   (b) ?   (b) ?

Summary Exercise (page 162)

1. *Marie Curie discovered radium.*

2. Correct

3. When I was a child, I was very sick.

4. I've lived in this house since 1989.

5. How long have you been married?

6. He's been working there for ten years.

7. Correct

8. I've typed this page five times.

9. I saw her two days ago.

10. Have you owned your car for a long time?

11. He has already gone shopping./He has gone shopping already.

12. I have never seen a flying saucer.

13. Correct

14. He's known about the problem all week/ for a week.

15. Have you eaten yet?

16. Correct

Chapter 7

Exercise 1 (page 165)

1. A: *Can I park*
   B: You can't park

2. Salesperson: May I help
   Customer: Could you suggest
   Salesperson: you could buy, you might want to

3. A: You shouldn't use
   B: How much should I use

4. A: visitors may not take
   B: May I check

5. A: Can you answer
   B: You should buy

6. A: Will you read
   B: you should take, you mustn't take

Exercise 2 (page 167)

1. You: *Can* (Also acceptable: Could/Would/Will)

2. You: Could/Would (Also acceptable: Can/Will)

3. You: Can/Will (Also acceptable: Could/Would)

4. You: Could/Would (Also acceptable: Can)

5. You: Will/Can (Also acceptable: Could/Would)

6. You: Could/Would (Also acceptable: Can)

7. You: Can/Will (Also acceptable: Could/Would)

8. You: Can/Will (Also acceptable: Could/Would)

9. You: Could/Would (Also acceptable: Can/Will)

10. You: Could/Would (Also acceptable: Can/Will)

Exercise 3 (page 168)

1. (a) *Will you meet me after class?/Can you meet me after class?*
   (b) Will you go shopping with me?/Can you go shopping with me?

2. (a) Would you please open the door?/Could you please open the door?
   (b) Would you please hold the elevator?/Could you please hold the elevator?
   (c) Would you please press 6?/Could you please press 6?

3. (a) Can you (please) answer the phone?/Will you (please) answer the phone?
   (b) Can you (please) get the mail?/Will you (please) get the mail?
   (c) Can you (please) cook dinner tonight?/Will you (please) cook dinner tonight?

4. (a) Can you (please) take out the trash?/Will you (please) take out the trash?
   (b) Can you (please) turn off the television?/Will you (please) turn off the television?
   (c) Can you (please) answer the doorbell?/Will you (please) answer the doorbell?

5. (a) Would you please reserve a hotel for me?/Could you please reserve a hotel for me?
   (b) Would you please call the airlines?/Could you please call the airlines?
   (c) Would you please check the schedule?/Could you please check the schedule?

6. (a) Could you please watch the children?/Would you please watch the children?
   (b) Could you please close the window?/Would you please close the window?
   (c) Could you please call me later?/Would you please call me later?

Exercise 4 (page 169)

Answers will vary. For example:

1. Situation: *Two strangers on a bus*
   Speaker: *Passenger A*
   Listener: *Passenger B*

2. Situation: Two roommates hanging up a picture
   Speaker: Roommate A
   Listener: Roommate B

3. Situation: Two people in a restaurant
   Speaker: Customer
   Listener: Waiter

4. Situation: Two friends in a cafeteria
   Speaker: Friend A
   Listener: Friend B

5. Situation: Two people in a bank
   Speaker: Teller
   Listener: Customer

6. Situation: Two people at home
   Speaker: Parent
   Listener: Child

7. Situation: Two people in a business office
   Speaker: Receptionist
   Listener: Client

8. Situation: Two people at home
   Speaker: Wife
   Listener: Husband

9. (〜〜) Would someone please open a window?
   Situation: Classroom
   Speaker: Instructor
   Listener: Student

10. (〜〜) Will you please pass the pepper?
    Situation: Home
    Speaker: Parent
    Listener: Child

Exercise 5 (page 173)

1. b, e
2. a, b, d, e, f, i
3. c, g, h
4. c, g, h
5. b, e, f, i

Exercise 6 (page 173)

Answers may vary. For example:

1. Patient: *May*
   Receptionist: *Certainly.*

2. You: Can
   Your friend: Sure.

3. Guest: Could
   Hostess: Yes, go right ahead.

4. Customer: Can
   Cashier: Yes.

5. Student: May
   OK.

6. Child: May
   Parent: Absolutely not.

7. You: Can
   Your sister: Sorry, but I lost my umbrella last week.

8. You: May
   Employer: Yes, certainly.

Exercise 7 (page 174)

Answers may vary. For example:

1. You: *Can I use your pencil for a minute?*
   Classmate: *Yeah, sure.*

2. You: May I leave this application with you?
   Secretary: Yes.

3. You: Could I please see the rest of the apartment?
   Landlord: Go right ahead.

4. You: Can I borrow your dictionary?
   Roommate: Yeah, sure.

5. You: May I see a copy of the employee handbook?
   Interviewer: Yes, certainly.

6. You: Can I call you later?
   Friend: Sorry, but I won't be home.

7. You: Can I have a drink of water?
   Friend: Sure.

8. You: Could I make an appointment with you?
   Professor: Certainly.

9. You: Can I pay by check?
   Gas station attendant: I'm sorry, but we don't accept checks.

10. You: Can I call you back later?
    Friend: OK.

11. You: Can I borrow your car for the weekend?
    Roommate: No way.

Exercise 8 (page 175)

Situations may vary. For example:

1. Meaning: *You can pay with a credit card.*
   Situation: *Getting gas at a service station*

2. Meaning: You can enter at that particular place.
   Situation: A sign at the entrance of a parking lot

3. Meaning: You cannot pay by check.
   Situation: A small grocery store

4. Meaning: You can swim if the lifeguard is on duty.
   Situation: A sign at a public swimming pool

5. Meaning: You cannot exit at that particular place.
   Situation: A sign in a parking lot

6. Meaning: You cannot exchange or return your purchase.
   Situation: Information stamped on a cash register receipt from a clothing store

7. Meaning: You can smoke in this section.
   Situation: A cafeteria

8. Meaning: You cannot make a right turn when the light is red.
   Situation: A traffic sign on a street corner

Exercise 9 (page 178)

Answers may vary. For example

1. You: *'d better*
2. You: could
3. You: ought to
4. Doctor: 've got to
5. You: should

6. You: might

7. You: must

8. You: ought to

Exercise 10 (page 179)

Answers may vary. For example:

1. B: *Maybe you ought to get a part-time job.*

2. B: You'd better renew them.

3. B: You could take some cough medicine before you go to sleep.

4. B: You could place an ad in the newspaper.

5. B: You should tie him up.

6. B: You ought to call a repair service.

7. B: Maybe you should try something else.

8. B: You'd better talk to your professor.

9. B: You should go to the lost and found.

10. B: You could make a reservation at that new Korean restaurant.

Exercise 11 (page 180)

Answers may vary. For example:

1. *Can I drink coffee?*
   Should I eat special food?
   Should I take an antacid?

2. May I go back to work?
   Can I jog?
   Should I take aspirin?

3. Should I stay home from work?
   Could I go swimming?
   Can I take an airplane trip?

4. Should I take cough medicine?
   Can I smoke?
   Can I go on vacation?

5. Can I take a shower?
   Could I drive my car?
   Can I walk around?

Exercise 12 (page 181)

1. *take 2 teaspoonfuls every 4 hours.*
   exceed 12 teaspoonfuls in 24 hours.
   take 1/2 teaspoonful every 4 hours.
   use the cough medicine if the plastic ring is broken.

2. apply sunscreen evenly to all exposed areas.
   reapply it often.
   get sunscreen in your eyes.

3. take 1 to 2 tablets every 4 hours.
   use pediatric strength or consult a physician.
   take 1/2 to 1 tablet every 4 hours.
   keep this and all medication out of the reach of children.

4. take 2 tablespoonfuls every 1/2 to 1 hour, if needed.
   take 1 teaspoonful every 1/2 to 1 hour.
   shake it well.

5. apply it sparingly.
   put it in your eyes or in your mouth.
   store it away from heat.

Exercise 13 (page 183)

Answers will vary.

Exercise 14 (page 183)

Answers will vary. For example:

1. *You'd better pull out the plug./You'd better not use the toaster anymore.*

2. You'd better put some air in your left rear tire.

3. You'd better not be late for your interview.

4. You'd better not call after 10:00 P.M.

5. You'd better close your car windows.

6. You'd better save your work.

7. You'd better call the manager.

8. You'd better go back and get your wallet.

Exercise 15 (page 186)

Answers to questions will vary.

1. A: *Should people smoke in restaurants?*
   B: *No, they shouldn't, because it bothers other customers.*
   A: *I agree. They shouldn't smoke because it's annoying.*

2. A: Should women with small children work?

3. A: Shouldn't buses have seatbelts?

4. A: Should men do housework?

5. A: Should women invite men to go out?

6. A: Should married couples live with their parents?

7. A: Should women fight in wars?

8. A: Should you phone your friends at dinnertime?

9. (～～) A: Shouldn't students go to school year-round?

10. (～～) A: Should teens drink before they are 21?

Exercise 16 (page 187)

Answers will vary. For example:

1. Situation: *You are eating dinner with your brother and you disapprove of his unhealthy eating habits.*

2. Situation: You are complaining to your friend about repeating a chemistry experiment.

3. Situation: You are disappointed that your guest is leaving.

4. Situation: You disapprove of your spouse's outfit.

5. Situation: Your friend is driving too fast.

6. Situation: You don't want to stop at the library on the way to a party, but your roommate left something there.

7. (～～) Must we see that movie?
   Situation: You don't want to see the movie that your spouse/friend wants to see.

8. (～～) Must you use so much sugar?
   Situation: You think your spouse/friend is using too much sugar.

Exercise 17 (page 188)

Answers will vary. For example:

1. *get up early on the weekend.*

2. rest

3. get water

4. get up at seven o'oclock

5. be 18 years old.

6. do my laundry

7. go to the motor vehicle facility.

8. call my aunt

9. must be 21 years old.

10. must have a passport.

11. should get a second opinion.

12. have to visit my relatives.

13. ought to call them often.

Exercise 18 (page 189)

Situations may vary. For example:

1. *you have to drive 55 mph or less.*
   Situation: *A highway*

2. you have to pay $4.00 to get in.
   Situation: A movie theater

3. an adult should supervise a child in this situation.
   Situation: An electric pony ride in a shopping mall

4. you have to show an identification card.
   Situation: A bar

5. you have to pay $5.00 extra if you register late.
   Situation: An adult education course catalog

6. you have to have exact change in that lane.
   Situation: An expressway toll booth

7. you should make a reservation.
   Situation: A restaurant

8. you have to pay cash.
   Situation: A discount store

9. you have to pay $1.00.
   Situation: A tollbooth before a bridge

10. you have to have no more than 12 items in this aisle.
    Situation: A supermarket

Exercise 19 (page 190)

Registration Information

1. *Students have to/have got to pay all fees before registering for courses.*

2. Before registration, all students have to/have got to present proof of immunization against diphtheria, tetanus, rubella, measles, mumps, and polio.

3. Students have to/have got to register before attending courses.

4. New students have to/have got to attend an orientation session during registration week.

Intermediate Grammar: From Form to Meaning and Use
© 1996 Oxford University Press. Permission granted to reproduce for classroom use.

Course Requirements

1. All students have to/have got to complete two semesters of physical education.

2. All new students have to/have got to take a swim test. Students who do not pass have to/have got to enroll in a swim course. Nonswimmers have to/have got to register in a beginning swim course.

3. All students have to/have got to take an English placement exam.

Exercise 20 (page 191)

Answers will vary.

Exercise 21 (page 192)

1. *must not*	6. must not
2. have to	7. must not; have to
3. don't have to	8. have to
4. don't have to	9. must not
5. must not	10. have to

Exercise 22 (page 193)

Answers may vary. For example:

1. *have secretarial skills; be energetic and willing to learn the travel business.*

2. work weekends, have experience; have a car.

3. be able to take charge, have bookkeeping and word-processing skills.

4. be friendly, be responsible; have experience.

5. be 18 years old, be able to work weekends; have experience; apply in person.

6. work 3 to 4 days a week, work weekends; smoke; be experienced, be reliable; have a car.

Exercise 23 (page 195)

Answers will vary. For example:

1. *I should clean out my closets, but I probably won't be able to because I have to go to the dentist.*

2. I absolutely must pay my phone bill. It was due five days ago.

3. I don't have to get a haircut, but I would like to if I have time.

Summary Exercise (page 197)

1. *You don't have to take it, but you can if you want to.*

2. Correct

3. Would/Could/Will you please hold this for me?

4. She can take this one.

5. NO SMOKING means that you must not smoke.

6. Correct

7. You must stop at a red light.

8. Does she have to go?

9. You should/have (got) to/must call an ambulance.

10. Do you have to take a driving test?

11. I really ought to study tonight.

12. Secretary: May/Can I help you?

13. You can't enter here.

14. Could you please open the door for me?

15. Correct

Chapter 8

Exercise 1 (page 201)

Answers will vary according to how the teacher stresses the words in each sentence.

Exercise 2 (page 202)

Answers to questions will vary. For example:

1. A: *At what age could you walk?*
   B: *I could walk when I was about a year old.*

2. At what age could you talk?

3. At what age could you read?

4. At what age could you write your name?

5. At what age could you say something in a foreign language?

6. At what age could you multiply two numbers?

7. At what age could you tie a bow?

8. At what age could you swim?

9. At what age could you drive a car?

10. (⁓⁓) At what age could you ride a bicycle?

Exercise 3 (page 205)

Answers to questions will vary. For example:

1. A: *Can you say the alphabet backwards?*
   B: *Yes, I can./No, I can't.*

2. A: Can you wiggle your nose?

3. A: Can you read in a car without getting sick?

4. A: Can you touch the end of your nose with your eyes closed?

5. A: Can you recite your phone number backwards?

6. A: Can you curl your tongue?

7. A: Can you stand on your head?

8. A: Can you remember your first teacher's name?

9. A: Can you raise one eyebrow without raising the other?

10. A: Can you cross your eyes?

11. A: Can you pull your fingers backwards to your wrist?

12. (〰) A: Can you pat your head and rub your stomach at the same time?

Exercise 4 (page 205)

Answers will vary.

Exercise 5 (page 206)

Answers will vary. For example:

1. Infants can't walk, but toddlers can.

2. eighteen-year-olds can vote, but twelve-year-olds can't.

3. Spiders can spin a web, but ants can't.

4. Judges can make rulings, but lawyers can't.

5. Jets can't land on buildings, but helicopters can.

6. Mice can't fly, but bats can.

7. Men can't give birth, but women can.

8. Computers can store information, but ordinary typewriters can't.

9. Cats can't bark, but dogs can.

10. Ducks can quack, but chickens can't.

11. Glass can shatter, but metal can't.

12. The earth can support life, but the moon can't.

Exercise 6 (page 206)

Answers to questions will vary. For example:

1. A: *What can you buy with a quarter?*
   B: *You can buy a piece of gum.*

2. A: Where can you get a driver's license?
   B: You can get a driver's license at the motor vehicle facility.

3. A: Where can you buy a hammer?
   B: You can buy a hammer at a hardware store.

4. A: Where can you find out about recycling trash?
   B: You can find out about recycling trash from the local government.

5. A: What number can you call in an emergency?
   B: You can call 911.

6. A: What can you do with a broken wristwatch?
   B: You can get it repaired.

7. A: Where can you buy a magazine?
   B: You can buy a magazine at the drugstore.

8. A: What can you do for free in this town?
   B: You can go to a park.

9. A: What can you buy at a department store?
   B: You can buy clothing at a department store.

10. A: Where can you get ten dollars in quarters?
    B: You can get ten dollars in quarters at a bank.

11. A: Where can you read newspapers from other cities?
    B: You can read newspapers from other cities at the library.

12. A: When can you go swimming around here?
    B: You can go swimming after Memorial Day.

Exercise 7 (page 207)

Answers will vary.

Exercise 8 (page 207)

Answers will vary.

Intermediate Grammar: From Form to Meaning and Use

Exercise 9 (page 208)

1. *For many years, we could take our vacations whenever we wanted.*
   Could *is also possible because of the long time period* for many years.

2. Could *is not possible because* yesterday *means it is a single event.*

3. When she was in college, she could read the newspapers and magazines from her country all the time in the library.
   Could is possible because of the long time period when she was in college.

4. I could buy groceries easily when I lived in that apartment.
   Could is possible because of the long time period when I lived in that apartment.

5. She could hear the marching band coming from a distance, and so she ran out to watch the parade.
   Before the verb of perception *hear, could* is always possible.

6. *Could is not possible because of the single event* on Monday.

7. Before she injured her knee, she could run five miles a day.
   Could is possible because of the long time period before she injured her knee.

8. *Could is not possible because of the single event* the morning after the storm.

9. I could see Central Park when I flew over New York.
   Before the verb of perception *see, could* is always possible.

10. *Could is not possible because of the single event* when the doorbell rang.

11. Could she remember what happened after the accident?
    Before the verb of perception *remember, could* is always possible.

12. *Could is not possible because of the single event* this morning.

Exercise 10 (page 209)

Answers will vary.

Exercise 11 (page 210)

1. A: *That may not be*
   B: It can't be

2. A: Could they arrive
   B: They might not arrive

3. A: Lee may not come
   B: He must not be; that shouldn't be; I'll be able to

4. A: he might not
   B: He may not have

5. A: We should arrive
   B: we might miss

Exercise 12 (page 213)

Answers may vary. For example:

1. B: *might*
   C: *must*

2. B: may/might/could
   C: must/have (got) to

3. B: must/has (got) to
   C: should

4. B: must/has (got) to
   C: may/might/could

5. B: may/might/could
   C: must/has (got) to

Exercise 13 (page 214)

Answers will vary. For example:

1. *She must be sick./She could be out of town.*

2. It might be a fire drill./There could be a fire.

3. He must be unhappy./He may have problems.

4. She must be busy./She might be sick.

5. I must have a cold./I might be allergic to something.

6. He must be having a hard day.

7. It might be a burglar./The children could be up.

8. She must have a secret admirer.

9. It must be out of order.

10. The baby must be sick./My neighbor must be unhappy.

Exercise 14 (page 215)

Answers will vary. For example:

1. B: *You must be exhausted.*

2. B: You must be hungry.

3. B: You must be nervous.

4. B: You must be happy.

5. B: You must be excited.

6. B: You must be angry.

7. B: You must be disappointed.

8. B: You must be worried.

9. B: You must be proud.

10. B: You must be upset.

Exercise 15 (page 216)

1. *Terry must be checking the patients' vital signs./ Terry should be checking the patients' vital signs.*

2. *it must be 7:45./it should be 7:45.*

3. she must/should be admitting new patients.

4. she must/should be meeting with the night nurses.

5. she must/should be discharging patients.

6. she must/should be giving patients medicine.

7. it must/should be 2:45.

8. it must/should be 10:00.

Exercise 16 (page 217)

Answers will vary.

Exercise 17 (page 217)

1. *He might have a cold./He may have a cold./ He could have a cold.*

2. It may rain./It might rain./It could rain.

3. He should be at home./He ought to be at home./ He must be at home./He has (got) to be at home.

4. She should be working./She ought to be working.

5. She may need help./She might need help./She could need help.

6. This has (got) to be the meeting place./This must be the meeting place.

7. He may be sleeping./He might be sleeping./He could be sleeping.

8. My keys should be on the table./My keys ought to be on the table./My keys must be on the table./ My keys have (got) to be on the table.

9. He should be in his office./He ought to be in his office.

10. I could need a new tire./I might need a new tire.

Exercise 18 (page 219)

Answers will vary. For example:

1. *She may not understand the questions, or she might not know the answers. She might not study enough, or she might not like to speak in class.*

2. She may/might not love him enough, or she may/might not be ready for marriage.

3. She may/might not like chocolate, or she may/might not want to eat sweets.

4. She may/might not be at home, or she may/might be sleeping.

5. He may/might not like movies, or he may/might not have enough money.

6. She may/might not be home, or she may/might not be able to answer the door.

7. He may/might not get enough sleep, or he may/might not feel well.

8. She may/might not like parties, or she may/might not have the time.

Exercise 19 (page 219)

(Sources: *The World Almanac and Book of Facts 1996* and *The 1995 Information Please Almanac*)

1. False. The literacy rate of Sweden is 100 percent.

2. False. The population of Japan is about 125 million.

3. False. North America is composed of three countries: Canada, the United States, and Mexico.

4. False. About 35 to 40 percent of the population are Ethiopian Orthodox Christians and 45 to 50 percent are Muslims.

5. False. Cosmologists say the universe may be 8 to 15 billion years old. They have determined this age by measuring the motions of galaxies. However, stellar astronomers disagree. They have found stars that are much older, perhaps 16 to 19 billion years old. Since stars cannot be older than the universe, they say the universe is at least 16 to 19 billion years old.

6. False. India now exports more rice than Italy. In 1993 India exported 628,000 metric tons compared with Italy's 574,000 metric tons. Note: Although India produces far more rice than Italy, in recent years Italy has exported more rice than India.

7. True. The butterfly stroke is one of several competitive strokes.

8. False. The correct answer is the reverse.

9. False. That is the definition for a tornado watch. A tornado warning means that at least one tornado has been detected by radar or sighted in your area.

10. True. China has 1.2 billion people. India is second with 937 million people. If the current rates of growth continue, by the year 2010, China will have about 1.3 billion people and India will have about 1.1 billion people.

11. True.

12. True.

Exercise 20 (page 220)

1. b   5. b
2. c   6. a
3. a   7. b
4. c   8. a

Exercise 21 (page 222)

1. *The exam should be easy.*

2. We may/might/could come later.

3. It could/might rain this afternoon.

4. The plane may/might/could be on time tonight.

5. He could/may/might be taking the express train this evening.

6. The flight will arrive at 8:10.

7. It shouldn't be cold today.

8. He should/ought to get the job.

Exercise 22 (page 223)

Answers will vary.

Exercise 23 (page 225)

1. A: *could have gone*
   B: might not have liked; must have been

2. A: shouldn't have driven
   B: should have taken

3. A: couldn't have left
   B: might have forgotten

4. A: must have had
   B: should have stopped by; could have heard

5. A: might have left
   B: couldn't have
   A: must have dropped
   B: could have put, might have locked

Exercise 24 (page 227)

1. (a) *He could have worked in a lab.*
   (b) He could have gone to medical school.
   (c) He could have entered a Ph.D. program.
   (d) (Answers will vary.) He could have worked for a drug company.

2. (a) He could have become a cook in a restaurant.
   (b) He could have opened a restaurant.
   (c) He could have worked in a hotel.
   (d) (Answers will vary.) He could have taught in a cooking school.

3. (a) She could have taught English in a high school.
   (b) She could have gone to law school.
   (c) She could have worked for a newspaper.
   (d) (Answers will vary.) She could have become a freelance writer.

4. (a) He could have become an art teacher.
   (b) He could have gotten a job in advertising.
   (c) He could have done graphic design.
   (d) (Answers will vary.) He could have worked in fashion design.

Exercise 25 (page 228)

Answers will vary.

Exercise 26 (page 229)

Answers will vary. For example:

1. B: *I couldn't have won the lottery because I didn't even buy a ticket.*

2. B: He couldn't have sent me a letter because he's not alive.

3. B: My Rolls Royce couldn't have run out of gas because I don't have one.

4. B: I couldn't have grown three inches taller this week because I'm not growing anymore.

5. B: My hair couldn't have turned green because I didn't do anything to it.

6. B: I couldn't have memorized all of Shakespeare's plays because I have a terrible memory.

7. B: I couldn't have lost a million dollars yesterday because I didn't have a million dollars.

8. B: I couldn't have swum the English Channel last week because I was in Tokyo.

9. B: I couldn't have robbed a bank last night because I never left my apartment.

10. B: I couldn't have solved a famous mathematical problem because I'm not very good in math.

Exercise 27 (page 230)

Answers to questions will vary. For example:

1. A: *Should he have brought an expensive gift?*
   B: *No, he shouldn't have.*
   A: Should he have brought flowers?
   B: Yes, he could have.
   A: Should he have brought a bottle of wine?
   B: Yes, he could have.
   A: Should he have brought his visiting relatives?
   B: No, he shouldn't have.
   A: (⌣⌣⌣) Should he have brought his favorite food?
   B: Yes, he could have.

2. A: Should he have whistled?
   B: No, he shouldn't have.
   A: Should he have snapped his fingers?
   B: No, he shouldn't have.
   A: Should he have clapped loudly?
   B: No, he shouldn't have.
   A: Should he have raised his hand when the waiter was looking at him?
   B: Yes, he should have.

A: (⌣⌣⌣) Should he have shouted "Waiter" across the room?
B: No, he shouldn't have.

3. A: Should he have ignored it?
   B: No, he shouldn't have.
   A: Should he have told the waiter?
   B: Yes, he should have.
   A: Should he have called the manager immediately?
   B: No, he shouldn't have.
   A: Should he have shouted at the waiter?
   B: No, he shouldn't have.
   A: (⌣⌣⌣) Should he have walked out without paying?
   B: No, he shouldn't have.

Exercise 28 (page 231)

Answers will vary. For example:

1. *I should have gone to the party.*
   I shouldn't have stayed home last night.

2. I should have used a timer.
   I shouldn't have cooked the rice so long.

3. I should have closed them.
   I shouldn't have left them open.

4. I should have studied.
   I shouldn't have watched television instead.

5. I should have bought fire insurance.
   I shouldn't have been so foolish.

6. I should have applied two months ago.
   I shouldn't have waited so long.

7. I should have obeyed the speed limit.
   I shouldn't have gone over the speed limit.

8. I should have saved some money.
   I shouldn't have spent so much.

9. I should have exercised more.
   I shouldn't have eaten so many sweets.

10. I should have taken the job.
    I shouldn't have worried about the boss.

Exercise 29 (page 232)

1. (a) *F*
   (b) *T*
2. (a) *F*
   (b) T
3. (a) T
   (b) ?
4. (a) ?
   (b) T
5. (a) T
   (b) ?
6. (a) F
   (b) T
7. (a) T
   (b) T
8. (a) T
   (b) ?
9. (a) T
   (b) T
10. (a) T
    (b) T

Summary Exercise (page 236)

1. *He may be working today.*
2. That could be Joe, but I'm really not sure.
3. Correct
4. The letter could have arrived this afternoon.
5. Correct
6. She must have had a cold yesterday.
7. Yesterday, I was able to take a walk at noon.
8. I shouldn't have asked him. I'm sorry that I did./ I should have asked him. I'm sorry that I didn't.
9. It may be too late.
10. He should have taken the exam.
11. You could have called me.
12. Correct
13. There ought to be some more in the kitchen.
14. B: It will be.

Chapter 9

Exercise 1 (page 240)

1. B: How about (the shirt) that you wore Saturday night?
2. A: You mean (the one) that has food all over it?
   B: Oh. Well, what about (the shirt) that you got for your birthday?

3. A: (The one) that you gave me or (the one) that my sister gave me?
   B: Wear (the one) that your sister gave you with (the suit) that you bought last month.
4. A: (The secretary) that I spoke to last week said 10:15, but (a letter) that I received a few days later said 10:30.
   B: Was (the book) that I gave you helpful?
5. A: Yes, especially (the part) that talked about staying calm.
   B: Is (the position) that you're applying for a new position?
6. A: No. In fact, I know (a man) whose wife had this job a few years ago, and I also know (the person) who has it now. She's leaving to work at (the new office) that they recently opened in Boston.

Exercise 2 (page 243)

Answers to questions will vary. For example:

1. A: *Which suitcase is yours?*
   B: *Mine is the one that has a green luggage tag.*
2. A: Which car is yours?
   B: Mine is the one that has a ski rack on top.
3. A: Which boots are yours?
   B: Mine are the ones that have red laces.
4. A: Which raincoat is yours?
   B: Mine is the one that has a blue scarf in the sleeve.
5. A: Which backpack is yours?
   B: Mine is the one that has a red name tag.
6. A: Which umbrella is yours?
   B: Mine is the one that has the green leaves on it.
7. A: Which keys are yours?
   B: Mine are the ones that have a globe key chain.
8. A: Which cake is yours?
   B: Mine is the one that has white icing.

Exercise 3 (page 244)

1. *We walked down the steps that led to the basement./We walked down the steps which led to the basement.*
2. *The professor who speaks Russian called me./ The professor that speaks Russian called me.*
3. My sister has a cat that/which has three kittens.
4. The little girl who/that hurt her knee was crying.

5. They gave us an exam that/which lasted an hour.

6. I spoke to two women who/that saw the accident.

7. My friend who/that was overweight went on a diet.

8. I called my aunt who/that lives in Albany.

9. She bought the sweater that/which cost thirty dollars.

10. Did you buy the socks that/which were on sale?

11. The child who/that was sick went home.

12. I took the notebooks that/which were lying on the desk.

Exercise 4 (page 245)

1. *A dermatologist is a doctor who treats skin problems.*

2. An orthopedist is a doctor who takes care of bone problems.

3. A obstetrician is a doctor who takes care of pregnant women.

4. An optometrist is a doctor who prescribes eyeglasses.

5. A cardiologist is a doctor who treats heart problems.

6. A pediatrician is a doctor who takes care of children.

7. A podiatrist is a doctor who treats foot problems.

8. An orthodontist is a dentist who corrects teeth problems with braces.

Exercise 5 (page 246)

Answers will vary. For example:

1. *that visits from outer space.*

2. who re-create dinosaurs.

3. who falls in love with a princess.

4. who explore outer space and encounter other species.

5. who has an adventure in New York City without his parents.

6. *Apollo 13* is the true story about three astronauts who fight to survive in a crippled spacecraft 200,000 miles from earth.

Exercise 6 (page 247)

1. A: *sits*
   B: asks

2. A: were
   B: looks

3. A: live
   B: own

4. A: were
   B: has

5. A: are
   B: have
   A: drive

6. A: treats
   B: does

7. A: finishes
   B: were

8. A: are
   B: wants

Exercise 7 (page 248)

Answers may vary. For example:

1. *Georgia O'Keeffe was a twentieth-century American artist who continued painting well into her eighties.*

2. (a) Gene therapy is a new branch of genetic engineering that may someday prevent hereditary diseases such as cancer.

   (b) Cancer is a disease that affects people of all countries and races.

3. Rosa Parks is an African-American who refused to give up her seat to a white passenger on a city bus./Rosa Parks is an African-American woman who is sometimes called the mother of the civil rights movement.

4. (a) Martin Luther King, Jr., was an African-American who led the civil rights movement in the 1960s.

   (b) Passive resistance is a nonviolent method of fighting that was used by Mahatma Gandhi.

5. (a) SATs are college entrance exams that help colleges decide whether or not to admit a student.

   (b) High school students who are preparing to apply for college take SATs.

6. (a) Eagles have been important symbols that represent strength and power to governments around the world.

   (b) The bald eagle is a large North American bird that is the national emblem of the United States.

7. (a) A phobia is an exaggerated fear that can sometimes prevent a person from leading a normal life.

(b) People who fear being in open spaces
have agoraphobia.

(c) People who fear being in closed places
have claustrophobia.

Exercise 8 (page 250)

1. *Let's look at some things that I've saved for
a long time.*
*Let's look at some things which I've saved for
a long time.*
Let's look at some things I've saved for a long time.

2. This is a trunk that/which/(omitted) your
grandmother used when she traveled.

3. Here's the dress that/which/(omitted) I wore
to my wedding.

4. I'll never forget the guests who/whom/that/
(omitted) I invited to my wedding.

5. A cousin who/whom/that/(omitted) I didn't even
know spilled wine all over my wedding dress.

6. A trophy that/which/(omitted) your father won
in high school is on the shelf.

7. A picture that/which/(omitted) I drew seventy
years ago is in this box.

8. I remember a high school teacher who/whom/
that/(omitted) I liked very much.

9. Here is a poem that/which/(omitted) I wrote
in her class.

10. A dog that/which/(omitted) I loved so much
is in the picture.

11. A lot of letters that/which/(omitted) your father
wrote in college are in this envelope.

12. Here are some gold coins that/which/(omitted)
my father gave to me seventy-five years ago.

Exercise 9 (page 251)

Answers to questions will vary. For example:

1. A: *Who is the person that you call most often?*
B: *My sister is the person that I call most often./
The person that I call most often is my sister.*

2. A: *What is a game that you liked to play as a child?*
B: *Hide and Seek is a game that I liked to play
as a child.*

3. Who is the relative that you resemble most?

4. Who is a friend that you'll never forget?

5. Who is the person that you call when you're
in trouble?

6. What is a possession that you can't live without?

7. What is a restaurant that you recommend?

8. Who is a teacher that you'll always remember?

9. What is a book that you like to read over
and over again?

10. What is a food that you have never tasted?

Exercise 10 (page 252)

Answers will vary.

Exercise 11 (page 252)

Answers will vary.

Exercise 12 (page 253)

Answers will vary.

Exercise 13 (page 254)

Answers may vary. For example:

1. *that he works with./he works with.*

2. that she listened to this morning./she listened to this
morning./which she listened to this morning.

3. that John is sitting on./John is sitting on./which
John is sitting on.

4. who she spoke to on Wednesday./that she spoke to
on Wednesday./she spoke to on Wednesday./whom
she spoke to on Wednesday.

5. that he hasn't heard about./he hasn't heard
about./which he hasn't heard about.

6. that she was born in./she was born in./which she
was born in.

Exercise 14 (page 255)

Answers may vary. For example:

1. *A man who my sister works with called me
last night.*
*A man that my sister works with called me
last night.*
A man my sister works with called me last night.

A man I always talk to at the supermarket called
 me last night.
A man I went to high school with called me
 last night.
A man I used to live next door to called me
 last night.

2. The movie we went to last night was great.
 The movie you told us about was great.
 The movie many people disapproved of was great.
 The movie you reported on in class was great.

3. Do you know the doctor John lives across from?
 Do you know the doctor Eva fell in love with?
 Do you know the doctor Joan is married to?
 Do you know the doctor I was waiting for?

4. Have you read the book the whole class is
 interested in?
 Have you read the book the teacher looked
 for last week?
 Have you read the book Julie wrote about?
 Have you read the book I brought in?

5. Today we're going to read the story we heard
 a lot about.
 Today we're going to read the story you listened
 to in the lab.
 Today we're going to read the story I was
 working on.
 Today we're going to read the story many people
 argue over.

Exercise 15 (page 256)

1. *Do you know the person she writes to every day?*

2. Do you know the music she listens to
 every evening?

3. Do you know the sports she's interested in?

4. Do you know the person she speaks to
 at midnight?

5. Do you know the small town she was born in?

6. Do you know the big city she grew up in?

7. Do you know the man she talks about a lot?

8. Do you know the person she's waiting for
 right now?

9. Do you know the doctor she goes to once a week?

10. Do you know the person she works with
 occasionally?

Exercise 16 (page 258)

1. *There's the man whose wife knows your mother.*

2. The doctor whose daughter wants to meet you
 lives there.

3. A woman whose son I work with owns this store.

4. I know the family whose house burned down
 right here.

5. This is the factory whose furnace exploded.

6. That's the man whose house my family rented
 last summer.

7. You're looking at an apartment building whose
 residents are all rich and famous.

8. The man whose beard is white helped me
 find my apartment.

9. The guy whose life I saved is crossing the street.

10. That's the school whose teachers are on strike.

Exercise 17 (page 259)

Answers will vary.

Exercise 18 (page 259)

1. *who/that/*(omitted)
2. whose
3. that/which
4. who/that
5. which
6. who/that
7. that/which
8. who/whom/that/(omitted)
9. whose
10. whom
11. who/that
12. that/which
13. who/whom/that/(omitted)
14. whose

Exercise 19 (page 261)

Answers will vary. For example:

1. *who lived in the sixteenth century*

2. who was a Greek philosopher

3. which is an Asian country

4. which is the capital of France

5. who was the sixteenth president of the United States

6. which border India and Tibet

7. which is in India

8. who was an Italian astronomer

9. which are found in China, Korea, and Japan

10. which is a planet

Exercise 20 (page 262)

Answers will vary.

Exercise 21 (page 263)

Answers will vary.

Exercise 22 (page 264)

1. *My parents, who used to live in New York City, moved to Florida a few years ago. nonrestrictive*

2. restrictive (no commas)

3. We live in the south, which is very warm and humid. nonrestrictive

4. My father, whose favorite sport is golf, retired from his job five years ago. nonrestrictive

5. restrictive (no commas)

6. restrictive (no commas)

7. I've invited my friend Jane Welch, who you met a long time ago. nonrestrictive

8. Pollution, which is still a major problem, was a political issue in the last presidential election. nonrestrictive

Exercise 23 (page 265)

1. (a) *F*   5. (a) F
   (b) *T*   (b) T

2. (a) F   6. (a) T
   (b) T   (b) F

3. (a) F   7. (a) F
   (b) F   (b) T

4. (a) T   8. (a) F
   (b) F   (b) T

Summary Exercise (page 268)

1. *I know the man whose daughter is blind.*

2. Correct

3. The book which I took doesn't have the answer.

4. The people who are waiting should leave first.

5. The building in which she works is very new./ The building which she works in is very new.

6. There's the man whose mother I know.

7. I don't remember the people who came late.

8. Correct

9. I spoke to the man who is very friendly.

10. My friend, who/whom I met in college, called me yesterday.

11. This is the only thing that he could do.

12. Kim, who is thirteen years old, swims very well.

13. We can probably replace the key that/which is lost.

14. The house, which I lived in for two years, was really beautiful.

15. The students with whom I work are very friendly.

16. Correct

Chapter 10

Exercise 1 (page 273)

Answers will vary.

Exercise 2 (page 274)

May 3

Dear Johanna,

I'm writing to tell you about Lynn's condition so that you can decide whether or not you should come while she is still in the hospital. Frankly, the news (is/are) not good. I'm afraid that her health (is/are) not improving very much. Her progress (is/are) very slow, but fortunately her spirits (is/are) still high. She is very friendly with the women who (is/are) in the room next to hers. She spends a lot of time talking to (her/them), and she reads a lot too. She broke her glasses on Friday, but she's managing well without (it/them). I ordered an extra pair for her, and (it/they) should be ready soon.

If you come, you'll probably want to go directly to the hospital. Don't worry about your belongings — you can leave (it/them) in my car until the evening. To save time, don't check your luggage. Take (it/them) with you on the plane and store (it/them) under your seat. Most of your stuff will probably fit by your (feet/foot), but if (it/they) (doesn't/don't), you can use the overhead compartment. After your plane arrives, if the traffic (is/are) light, it'll only take fifteen minutes to get to the hospital from the airport by taxi.

If you want more information about Lynn's condition, you can probably get (it/them) from the doctor when you come. He doesn't offer a lot of details unless you ask for (it/them). His advice (is/are) usually helpful, however. Most important, I appreciate his honesty. I'm sure you'll appreciate (it/them) too, even if the information (is/are) not always optimistic.

Call me to let me know about your plans. Take care.

Love,

Maria

P.S. Bring your jeans. You'll need (it/them) when I take you for a long, refreshing hike in the woods. You'll need the fresh air after a day or two in the hospital!

Exercise 3 (page 276)

(top left) Get cash[NC] for trash[NC]! Sell us your cans[C], bottles[C], and newspapers[C]. Clean up your neighborhoods[C] now! Remember, don't throw away junk[NC]! Call 785-1123.

(middle left) Needed: We're looking for volunteers[C] to participate in a psychology experiment[C]. We'll pay $25.00 for two hours[C]. Make money[NC] and have fun[NC] for just a little work[NC]! For more details[C], call Chris at 345-9898.

(bottom left) Students[C]: Are you looking for a part-time job[C]? Would you like to earn money[NC]? Would you like to be a baby-sitter[C], a messenger[C], or an office assistant[C]? We have several positions[C] available. Call 345-0403.

(top right) Tickets[C] available: Bus tickets[C] are still available for a trip[C] to Chicago on April 15. We will leave at 6:30 A.M. and return around 1:00 A.M. Call 345-9871 for reservations[C] and information[NC].

(middle right) Attention students[C]: Do you have health insurance[NC], or is it too expensive? If you are concerned about rising medical costs[C], come to a meeting[C] on March 25, at 7:30 P.M. at Ives Hall. Bring your friends[C]. Remember, good health[NC] is very important! Additional information[NC] is available at the Student Union.

(bottom right) Blood donations[C] requested: Donate blood[NC] to the Community Blood Bank. Call 345-9990 for an appointment[C]. We need as much help[NC] as we can get!

Exercise 4 (page 279)

1. wine, a wine
2. hairs, hair
3. chocolates; chocolate
4. A: beer
   B: beers
5. cheese; cheeses
6. lamb, lambs
7. crime, a crime
8. coffees, coffee
9. light; lights
10. Indonesian, Indonesians

Exercise 5 (page 280)

1.

Answers may vary. However, the first choice would be more likely for an individual ad. For example:

1 tricycle/tricycles	1 stroller
plants/1 plant	jewelry
lamps/1 lamp	dishes
farm equipment	1 mattress/mattresses
computer games	carpeting
books	bookshelves
magazines	1 computer
furniture	1 double bed/double beds
clothing	
toys	

2.

Answers will vary.

Exercise 6 (page 280)

Answers will vary. For example:

1. *a shopping list, money, coupons, recycled plastic bags.*

2. towels, a bathing suit, sunscreen, water, sandwiches, snacks.

3. a tent, a flashlight, food, cooking equipment, clothes.

4. a birth certificate, money, a photograph.

5. soccer shoes, shin guards, a soccer ball, water, a sweatshirt.

6. a toothbrush, clothing, pajamas, a hairbrush.

Exercise 7 (page 281)

1.

> Smog is a form of air pollution. The term was first used in 1905 to describe the combination of *smoke* and *fog (sm + og)* that occasionally hung over London and other British cities.
>
> Today, smog also refers to a condition caused by the interaction of sunlight with exhaust gases from cars and factories. Heavy concentrations of smog are poisonous. In 1948, 20 people died and nearly 6,000 became ill from a photochemical smog in Pennsylvania. About 4,000 Londoners died as a result of a thick smog in 1952. Smog also destroys plant life and causes building material to deteriorate faster than usual.

1. smog
2. noncount
3. a photochemical smog; a thick smog
4. count
5. It has the indefinite article *a* before it.

2.

> Slang is an informal kind of language in which words and phrases are used in new and unusual ways. People use slang more often in speaking than in writing. They use it more often with friends than with strangers. Slang has a wide variety of uses. Many people use it because they want to seem fashionable and modern. Others use slang because it is frank and informal, it expresses friendliness, and it puts people at ease.

1. slang
2. noncount
3. It is singular and it doesn't have any articles with it.

Exercise 8 (page 282)

Answers to numbers 7–10 will vary. For example:

1. *mail*

2. clothing

3. fruit

4. livestock

5. luggage

6. money

7. *tables,* beds

8. trains, planes

9. necklaces, earrings

10. used bags, used paper, used cartons

Summary Exercise (page 284)

1. *In many families, husbands and wives both work and share the child care responsibilities.*

2. There is pollution in many cities around the world.

3. Correct

4. She gave me good advice.

5. She brought a notebook/notebooks, pencils, and a pen.

6. His teeth are loose.

7. An oak tree fell down during the storm.

8. Did you see them in the living room?

9. Would you like to be a computer programmer or an engineer when you graduate?

10. Correct

Chapter 11

Exercise 1 (page 286)

Questions and answers will vary. For example:

1. A: *Is there much pollution in Mexico City?*
   B: *Yes, there is. There's a great deal of pollution./
   No, there isn't. There's not much pollution./
   No, there isn't. There's no pollution./
   No, there isn't. There is not any pollution at all.*

2. A: Is there much traffic in ___?

3. A: Are there many subways in ___?

4. A: Are there many taxicabs in ___?

5. A: Is there much crime in ___?

6. A: Are there many police in ___?

7. A: Are there many hospitals in ___?

8. A: Is there much cold weather in ___?

9. A: Are there many hurricanes in ___?

10. A: Is there much sunshine in ___?

Exercise 2 (page 287)

Answers to questions will vary. For example:

1. A: *How many classes per week are there?*
   B: *Five.*

2. How many hours per class are there?

3. How many weeks per semester are there?

4. How much homework is there?

5. How many students per class are there?

6. How many exams are there?

7. How many textbooks are there?

8. How much writing is there?

9. How much computer lab work is there?

10. (⁓) How many speeches are there?

Exercise 3 (page 289)

1. *very few*

2. very few

3. a little

4. a little

5. A: a little
   B: very little

6. very little

7. a few

8. very little

9. A: very little
   B: very few

10. B: very little

Exercise 4 (page 290)

Answers will vary. For example:

In my ideal city, there are not too many people and there is not much crime. There is very little unemployment and there are plenty of available jobs.

There is a great deal of public transportation; for example, quite a few buses and a lot of trains. Actually, there is not too much traffic because there are only a few taxicabs and there are no private automobiles in the downtown area.

My ideal city has a lot of parks and museums, plenty of restaurants, and only a few hotels. It has only a few tourists.

As for the climate, it has a lot of sunshine, not too much rain, no snow, and only a little cold weather. It has no pollution.

My ideal city has only a few shopping malls. There are a lot of department stores and plenty of smaller shops. It has no skyscrapers, only a few apartment buildings, and plenty of private homes.

My ideal city is a nice place to live and work. People have a lot of fun there.

Exercise 5 (page 291)

Answers will vary.

Exercise 6 (page 292)

Answers will vary. For example:

a bag of apples	a box of spaghetti
two cartons of eggs	a box of cereal
a jar of peanut butter	a package of napkins
a quart of orange juice	a roll of toilet paper
a tube of toothpaste	a bottle of shampoo
a box of crackers	a box of tissues
three containers of yogurt	a package of light bulbs
a bag of potatoes	a bottle of vitamins
a box of trash bags	two cans of tomato sauce
a pound of rice	a jar of salsa
a pound of flour	a package of tortilla chips

Exercise 7 (page 294)

1. A: *How much is milk?*
   B: *It's ninety-nine cents a quart.*

2. A: *How much are bananas?*
   B: *They're fifty-nine cents a pound.*

3. A: How much are grapes?
   B: They're a dollar sixty-nine a pound.

4. A: How much is lettuce?
   B: It's ninety-nine cents a head.

5. A: How much are carrots?
   B: They're thirty-nine cents a pound.

6. A: How much is broccoli?
   B: It's a dollar fifty-nine a pound.

7. A: How much are tomatoes?
   B: They're a dollar twenty-nine a pound.

8. A: How much is ground beef?
   B: It's a dollar eighty-nine a pound.

9. A: How much is chicken?
   B: It's ninety-nine cents a pound.

10. A: How much is steak?
    B: It's $4.29 a pound.

11. A: How much are crackers?
    B: They're $1.99 a box.

12. A: How much is soap?
    B: It's 79¢ a bar.

13. A: How much are chocolate chip cookies?
    B: They're $2.19 a package.

14. A: How much is detergent?
    B: It's $4.49 a bottle.

15. A: How much is toilet paper?
    B: It's $1.29 a package.

16. A: How much is toothpaste?
    B: It's $2.29 a tube.

17. A: How much are batteries?
    B: They're $2.09 a package.

18. A: How much is rice?
    B: It's 69¢ a pound.

19. A: How much is spaghetti?
    B: It's 79¢ a box.

20. A: How much is salsa?
    B: It's $1.29 a jar.

Exercise 8 (page 296)

Have you ever eaten coconut? You probably have, but you may not be very familiar with coco palms. Coconuts come from coco palms, which are trees that grow in tropical regions. Coco palms are very unusual because all of the parts of the tree have a commercial value. For example, coconuts are an important food in tropical regions, and coconut milk, which comes from inside the coconut, is a nutritious drink. Coconut oil, the most valuable product of all, also comes from coconuts. Some of the other parts of the tree that are eaten include the buds and the young stems. Besides food, the tree is also used for manufacturing commercial products. The leaves are used for making fans and baskets, and the fibers from the husks and trunks are made into mats, cord, and rope. The hard shells and the husks are used to make fuel, and the trunks are used for timber. Finally, even the roots are used. They are chewed as a narcotic.

Exercise 9 (page 299)

1. *a*
2. the; a
3. the; a
4. the; a; an, a
5. an; the
6. the; the; The, a; the, the
7. the; an, the
8. the; the
9. a; a
10. a; a

Exercise 10 (page 300)

1. A: *I bought a shirt and a pair of pants.*
   B: *What color is the shirt?*

2. A: How much do you pay the baby-sitter?

3. B: Who owns the dog?

4. B: Is the park nearby?

5. B: Well, what time does the football game start?

6. B: Can you carry the others?

7. B: How much did the jacket cost?

8. A: Are the wallets on sale?

9. B: Well, what does the letter say?

10. B: Where did you put the umbrella?

Exercise 11 (page 301)

Answers will vary. For example:

1. *The women are sisters. They're sending a gift to their mother./The women are friends. One of them is getting married soon. They're discussing the wedding.*

2. The young men are students. They're talking about a textbook they need for class.

3. They're married and they're going to buy a gift together. The wife took some money out of the bank.

4. Three co-workers are eating lunch. One of the women was supposed to bring her recent wedding photos.

5. They're husband and wife. The husband was supposed to pay the electric bill last month. He forgot, and there is a large penalty on this month's bill.

6. Two friends were planning to go to a concert. One of them promised to buy the tickets.

7. They're co-workers. They're all working on a certain business deal together.

8. Two psychology majors are working on an experiment together. They need to advertise for volunteers.

Exercise 12 (page 303)

Answers will vary.

Exercise 13 (page 303)

1. The driver
2. The waiter
3. The mechanic
4. the computers
5. The star
6. The teacher
7. the drawers
8. the engine

Exercise 14 (page 304)

Grandma's Chicken Soup

Put chicken in (the) large pot. Cover (a) chicken with (the) water. Cut up (the) onion, (the) carrot, and (the) celery. Add (the) vegetables to (the) water. Also add (the) garlic, (the) parsley, (the) salt, and (the) pepper. Boil (the) ingredients for 10 minutes. Lower (the) heat and simmer (the) ingredients slowly for 1 hour. Skim (the) fat occasionally. Remove (the) chicken from (the) pot. When it has cooled, remove (the) skin and cut (the) chicken from (the) bones. Strain (the) soup and discard (the) vegetables. Put (the) chicken back into (the) liquid. Reheat and serve. You may add (the) pasta if you like.

Old-Fashioned Chocolate Chip Cookies

Preheat (the) oven to 375° Fahrenheit. In (a) small bowl, combine (the) flour, (the) baking soda, and (the) salt. Set these aside. In (a) large mixing bowl, combine (the) butter, (the) sugar, (the) brown sugar, and (the) vanilla extract. Beat until creamy. Beat in (the) eggs. Gradually add (the) flour mixture. Stir in (the) chocolate

$\overset{\text{(the)}}{\text{chips}}$ and $\overset{\text{(the)}}{\underset{\wedge}{\text{nuts}}}$. Drop $\underline{\text{tablespoonfuls}}$ of $\overset{}{\underset{\wedge}{\text{batter}}}$ onto

ungreased $\underline{\text{cookie sheets}}$. Bake for 10–12 minutes.

$\overset{\text{the}}{\text{Remove}} \underset{\wedge}{\underline{\text{cookies}}}$ from $\overset{\text{the}}{\underline{\text{cookie sheets}}}$ with $\overset{\text{a}}{\underset{\wedge}{\text{spatula}}}$

$\overset{\text{The}}{\text{while still warm.}} \underset{\wedge}{\text{Recipe}}$ makes about 5 dozen $\underline{\text{cookies}}$.

Exercise 15 (page 305)

5, 3, 1, 4, 6, 2

Exercise 16 (page 305)

Answers will vary. For example:

1. *I went to the supermarket last night — the A & P near my house.*

2. I went to the bank — the Harris Bank near school.

3. I bought the newspaper — the *Chicago Tribune*.

4. The mayor — Mayor Daley — is going to speak on television tonight.

5. I didn't feel well yesterday, so I went to the doctor — Dr. Nelson.

6. (Answers will vary.)

7. No. You don't have to know the exact name. You can assume it's the supermarket your friend always goes to, the bank he or she always goes to, etc.

8. (a) *A bank* suggests that it's not your usual bank. You may have gone to a different bank. (b) *The bank* suggests it's a bank that you usually go to, one that you're more familiar with.

Exercise 17 (page 307)

Answers will vary.

Exercise 18 (page 307)

Answers will vary.

Exercise 19 (page 308)

Answers will vary. For example:

1. *A begonia is a flower.*

2. *A spatula is a cooking utensil.*

3. An elm is a tree.

4. A mango is a tropical fruit.

5. A screwdriver is a tool.

6. A shark is a large sea fish.

7. A crib is a bed for infants.

8. A penny is a coin.

9. An herb is a plant.

10. A square is a four-sided shape.

11. A bibliography is a list of books.

12. A moth is an insect.

13. A calculator is an electronic device.

14. An astronomer is a scientist.

Exercise 20 (page 308)

Answers will vary. For example:

1. *My neighbor has a cat that always digs up my flower garden.*

2. I had an exhausting vacation with my family last month.

3. However, the dinner party I went to last week was great.

4. The supermarket near my house even has a post office and an ATM.

5. The teacher that I had last year was very patient.

6. When I buy a car, I bring someone to help me.

Exercise 21 (page 309)

Answers will vary.

Exercise 22 (page 309)

1. (omitted), *a*

2. the; (omitted), (omitted)

3. (omitted); a

4. (omitted); The

5. (omitted); The; a

6. (omitted), (omitted); the, (omitted); the; the

7. (omitted); (omitted)

8. (omitted); a

1. *How many pencils do you need?*

2. Please buy a bag of potatoes at the supermarket.

3. Correct

4. A lot of water spilled on the floor.

5. I'd like two pounds of ground beef, please.

6. Life is not always easy.

7. Calcium is a mineral.

8. Correct

9. Correct

10. I spoke to the/a bank manager about my problem.

11. Correct

12. I need a new coat.

13. I'll buy three packages of crackers.

14. When you get to my house, you don't have to ring the doorbell.

Chapter 12

Exercise 1 (page 314)

1. B: *cheaper, healthier*

2. B: taller, thinner, curlier
   A: lighter

3. B: more challenging, more refreshing; more strenuous

4. A: more annoyed
   B: angrier; simpler

5. B: earlier
   A: later, more expensive

6. Doctor: worse; more serious
   Relative: better
   Doctor: longer; more accurate; more tired

Exercise 2 (page 317)

Answers to questions will vary. For example:

1. A: *Which is better, a bath or a shower?*
   B: *A bath, because it's more relaxing.*

2. A: *Which is worse, a headache or a toothache?*
   B: *A toothache, because it's usually more painful.*

3. A: Which is better, classical music or jazz?

4. A: Which is better, soccer or American football?

5. A: Which is better, coffee or tea?

6. A: Which is worse, rain or snow?

7. A: Which is better, a romance novel or a mystery?

8. A: Which is worse, a written exam or an oral exam?

9. A: Which is worse, a hurricane or a tornado?

10. A: Which is worse, poverty or loneliness?

11. A: Which is worse, the chicken pox or pneumonia?

12. A: Which is worse, a broken arm or a broken leg?

Exercise 3 (page 317)

1. *You look (much) better now. You look more energetic.*

2. You look (much) taller now. You look more grown-up.

3. You look (much) healthier now. You look stronger.

4. You look (much) more wide awake now. You look more alert.

5. You much (much) happier today. You look more cheerful.

6. You look (much) more relaxed now. You look calmer.

Exercise 4 (page 318)

Answers will vary.

Exercise 5 (page 319)

1. A: *the slowest, the most careful*
   B: the fastest

2. A: the most popular, the cheapest
   B: the best

3. A: the most painful
   B: the most competent

4. A: the most suitable
   B: the nicest, the most comfortable

5. A: the most reliable
   B: the nearest; the worst

Exercise 6 (page 321)

Answers will vary. For example:

1. *The most beautiful park is Memorial Park.*
2. *The least expensive supermarket is Joe's.*
3. The best…
4. The nearest…
5. The nicest…
6. The most/least crowded…
7. The most popular…
8. The most interesting…
9. The worst…
10. The cheapest…

Exercise 7 (page 322)

Answers will vary. For example:

1. *San Francisco is one of the most beautiful cities I know.*
2. Joe is one of the funniest people I know.
3. Bonnie is one of the most talented musicians I know.
4. That lecture was one of the most boring lectures I have ever attended.
5. A Ferrari is one of the most expensive cars there is.
6. Chick Corea is one of the most unusual pianists I have ever heard.
7. Skiing is one of the most exciting sports there is.
8. She is one of the thriftiest people I know.
9. A free concert at Orchestra Hall is one of the most crowded events I have attended.
10. She is one of the smartest people I know.

Exercise 8 (page 322)

Answers will vary.

Exercise 9 (page 323)

Answers to questions will vary. For example:

1. A: *How much is a pound of apples?*
   B: *About as much as a pound of pears.*

2. About as big as this town.
3. About as much as a stereo.
4. About as tall as I am.
5. About as large as a soccer ball.
6. About as heavy as a quart of water.
7. About as high as this building.
8. About as strong as my sister.

Exercise 10 (page 324)

1. *I'll work as fast as I can.*
2. I'll work as hard as I can.
3. I'll come home as early as I can.
4. I'll drive as carefully as I can.
5. I'll return as soon as I can.
6. I'll bring as many as I can.

Exercise 11 (page 325)

Answers will vary. For example:

1. *I still work as hard as I did ten years ago.*
2. *I'm not as poor as I was ten years ago.*
3. I don't get up as early as I did ten years ago.
4. I'm not as energetic as I was ten years ago.
5. I'm still as happy as I was ten years ago.
6. I don't eat out as frequently as I did ten years ago.
7. I still feel as healthy as I did ten years ago.

Exercise 12 (page 326)

1. *less pollution than*
2. fewer calories than
3. more money than
4. less value than
5. more people than

Exercise 13 (page 327)

1. *is the state with the most people.*
2. *is the state with the least land area.*

3. is the state with the most lakes.

4. is the state with the least income.

5. is the state with the most islands.

6. is the state with the least rainfall.

7. is the state with the fewest people.

8. is the state with the most land area.

Exercise 14 (page 327)

1. *John is the same weight as Tom.*

2. The book is the same price as the videocassette.

3. My office building is the same height as yours.

4. This paper is the same width as that one.

5. The pool is the same depth as the lake.

6. This book is the same length as my math book.

Exercise 15 (page 328)

There is more pollution than there was four years ago.
There are fewer educational programs than there were
   four years ago.
There is more poverty than there was four years ago.
There is more hunger than there was four years ago.
There is more crime than there was four years ago.
There is less employment than there was four
   years ago.
There are more strikes than there were four years ago.
There is less available housing than there was four
   years ago.
There is more traffic than there was four years ago.
There are fewer business opportunities than there were
   four years ago.
There are more public health problems than there were
   four years ago.
There are more homeless people than there were four
   years ago.

Exercise 16 (page 329)

Carrots have the most vitamin A.
Onions have the least vitamin A.
Sweet potatoes have the most calories.
Spinach has the fewest calories.
Peas have the most vitamin C.
Carrots have the least vitamin C.
Peas have the most iron.
Celery has the least iron.
Spinach has the most calcium.
Peas have the least calcium.

Celery has the most sodium.
Peas have the least sodium.
Sweet potatoes have the most carbohydrates.
Spinach has the fewest carbohydrates.

Exercise 17 (page 330)

Answers will vary.

Exercise 18 (page 330)

Answers will vary.

Exercise 19 (page 330)

Answers will vary.

Exercise 20 (page 331)

Answers may vary. For example:

	Supergrand	Seagull
age	+ *newer*	– *older*
price	– *more expensive*	+ *cheaper*
size	– smaller	+ bigger
storage	– less storage	+ more storage
total mileage	– more total mileage	+ less total mileage
gas mileage	+ more gas mileage	– less gas mileage
color	– worse color	+ better color
condition of body	+ less rust	– more rust
condition of interior	+ better interior	– worse interior
financing	+ better financing	– worse financing
extras	+ more extras	– fewer extras

Exercise 21 (page 332)

Answers to numbers 4–6 will vary. For example:

1. B: *so*

2. B: such a

3. B: such; so

4. B: so, I fell asleep at 8:30.

5. B: so, I'd like to see it again.

6. A: such, I feel very lonely now.

Exercise 22 (page 334)

Answers will vary.

Exercise 23 (page 335)

Answers will vary.

Summary Exercise (page 338)

1. *My cold was so bad that I went home.*
2. She is taller than I am.
3. We had such good weather that we stayed for a long time.
4. Correct
5. This one is prettier than that one.
6. I have as much as he does.
7. It's the most expensive restaurant in town.
8. Correct
9. I don't think that I'm as friendly as she is.
10. My hair is the same length as my sister's hair.
11. I work better in the morning than in the afternoon.
12. It was the most interesting one of them all.

Chapter 13

Exercise 1 (page 340)

1. A: *had*
   B: *did*
2. A: wasn't/weren't
   B: could
3. A: had
   B: worked
4. B: didn't rain
5. B: could
6. (Answers will vary.)

Exercise 2 (page 342)

Answers will vary. For example:

1. *I wish I didn't live in such a small apartment./ I wish I could move./I wish I had more space./ I wish I could afford a bigger apartment.*
2. I wish I had more money.
3. I wish I was/were in a different class.
4. I wish I wasn't/weren't so busy.
5. I wish I lived in a small town.
6. I wish I had my family nearby.
7. I wish I could exercise more.
8. I wish I had a compass.

Exercise 3 (page 342)

Answers will vary. For example:

1. Roommate B: *I could, but I have to leave right now.*
2. Salesclerk: I did, I just sold the last one.
3. Student B: I could, I lent them to someone else this morning.
4. Friend B: I did, I have a dentist appointment.
5. Parent: there were, you ate the last one yesterday.
6. Spouse B: it was/were, it's quite cool.

Exercise 4 (page 343)

Answers will vary. For example:

1. *I wish you'd take a walk with me.*
2. I wish you'd take better care of yourself.
3. I wish you'd come to the next concert with me.
4. I wish you'd take a vacation.
5. I wish you'd stay longer.
6. I wish you wouldn't quit school/leave.

Exercise 5 (page 344)

1. *I wish he wouldn't make so much noise in the morning./I wish she would be quieter in the morning.*
2. I wish he/she wouldn't use up all the hot water.
3. I wish he/she wouldn't stay in the bathroom so long.

4. I wish he/she'd write down phone messages.

5. I wish he/she wouldn't smoke.

6. I wish he/she wouldn't leave dirty clothes in the living room.

7. I wish he/she'd clean up the kitchen.

8. I wish he/she wouldn't talk on the phone for hours.

9. I wish he/she'd buy his/her own food.

10. I wish he/she'd turn the lights off.

Exercise 6 (page 345)

Answers will vary. For example:

1. A: *I hope I can. I have to work until 8:30, but I think I can come afterwards.*
   B: *I wish I could, but I have to work until 8:30 and then I'll probably be too tired.*

2. A: I hope I can. I'll have to work more hours to make enough money.
   B: I wish I could, but it's too expensive.

3. A: I hope I can. I'm working very hard and I think I can do it.
   B: I wish I could, but I don't think it's possible.

4. A: I hope I can. I just have to find a ride.
   B: I wish I could, but I don't think I'll be able to find a ride.

5. A: I hope I can if I get home early enough.
   B: I wish I could, but I probably won't get home on time.

6. A: I hope I can soon. I'll have more time in a few weeks.
   B: I wish I could, but I don't have the time.

Exercise 7 (page 347)

Answers will vary.

Exercise 8 (page 348)

Answers will vary. For example:

1. *I'd have to walk to work.*

2. I'd be a great basketball player.

3. I'd call ahead to let them know.

4. I'd stay home.

5. I spilled food on myself in a restaurant.

6. the working conditions were bad.

7. telephone solicitors didn't call at dinner time.

8. I could afford it.

Exercise 9 (page 349)

Answers will vary.

Exercise 10 (page 349)

Answers will vary.

Exercise 11 (page 350)

Answers will vary. For example:

1. B: *If I were you, I'd call the business office.*

2. B: If I were you, I wouldn't pay the rent.

3. B: If I were you, I'd speak to the instructor.

4. B: If I were you, I'd cancel one of them.

5. B: If I were you, I'd tell her what time to call.

6. B: If I were you, I'd look for a new job.

7. B: If I were you, I'd ask a friend to help.

8. B: If I were you, I'd call the company.

9. B: If I were you, I'd talk to your landlord.

10. B: If I were you, I'd complain to the police department.

Exercise 12 (page 351)

Answers will vary. For example:

1. A: *Would you mind if I picked you up earlier?*
   B: *No, that's OK.*

2. A: Would it be OK if I called you back later?
   B: Sure.

3. A: Would it bother you if I listened to the news?
   B: No, not at all.

4. A: Would you mind if I opened the window?
   B: No, go right ahead.

5. A: Would it be OK if I borrowed your book?
   B: Sure.

6. A: Would you mind if I stopped for gas?
   B: No problem.

Exercise 13 (page 352)

1. (a) *F*
   (b) *T*
2. (a) *F*
   (b) *F*
3. (a) *T*
   (b) *F*
4. (a) T
   (b) T
5. (a) F
   (b) T
6. (a) T
   (b) F

Summary Exercise (page 354)

1. *I wish I could go with you, but I have to baby-sit.*
2. What would you do if there were/was a fire in your kitchen?
3. I can't play the piano, but I wish I could.
4. Correct
5. Correct
6. If I knew the answer, I wouldn't ask you.
7. I wish you'd stop smoking so much.
8. If I were you, I'd return it to the store.
9. Correct
10. I hope you'll call me back later.
11. I wouldn't be able to do the job if she weren't helping me.
12. Do you wish you were there right now?

Chapter 14

Exercise 1 (page 356)

1. A: *staying home all weekend*
   B: *complaining*
2. A: driving, taking my medicine; leaving for vacation
   B: spending more time
3. A: quitting my job
   B: working there
   A: going back to school
4. A: Swimming
   B: taking hot baths
5. A: passing the exam
   B: studying so hard; going to bed
   A: worrying

Exercise 2 (page 358)

Answers will vary. For example:

1. *Running*
2. Skydiving
3. Swimming
4. Smoking
5. Drunk driving
6. *Going to a concert*
7. Studying for final exams
8. Driving in a big city
9. Turning your thermostat down
10. Taking a long vacation
11. *is hard when I'm tired.*
12. isn't easy.
13. bores me to death.
14. saves a lot of time.
15. is a good habit to form.

Exercise 3 (page 358)

Answers will vary.

Exercise 4 (page 359)

Answers to questions will vary. For example:

1. A: *Which is more fun, swimming or skiing?*
   B: *I think skiing is more fun than swimming.*
2. A: Which is more relaxing, taking a hot bath or sunbathing?
3. A: Which is more fun, staying in a hotel or going camping?
4. A: Which is more exciting, riding a motorcycle or skydiving?
5. A: Which is worse, missing a plane or losing your luggage?
6. A: Which is more important, enjoying your work or making a lot of money?
7. A: Which is more useful, learning to cook or learning to drive?
8. A: Which is easier, learning mathematics or learning a second language?

Exercise 5 (page 360)

Answers will vary.

Exercise 6 (page 361)

1. A: *writing*
   B: *postponing*
2. A: helping
   B: doing
3. A: drinking
   B: having; smoking
4. A: waiting
   B: spending
   A: going; relaxing, shopping
5. A: visiting
   B going; not buying, looking

Exercise 7 (page 363)

Answers to questions will vary. For example:

1. A: *What do you enjoy doing on Sundays?*
   B: *I enjoy sleeping late. What about you?*
   A: *I enjoy taking long walks.*
2. A: What do you avoid doing?
3. A: What do you dislike doing?
4. A: What do you enjoy doing after work?
5. A: What do you miss doing in this country?
6. A: What do you regret not doing recently?
7. A: What do you often postpone doing?
8. A: What do you have trouble doing?

Exercise 8 (page 364)

Requests and responses will vary. For example:

1. A: *Would you mind putting out your cigarette?*
   B: *No, not at all. I didn't know it was bothering you.*
2. A: Would you mind fixing the horn too?
   B: No problem.
3. A: Would you mind stopping at the drugstore on our way home?
   B: No, not at all.
4. A: Would you mind helping me?
   B: No, I'll be right with you.

5. A: Would you mind repeating that, please?
   B: No problem.
6. A: Would you mind lending me the notes from last week?
   B: No, I'd be glad to.

Exercise 9 (page 366)

Answers will vary. For example:

1. *By writing a check.*
   By using a credit card.
   By using an ATM card.
2. By using a spare key.
   By breaking the window.
3. By asking someone to tie them.
4. By using a phrase book.
   By using a dictionary.
5. By using a microwave.
   By making a cold meal.
6. By asking someone to wake you.
   By having children.

Exercise 10 (page 366)

1. *Instead of dieting, start an exercise program.*
   Besides dieting, you need exercise too.
   In addition to dieting, you need exercise too.
2. Instead of leaving your house at eight o'clock, leave fifteen minutes earlier.
   In addition to/Besides leaving earlier, you should also walk faster.
3. Shop at a discount store instead of shopping at the local supermarket.
   In addition to/Besides buying sale items, use grocery store and manufacturers' coupons.
4. Instead of worrying about it, relax and listen to soft music.
   In addition to/Besides relaxing before bedtime, read a book until you feel sleepy.
5. Instead of responding angrily, leave the room.
   In addition to/Besides working, you need to enjoy life more.
6. Instead of saying yes, say, "I'd love to help you, but I really can't."
   In addition to/Besides saying no, say, "I'm very sorry, but I can't."

Exercise 11 (page 368)

Answers to questions will vary. For example:

1. A: *What are you tired of doing?*
   B: *I'm tired of cooking dinner every night. What about you?*
   A: *I'm tired of studying so much.*

2. A: What are you good at doing?

3. A: What do you often think about doing?

4. A: What are you interested in doing?

5. A: What are you afraid of doing?

6. A: What are you used to doing after dinner?

7. A: What do you look forward to doing next year?

8. A: What do you worry about doing?

Exercise 12 (page 368)

Answers will vary. For example:

1. *Before taking a trip, check your car to see if it is working properly.*

2. After dialing a wrong number, say, "I'm sorry, I must have dialed the wrong number."

3. Instead of cooking dinner, go out to a restaurant or ask your spouse/roommate to cook dinner.

Exercise 13 (page 370)

1. A: *to leave*
   B: *to move out*, to start; to be

2. A: not to arrive
   B: to help
   A: to clean up; to arrive, to hang up

3. A: to complete
   B: to do; to finish, to take

4. A: to go
   B: to leave

5. A: to move
   B: not to move
   A: to pay

Exercise 14 (page 372)

Answers to questions will vary. For example:

1. A: *Do you expect to travel or stay home next summer?*
   B: *Stay home.*

2. A: Do you hope to get high grades or get passing grades?

3. A: Do you need to study hard or study a little?

4. A: Do you plan to go out or stay home this weekend?

5. A: Do you want to stay in your apartment or find a new apartment?

6. A: Do you expect to get a lot of mail or get a little mail today?

Exercise 15 (page 372)

1. B: *hope to.*

2. B: expect to.

3. B: hope to.

4. B: don't want to.

5. B: plan to

6. B: need to.

Exercise 16 (page 373)

Answers will vary according to which situation is chosen. For example:

1. *to run for president.*

2. to win.

3. to get a lot of votes.

4. to accept defeat.

5. to change the government overnight.

6. to retire at the end of my term.

7. to accomplish many things.

8. to select a running mate.

9. to make a difference.

10. to accept what I cannot change.

11. to win this race.

12. to think I won't win.

Exercise 17 (page 374)

1. *to see it.*
2. *seeing it.*
3. seeing it.
4. to see it.
5. seeing it.
6. to see it?
7. to see it.
8. to see it.
9. to see it.
10. seeing it.
11. to see it.
12. seeing it?
13. to see it.
14. seeing it.
15. seeing it.
16. to see it?

Exercise 18 (page 376)

1. A: *I love to ski. What about you?*
   B: *I like to ski, but I prefer to stay indoors in the winter.*

2. A: I hate driving in traffic.
   B: Then you should continue taking the bus home.

3. A: Karen began to smoke as a teenager.
   B: Well, she'll probably continue to cough until she gives up the habit.

4. A: It started raining a few minutes ago.
   B: Let's wait for a while. I don't like walking in the rain.

5. A: I hate to wait in line.
   B: So do I. That's why I prefer shopping at night when there are fewer people.

Exercise 19 (page 378)

1. A: *getting up/to get up;* getting out, doing
   B: getting up; worrying, to do.

2. A: shopping; watching/to watch, to buy
   B: fighting/to fight
   A: looking at
   B: to go; going/to go
   A: to go; being
   B: going; having/to have

3. sightseeing; to check, going
   A: getting/to get
   B: getting/to get

4. A: to feel; to stay home; finding/to find
   B: eating out/to eat out; avoiding/to avoid; cooking

Exercise 20 (page 379)

Answers will vary. For example:

1. *to make a plan before you begin.*
2. *getting some help.*
3. renting a carpet cleaning machine.
4. to start early.
5. to buy ammonia.
6. surveying each room.
7. inhaling ammonia or bleach.
8. getting this done.
9. to take too many breaks.
10. to wash the windows.

Exercise 21 (page 380)

Answers will vary.

Exercise 22 (page 381)

Answers to questions will vary. For example:

1. A: *Is it unhealthy to worry a lot?*
   B: *Yes, it is.*

2. A: *Does it cost a lot to go to college?*
   B: *Yes, it does.*

3. A: Is it polite to phone people late at night?

4. A: Is it necessary to sleep eight hours every night?

5. A: Does it cost much to travel to your relatives?

6. A: Is it important to graduate from high school?

7. A: Does it take a long time to get a driver's license?

8. A: Is it a good idea to get married?

9. A: Is it unhealthy to eat a lot of eggs?

Exercise 23 (page 382)

1. *It's not easy to raise children.*
2. It's a bad idea to study all night.
3. It takes too much time to walk to work.
4. It's important to get exercise.
5. It's dangerous to smoke cigarettes.
6. It's useful to know a foreign language.

Intermediate Grammar: From Form to Meaning and Use
© 1996 Oxford University Press. Permission granted to reproduce for classroom use.

Exercise 24 (page 382)

Answers will vary.

Exercise 25 (page 384)

Answers will vary. For example:

I spent a lot of time doing errands this morning. First I went to the bank *to get some money* and I went to the post office to mail a letter. Then I stopped at the dry cleaners to pick up my suit, and I went to the drugstore nearby to buy some shampoo. After that, I stopped at the library to return some books, and then I went to the supermarket to get some groceries. On the way back home, I stopped at the gas station to get some gas. Finally, I went home to rest.

Exercise 26 (page 384)

Answers will vary. For example:

1. *To stay healthy, to feel good, to lose weight.*
2. To relax, to escape their problems.
3. To stay awake.
4. To take care of their teeth.
5. To cook, thaw, or reheat food quickly.
6. To get better jobs, to improve themselves.
7. To save for emergencies, to save for retirement.
8. To get books, to do research.
9. To find out the news.
10. To be able to attend an American university, to do business in the United States, to get better jobs.
11. To learn about other cultures, to see new places.
12. (⌒⌒) Why do people start wars?

Exercise 27 (page 385)

Answers will vary.

Exercise 28 (page 385)

1. *F*	6. T
2. F	7. F
3. T	8. T
4. T	9. F
5. F	10. F

Summary Exercise (page 388)

1. *Playing tennis is good exercise.*
2. Please remember to take out the trash tomorrow morning.
3. Correct
4. We don't want to leave, but we need to.
5. I arrive early in order not to miss her speech.
6. Did you decide to stay here?
7. We're looking forward to seeing them this weekend.
8. It's easy to take the bus downtown.
9. Correct
10. It's beginning to rain again.
11. When do you expect to get your degree?
12. I went to the supermarket to buy/in order to buy some milk.
13. Before leaving for work, close the windows.
14. Would you mind helping me with this, please?
15. I used to write a lot of letters when I lived far away from my family.

Chapter 15

Exercise 1 (page 391)

1. A: *had already begun*
   B: had happened
   A: had already ended, 'd wanted
2. B: 'd already seen, had read, had gone
3. A: Had you made
   B: 'd already arranged, hadn't registered

4. A: had come in
   B: had broken down; 'd been

5. A: had changed; had gained, had turned; had lost
   B: 'd just graduated

Exercise 2 (page 392)

Answers to questions will vary. For example:

1. A: *Before you started this course, had you ever taken any other English courses?*
   B: *Yes, I had. I'd studied English for a year in high school.*

2. A: Before you started this course, had you ever studied English grammar?

3. A: Before you started this course, had you ever read any English-language newspapers?

4. A: Before you started this course, had you ever spoken on the phone in English?

5. A: Before you started this course, had you ever written any letters in English?

6. A: Before you started this course, had you ever seen any movies in English?

7. A: Before you started this course, had you ever read any English-language books?

8. A: Before you started this course, had you ever made any English-speaking friends?

9. A: Before you started this course, had you ever ordered from a menu in English?

10. A: Before you started this course, had you ever watched any TV programs in English?

Exercise 3 (page 394)

1. 2; 1; *He had had a headache until he took some aspirin.*

2. 2; 1; The sink overflowed after I had left the water running.

3. 1; 2; I failed the exam because I hadn't studied.

4. 1; 2; By the time they got divorced, they had been married for five years.

5. 1; 2; He called the police after he had been robbed.

6. 2; 1; She had been worried until the doctor said she was very healthy.

7. 1; 2; When she had slept for ten hours, she felt rested.

8. 2; 1; He had never held a newborn baby until his wife gave birth.

Exercise 4 (page 396)

1. (a) *Brian had never held a newborn baby before.*
   (b) He'd never diapered a baby before.
   (c) He'd never bathed a baby before.

2. (a) She'd never been on her own before.
   (b) She'd never lived in a dormitory before.
   (c) She'd never done her own laundry before.

3. (a) He'd never used an electronic cash register before.
   (b) He'd never packed groceries before.
   (c) He'd never gotten a paycheck before.

4. (a) She'd never started a car before.
   (b) She'd never driven a car before.
   (c) She'd never been so scared before.

Exercise 5 (page 396)

Answers will vary.

Exercise 6 (page 397)

Answers will vary. For example:

1. *The painters had already painted the apartment.*
   They hadn't cleaned the carpet yet.
   They had already fixed the refrigerator.
   The plumbers hadn't repaired the pipes yet.

2. He'd already completed the English requirement.
   He hadn't taken a math course yet.
   He'd already passed the writing test.

3. The class hadn't checked the homework yet.
   The teacher hadn't given a new assignment yet.
   The class had already begun a new chapter.

4. He'd already answered the classified ads.
   He hadn't gone to an employment agency yet.
   He'd already sent letters of inquiry.

Exercise 7 (page 399)

1. A: *had you been doing*
   B: 'd been jogging, 'd been playing

2. A: 'd been stealing
   B: had this been going on
   A: had been watching

3. A: 'd been waiting
   A: 'd been looking

4. B: 'd been losing
   A: 'd been hoping

5. B: had been bothering; 'd been working

Exercise 8 (page 401)

1. *When Julia went back to school, she had been working for two years.*
   When Julia went back to school, she had been working since 1992.

2. When the receptionist called his name, Steve had been waiting for half an hour/since 2:00 P.M.

3. When Brigette came to the United States, she'd been studying English for a year/since 1993.

4. When Michael was offered a job in Thailand, he'd been living in Indonesia for five months./since April.

5. When the electricity went off, the chicken had been baking for fifteen minutes./since 5:30.

Exercise 9 (page 401)

Answers will vary. For example:

1. *he had been sleeping poorly.*

2. he'd been sleeping.

3. I'd been making too many mistakes.

4. he'd been smoking.

5. we'd been running.

6. she'd been staying out past curfew.

7. she'd been sleeping during first period class.

8. my old one had been burning the toast.

Exercise 10 (page 402)

Answers will vary. For example:

1. *...she had been crying./...she had been suffering from allergies./...she had been chopping onions.*

2. ...he'd been dieting./he'd been exercising regularly.

3. ...he'd been sleeping.

4. ...he'd been drinking.

5. ...somebody had been smoking.

6. ...he'd been shopping for a birthday present.

7. ...they'd been talking about you.

8. ...he'd been lying.

Exercise 11 (page 403)

Answers will vary.

Exercise 12 (page 404)

1. A: *Does he ever wish, had chosen*
   B: wishes, 'd gone

2. A: wish, 'd come
   B: wish, 'd told

3. A: wishes, 'd seen
   B: wish, 'd shown

4. A: Do you ever wish, 'd learned to ski
   B: wish, 'd been in the Olympics

Exercise 13 (page 405)

Answers will vary. For example:

1. *I wish I'd lent him the money.*
   I wish I'd helped him.

2. I wish I'd been calmer.

3. I wish I'd told the truth.

4. I wish I'd taken your advice and called the doctor.

5. I wish I'd taken my sunglasses.

6. I wish I'd made some plans for the weekend.

7. I wish I'd remembered her birthday.

8. I wish I'd waited before accepting the first job.

Exercise 14 (page 405)

1. B: *I wish it weren't.*   6. B: I wish I had.

2. B: *I wish we had.*   7. B: I wish it weren't.

3. B: I wish he hadn't.   8. B: I wish he didn't.

4. B: I wish it weren't.   9. B: I wish they had.

5. B: I wish it hadn't.   10. B: I wish I had.

Exercise 15 (page 407)

Answers will vary.

Exercise 16 (page 408)

Answers will vary.

Exercise 17 (page 409)

Answers will vary. For example:

1. B: *(If I were/had been you,) I would have gone to see the instructor.*
2. B: (If I were/had been you,) I wouldn't have lent it to him.
3. B: (If I were/had been you,) I would have told the manager.
4. B: (If I were/had been you,) I would have called him again.
5. B: (If I were/had been you,) I would have told him/her.
6. B: (If I were/had been you,) I would have asked to speak to a supervisor.

Exercise 18 (page 410)

Answers will vary.

Exercise 19 (page 410)

1. (a) *F*   4. (a) T
   (b) F   (b) F

2. (a) F   5. (a) F
   (b) T   (b) T

3. (a) F
   (b) T

Summary Exercise (page 413)

1. *Why hadn't she called you before she left?*
2. Correct
3. If we'd arrived earlier, we wouldn't have missed the bus.
4. When I entered the building, the window had already been broken.
5. I've been waiting for an hour.

6. Correct
7. I wish you'd gone/you had gone to the doctor.
8. She'd already answered the door when I got there.
9. What would you have done if they had lied?
10. Correct
11. I wish I had seen her yesterday.
12. If I had taken the exam, I would have passed it.

Chapter 16

Exercise 1 (page 416)

1. *A*
2. *P* It's <u>being cooked</u>.
3. P He's <u>been weighed</u>.
4. A
5. A
6. A
7. P They <u>were fired</u>.
8. A
9. P We're <u>forbidden</u> to take it.
10. A
11. P You'll <u>be called</u> again about it.
12. P It <u>could be refilled</u>.
13. A
14. P She's <u>been injured</u>.

Exercise 2 (page 419)

1. (a)✔   6. (a)✔
   (b)✔   (b)✔

2. (a)✔   7. (a)
   (b)   (b)✔

3. (a)✔   8. (a)✔
   (b)✔   (b)✔

4. (a)   9. (a)
   (b)✔   (b)

5. (a)✔   10. (a)
   (b)   (b)✔

Intermediate Grammar: From Form to Meaning and Use

Exercise 3 (page 422)

When glass *is made*, certain materials <u>are melted</u> together and then <u>cooled</u>. The materials <u>are heated</u> in large furnaces that <u>are usually built</u> of ceramic blocks. When the bubbles <u>are removed</u> from the hot mixture, the hot liquid is <u>poured</u> into molds and <u>formed</u> into different shapes.

Exercise 4 (page 422)

A: *'s the trash collected*
B: 's picked up; is recycled
A: are the recycled items collected
B: are collected; are taken away, 's paid
A: 's done
B: 's separated, sold

Exercise 5 (page 423)

1. *The medicine was taken by the patient.*

2. *The patient took the medicine.*

3. The glass was dropped by the child.

4. The concert was attended by thousands of people.

5. The cake cost quite a bit.

6. Soccer was played on Sundays at 2:00 P.M.

7. We canceled the appointment.

8. The waiter took the order.

9. The car was repaired by two mechanics.

10. The baby cried for an hour.

11. The package was mailed by the woman early in the morning.

12. The shoes were bought at the mall.

Exercise 6 (page 424)

Answers for locations will vary. For example:

1. *Reservations are required.*
   Location: *In a restaurant*

2. Credit cards are accepted.
   Location: In a drugstore

3. Volunteers are needed.
   Location: A bulletin board

4. An ID is required.
   Location: In a liquor store

5. Lottery tickets are sold here.
   Location: In a supermarket

6. Chinese is spoken here.
   Location: In a travel agency

7. Satisfaction is guaranteed.
   Location: In a shoe repair shop

8. Parking is prohibited.
   Location: In front of a public building

9. No cameras are allowed.
   Location: In a museum

10. Prices are reduced.
    Location: In a department store

11. Checks are cashed here.
    Location: In an airport currency exchange

12. Children under 12 are admitted free.
    Location: In a zoo

Exercise 7 (page 425)

Answers to numbers 6–10 will vary. For example:

1. *is made*

2. is trained

3. are found

4. is celebrated

5. is made; is produced

6. *is found in coffee.*

7. is celebrated in September.

8. is used in cooking.

9. is worn by men on formal occasions.

10. is used in Indian cooking.

Exercise 8 (page 426)

1. *False. Oxygen isn't carried by white blood cells. It's carried by red blood cells.*

2. *True.*

3. False. Nitrogen isn't required for a fire to burn. Oxygen is required for a fire to burn.

4. False. Microwaves aren't used in refrigerators. They're used in ovens.

5. True.

6. False. Earthquakes aren't measured by a device called a polygraph. They're measured by a device called a seismograph.

7. False. The telephone wasn't invented in ancient times. It was invented in modern times.

8. False. Antibiotics weren't developed to kill viruses. They were developed to kill bacteria.

9. False. Rice isn't grown in cold, dry climates. It's grown in warm, wet climates.

10. True.

11. False. Cholesterol isn't needed for strong bones. Calcium is needed for strong bones.

12. True.

Exercise 9 (page 427)

1. *Several homes were damaged.*
   One major road was closed for an hour.
   Twelve people were injured.
   One person was killed.
   Many windows were shattered.
   One building was destroyed.
   One person was hospitalized.
   No major power lines were affected.

2. Some schools were closed.
   Several businesses were shut down.
   Many public events were canceled.
   More doctors were needed.
   Several new treatments were tried.
   Many flu shots were given.
   Hundreds of people were treated.

Exercise 10 (page 428)

1. (a)   5. (b)
2. (b)   6. (b)
3. (a)   7. (a)
4. (a)   8. (a)

Exercise 11 (page 430)

1. (a) *will be offered*
   (b) will be posted
   (c) will be announced
   (d) will be canceled

2. (a) will be shipped
   (b) will be added
   (c) will be sent
   (d) will be credited
   (e) will be refunded

3. will be answered; will not be repeated

Exercise 12 (page 432)

The building where I work *is being renovated* right now, and a number of changes are being made. For example, all of the offices are being painted and the carpeting is being replaced. New shelves are being built and a new computer system is being installed. And finally, a new kitchen is being added for the staff. A refrigerator, microwave, and sink are being put in near the lounge.

Exercise 13 (page 433)

Last month, while I was trying to complete an important project at work, the building was being renovated, and a number of changes were being made. For example, all of the offices were being painted and the carpeting was being replaced. New shelves were being built and a new computer system was being installed. And finally, a new kitchen was being added for the staff. A refrigerator, microwave, and sink were being put in near the lounge.

Exercise 14 (page 433)

1. *The exam has been canceled by the teacher.*

2. *The company has manufactured the product.*

3. This book has been translated into many languages.

4. The senator has been called dishonest.

5. The man has eaten the steak.

6. A new prescription has been recommended by the doctor.

7 The computer has been used by the whole class.

8. The school newspaper has received an award.

Exercise 15 (page 433)

1. A: *Have you been invited to any parties lately?*
   B: *Yes, I have.*

2. A: Will your apartment be painted this year?
   B: Yes, it will./No, it won't.

3. A: Has your class been canceled recently?
   B: Yes, it has./No, it hasn't.

4. A: Is your telephone being used right now?
   B: Yes, it is./No, it isn't.

5. A: Had you ever been robbed before?
   B: Yes, I had./No, I hadn't.

6. A: Will your rent be raised soon?
   B: Yes, it will./No, it won't.

7. A: Is this course being taught by a man?
   B: Yes, it is./No, it isn't.

8. A: Was this English course being given last semester?
   B: Yes, it was./No, it wasn't.

Exercise 16 (page 434)

1.

When John arrives at the emergency room, his arm will be examined and he will be sent for an X ray. After his arm is x-rayed, he will be told whether it is broken. If his arm is broken, he will be sent back to the emergency room, where a cast will be put on his arm. First, his arm will be put in the proper position. Then, a cotton sleeve will be put over his arm and it will be wrapped with wet bandages.

(The agent is not needed here because the focus is on the patient and the patient's arm. The agent *they* is vague, and therefore the active version sounds less informative.)

2.

Each subject will be given two lists of words by the research assistant. The subjects will be asked to read each list once. Then they will be shown some pictures and (they) will be asked to press a bell...

(The agent is needed in the first sentence since it is new information. Once the agent is given, it is not needed in the remaining sentences because it is understood. The active description is focused more on the research assistant and his actions. The passive version focuses on the subjects and what they are going to do.)

Exercise 17 (page 435)

1. (a) *The guests were being greeted.*
   (b) The bride and groom were being photographed.
   (c) Drinks were being served.

2. (a) The rooms were being painted.
   (b) The carpets were being cleaned.
   (c) The appliances were being repaired.

3. (a) The wine was being chilled.
   (b) The salad was being prepared.
   (c) The table was being set.

4. (a) One person was being lifted into an ambulance.
   (b) A man was being given oxygen.
   (c) Two witnesses were being questioned by the police.

Exercise 18 (page 436)

1. *Two children have been/were injured in a train accident.*

2. A new cancer treatment has been/was discovered.

3. The president's trip has been/was postponed. New plans have been/were announced.

4. A building has been/was damaged by an explosion.

5. A site has been/was selected for a recycling plant.

6. A restaurant has been/was closed by the health department.

7. A local bank has been/was robbed. Two people have been/were killed.

8. Higher wages have been/were demanded by strikers.

9. A golfer has been/was struck by lightning.

10. Three journalists have been/were released from jail.

11. A teenager has been/was charged with burglary.

12. A man has been/was hospitalized after a motorcycle crash.

Exercise 19 (page 437)

Answers will vary.

Exercise 20 (page 437)

1. *The office was being painted yesterday.* (The agent is obvious from the meaning of the sentence.)

2. *The house will be painted by a painter from Dryden.* (The sentence tells us something about the agent.)

3. The prices at the farmer's market are always being reduced. (The agent is obvious from the meaning of the sentence.)

4. At the meeting, the new regulations will be announced by the president. (The agent is necessary because the sentence tells us something about the agent.)

5. Applications for summer employment are being accepted at the supermarket. (The agent, impersonal *they*, doesn't add any important information to the sentence. It is unnecessary.)

6. When a pipe burst in our house, our new carpet was ruined. (The agent is obvious from the meaning of the sentence.)

7. The strikers will be arrested if they don't leave. (The agent is obvious from the meaning of the sentence.)

8. At that moment, the door was being unlocked. (It's obvious that somebody was unlocking the door; the agent doesn't add any information to the sentence. It's unnecessary.)

9. My aunt's car was being repaired at the service station. (The agent is obvious from the meaning of the sentence.)

10. Many accidents are caused by people who drink alcohol. (The agent is necessary because it tells which people.)

11. Many books are being written about health and nutrition. (The agent is obvious from the meaning of the sentence.)

12. Next semester, undergraduates will be required to take five courses each semester. (The agent is obvious from the meaning of the sentence.)

Exercise 21 (page 439)

1. (a) *should be refrigerated*
   (b) cannot be refilled
   (c) should be kept
   (d) must be discarded
   (e) may be stored
   (f) should not be frozen

2. (a) *should be examined*
   (b) must be reported
   (c) must be accompanied
   (d) should be sent
   (e) must be paid
   (f) can be placed

Exercise 22 (page 439)

1. B: *must have been damaged*

2. B: could have been sent

3. B: shouldn't have been planted

4. B: must have been delayed

5. B: couldn't have been accepted

6. B: must have been transferred

7. B: should have been notified

8. A: could have been saved
   B: couldn't have been helped

Exercise 23 (page 441)

1. *Membership passes must be shown at the gate.*

2. Guest passes can be bought at the main office.

3. The number of guests may be limited on weekends.

4. Children under 12 are not admitted unless they are accompanied by an adult.

5. Small children must be supervised at all times.

6. A shower must be taken before entering the pool.

7. The lifeguard must be obeyed at all times.

8. Diving is permitted in designated areas only.

9. Smoking, gum-chewing, and glass bottles are prohibited.

10. Food may be eaten in the picnic area only.

Exercise 24 (page 442)

1. A: *Should smoking be permitted in public places?*
   B: *Yes, it should./No, it shouldn't.*

2. A: Should bicyclists be allowed on busy streets?
   B: Yes, they should./No, they shouldn't.

3. A: Should violence be banned from television?
   B: Yes, it should./No, it shouldn't.

4. A: Should guns be sold in stores?
   B: Yes, they should./No, they shouldn't.

5. A: Should pilots be tested for drugs and alcohol?
   B: Yes, they should./No, they shouldn't.

6. A: Should women be paid the same wages as men?
   B: Yes, they should./No, they shouldn't.

7. A: Should men be given parental leave?
   B: Yes, they should./No, they shouldn't.

8. A: Should animals be used for medical research?
   B: Yes, they should./No, they shouldn't.

9. A: Should children be given an allowance?
   B: Yes, they should./No, they shouldn't.

10. (﹏) A: Should teenagers be allowed to drive?
    B: Yes, they should./No, they shouldn't.

Exercise 25 (page 442)

Answers will vary. For example:

1. *It could have been delivered incorrectly.*
   It may have been sent to the wrong address.
   It might have been lost.

2. It could have been delayed.

3. They might have had an argument.

4. The paper may have been copied.

5. His house might have been robbed.

6. It could have been stolen.

Exercise 26 (page 443)

1. *(b)*   5. (b)
2. (a)   6. (b)
3. (a)   7. (b)
4. (b)   8. (b)

Summary Exercise (page 445)

1. *These pills should be taken every four hours.*

2. They were questioned by the police.

3. The letter should have been delivered in the afternoon.

4. The bell was rung several times.

5. Correct

6. A young man has been put/was put in prison.

7. This carpet is being cleaned/was being cleaned by a professional carpet cleaner.

8. The show must have been canceled.

9. The mail has been sent/was sent to the wrong address.

10. Correct

11. He was dead/He died at the age of twenty.

12. Will the new road be built soon?

13. The phone was being used when I needed it.

14. It will not be needed any longer.

15. Correct

Chapter 17

Exercise 1 (page 449)

1. A: *Eric went*
   B: he came back/he's coming back

2. A: The mail didn't come/hasn't come
   B: happened; the post office closes

3. A: you want to go; it costs
   B: we should go; I should be ready

4. A: the chemistry exam is
   B: it is, it is

5. A: they are
   B: you did

6. A: this costs
   B: he is

Exercise 2 (page 450)

Answers to questions will vary. For example:

1. Witness 1: I'm not sure who was driving it.

2. Witness 1: I can't remember what time it occurred.

3. Witness 2: I have no idea what the license plate number was.

4. Witness 2: I'm not sure where the bicyclist was.

5. Witness 3: I don't know what the truck looked like.

6. Witness 3: I'm not certain how many people were in the truck.

7. Witness 4: I can't remember what I was doing at the time of the accident.

8. Witness 4: I have no idea how fast the truck was going.

9. Witness 5: I'm not sure what color the truck was.

10. Witness 5: I don't know what the driver looked like.

Exercise 3 (page 451)

Answers will vary.

Exercise 4 (page 452)

Answers to questions will vary. For example:

1. A: *Excuse me. Can you please tell me where the restroom is?/Excuse me. Could you please tell me where the restroom is?*
   B: *It's downstairs on the left.*
   A: *Excuse me. Could you please tell me where the baggage claim is?*
   B: *It's straight ahead on your right.*

2. A: Pardon me. Do you know what time it is?
   A: Excuse me. I'd like to find out where I can find a bus schedule.

3. A: Pardon me. Do you know the price of this shirt?
   A: Excuse me. I was wondering if you could tell me what size these socks are.

4. A: Pardon me. I'd like to find out where the manager is.
   A: Excuse me. Can/Could/Would you tell me how much the broccoli is?

5. A: Excuse me. Can/Could/Would you please tell me where I can/could get a new ID card?
   A: Pardon me. Can/Could/Would you please tell me where I can/could pay my tuition bill?

Exercise 5 (page 453)

Answers will vary. For example:

1. A: *is open today?*
   B: *it is or not.*

2. A: it's going to rain.

3. A: the manager is calling a staff meeting today?
   B: she is

4. A: the lettuce is on sale?
   B: it is

5. A: you have any seats for April 6.
   B: there are any for the next day either

Exercise 6 (page 454)

Answers will vary.

Exercise 7 (page 455)

Answers will vary.

Exercise 8 (page 456)

Answers will vary. For example:

1. *Do you know if the assignment is due tomorrow?*

2. Do you have any idea if the library is closed during vacation?

3. Do you know if the teacher is going to show a film today?

4. I was wondering if you could please repeat that.

5. Can/Could you please tell me if you had any trouble with the last assignment?

6. Do you know if the new language lab is open yet?

7. Do you have any idea if I missed anything important yesterday?

8. I was wondering if you can/could give me a ride home this afternoon.

Exercise 9 (page 456)

Answers will vary.

Exercise 10 (page 457)

1. *Did you notice that he was angry?*

2. We doubt she is coming.

3. They predict it will happen soon/will soon happen.

4. I guess that I need some help.

5. I remembered that my rent was due tomorrow.

6. He proved he could do it.

7. I assume you can register tomorrow.

8. Do you believe that he is guilty?

Exercise 11 (page 460)

Answers will vary.

Exercise 12 (page 460)

Answers will vary.

Exercise 13 (page 460)

1. *I thought that something happened.*
   I thought that he had won.
   I thought that... we were going to complain.
   I thought that Joe could win.
   I thought that water freezes at 32° Fahrenheit.

2. She doubts that he'll change.
   She doubts that it's raining.
   She doubts that something happened.
   She doubts that he had won.
   She doubts that we were going to complain.
   She doubts that Joe could win.
   She doubts that water freezes at 32° Fahrenheit.

3. I hoped that he had won.
   I hoped that we were going to complain.
   I hoped that Joe could win.
   I hoped that water freezes at 32° Fahrenheit.

4. They realized that he'll change.
   They realized that it's raining.
   They realized that something happened.
   They realized that he had won.
   They realized that we were going to complain.
   They realized that Joe could win.
   They realized that water freezes at 32° Fahrenheit.

Exercise 14 (page 462)

1. A: I don't think that the new manager is doing a good job.
   B: Me neither. He told me to come in early yesterday for a meeting, and he forgot to show up.
   A: You're kidding. Julia said the same thing happened to her on Tuesday. I wonder whether we should complain to Allison. She hired him.
   B: I'm not sure if we should say anything yet. I asked Tom what he thought. He suggested that we wait one more week.

2. A: Did you hear the news? Channel 7 reported that the superintendent resigned.
   B: I know. I wonder if something happened. Everyone says she was pleased with the way things were going.
   A: Yesterday's news mentioned that she hadn't been feeling well lately. Maybe it's something serious and she was advised to step down.

3. A: Did you speak to the travel agent?
   B: I asked whether I needed to change the flight. He said he'd take care of it, and he admitted that he'd made a mistake. He assured me that everything would work out.
   A: Let's hope so. I told you to be careful during the holiday season. They're so busy that they often make mistakes.

Exercise 15 (page 464)

1. Martha: *how you were feeling; if we could come over for dinner Sunday.*
   John: we were/are busy on Sunday.
   Martha: I thought we could, but I'd have to check with you first.

2. A: to use fresh herbs.
   B: to make the sauce a day ahead.

3. A: what Jim's letter says.
   B: he's having a great time; he's going to come home on the twenty-ninth at 6:30 P.M., he hopes Nina can pick him up at the airport.
   A: to pick Jim up at the airport at 6:30 P.M. on the twenty-ninth.

4. B: to get some rest for a few days.
   A: if you need/needed an X ray
   B: to wait until Monday and then call his office.

Exercise 16 (page 468)

1. *She told me that he was leaving.*
   She told him to stay.
   She told... them that they were next.

2. He explained to the woman that it was impossible.
   He explained I was tired.
   He explained that the bridge was open.
   He explained that it was too late.
   He explained to me that I should try.

3. They require him to stay.
   They require that the student take an exam.

4. I admitted to the woman that it was impossible.
   I admitted I was tired.
   I admitted that the bridge was open.
   I admitted that it was too late.

5. We asked him to stay.
   We asked that the student take an exam.
   We asked if he was leaving.

6. He suggested to the woman that it was impossible.
   He suggested I was tired.
   He suggested that the bridge was open.

He suggested that it was too late.
He suggested that the student take an exam.
He suggested to me that I should try.

7. You said to the woman that it was impossible.
You said I was tired.
You said that the bridge was open.
You said that it was too late.
You said to me that I should try.

8. I answered I was tired.
I answered that the bridge was open.
I answered that it was too late.

Exercise 17 (page 469)

Answers may vary. For example:

1. Person B: *Excuse me. I didn't hear you.*
Person A: *I said that class is canceled today.*

2. B: I'm sorry. What did you say?
A: I asked where the stamps are/were.

3. B: Excuse me. I didn't hear you.
A: I asked if you're/you were going with us tonight.

4. B: Could you repeat that, please?
A: I asked whether I could give you a check.

5. B: Could you please say that again?
A: I said to take this to the front desk.

6. B: Excuse me. I didn't hear you.
A: I said your mother called this afternoon.

7. B: I'm sorry. What did you say?
A: I asked if you finished/had finished
your homework.

8. B: Could you please say that again?
A: I said not to worry about the report.
You can/could finish it tomorrow.

Exercise 18 (page 470)

Answers may vary. For example:

1. *not to quit her job until she knows what she wants
to do.*

2. Her husband says she should think about getting
another degree.

3. Her mother suggested that she find out about
different types of graduate programs.

4. Her father told her not to quit, just to take a leave
of absence for a year.

5. Her aunt advises that she quit her job and have
a baby.

6. Her uncle says to do whatever makes her happy.

7. Her sister recommended that she ask for a raise.

8. Her brother-in-law told her to go to an
employment agency.

9. Her colleague suggested that she ask to teach
a different grade next year.

10. Her neighbor advised her to try to get a job
in his/her company.

Exercise 19 (page 471)

Answers may vary. For example:

1. (a) *Nora Green called on Monday. She said to call
her back.*
(b) Joe's Repair Shop called on Monday. They said
your TV would be ready (on Monday) at noon.

2. (a) Bob called on Tuesday. He said he would call
back later that day.
(b) Richard Smith called on Tuesday. He said he
wanted to speak to you about an insurance
policy. His number is 324-1221.

3. (a) Jill called on Wednesday. She said she was just
calling to say hello and that she'd be home all
that evening.
(b) Stuart Lee called on Wednesday. He said he had
been calling for several days. He asked if
anything was wrong and he said to call him
back soon.

4. (a) Eric Martin called today to remind you about
the board meeting on the twenty-ninth. He said
to call him back if you have any questions.
(b) Gibson's called today. They said they'll be able to
deliver the desk you ordered on Monday, March
27. They said to call if that date is inconvenient.

Exercise 20 (page 472)

Answers may vary. For example:

*The weather report said that a cold front will move in
from the west tonight. It predicted that* the temperatures
will/would drop into the fifties. It said that the skies
will/would turn cloudy tomorrow with a 30 percent
chance of afternoon showers. It predicted that the
temperatures will/would remain in the fifties all day

Intermediate Grammar: From Form to Meaning and Use

(Saturday). The weather report said that on Sunday we can/could expect sunny skies, and it predicted that Sunday will/would be warmer than Saturday, with highs in the upper sixties.

Exercise 21 (page 472)

Answers will vary.

Exercise 22 (page 473)

Answers will vary.

Exercise 23 (page 473)

Answers will vary.

Exercise 24 (page 473)

Answers will vary.

Summary Exercise (page 475)

1. *I wonder where he is.*

2. Correct

3. She told me that it was too late.

4. B: Yes, I think so./Yes, I think (that) she is.

5. Correct

6. I think she told me the truth.

7. I didn't realize that she was absent.

8. She thought he would come later./She thinks he will come later.

9. They told me why she left.

10. Correct

11. They said that the store was closed./They told us/me that the store was closed.

12. Do you know whether or not he's staying?/ Do you know if he's staying (or not)?

13. Please tell me if you want to come or not./ Please say if you want to come or not.

14. They recommended that she leave early.

15. She asked if I wanted a ride home.